PACIFIC YOUTH

LOCAL AND GLOBAL FUTURES

PACIFIC YOUTH

LOCAL AND GLOBAL FUTURES

EDITED BY HELEN LEE

PRESS

PACIFIC SERIES

Published by ANU Press
The Australian National University
Acton ACT 2601, Australia
Email: anupress@anu.edu.au

Available to download for free at press.anu.edu.au

ISBN (print): 9781760463212
ISBN (online): 9781760463229

WorldCat (print): 1125205462
WorldCat (online): 1125270333

DOI: 10.22459/PY.2019

Cover design and layout by ANU Press

Cover photograph: 'Two local youths explore their backyard beach in Tupapa, Rarotonga' by Ioana Turia

Contents

1

Pacific Youth, Local and Global

Helen Lee and Aidan Craney

Introduction

Pacific Youth: Local and Global Futures was conceived as a follow-up to the collection that was edited by Gilbert Herdt and Stephen Leavitt (1998a), *Adolescence in Pacific Island Societies.* As with that earlier book, it contains a series of rich ethnographic case studies of youth across the Pacific, adding a focus on youth in the diaspora. The case studies consider the contemporary situation of youth and their uncertain futures, with a stronger focus on social change than the more 'traditional' emphasis of the contributions to the 1998 volume. In the two decades since that earlier publication, the local and, to varying extents, what is perceived as traditional has continued to shape the everyday lives of Pacific youth, but they now live in a globalised, interconnected world that has changed remarkably in that time.

The chapters in this collection cluster around some key themes that emerged during sessions at the annual conferences of the Association for Social Anthropology in Oceania (ASAO) in 2017 and 2018. These include education and employment and how these are linked to social inequalities; the marginalisation of youth and the focus in recent years on trying to encourage their political and civil engagement; youth 'problems', such as substance abuse, crime and violence; and the experiences of youth in the diaspora. These themes also recur throughout the youth-focused work within the expanding and interdisciplinary field of Pacific studies and in the numerous reports on Pacific youth for governments and non-government organisations—resulting in strategies and policies that have been produced for many years, mostly with remarkably little effect on young people's daily lives.

Who Are 'Pacific Youth'?

In their introduction to *Adolescence in Pacific Island Societies*, Herdt and Leavitt (1998b) recognised that 'adolescence' is a Western category that is constructed from a specific period of physical and social maturation. Although they use the term throughout their introduction, several of the chapter authors clarify that the category does not fit well for their case studies. In two of the case studies based in Papua New Guinea (PNG) (Biersack 1998; Lepowsky 1998), 'youth' is used instead and is shown to extend into the late 20s. In Rotuma, 'youth' can extend even beyond the 20s and it encompasses all those who are unmarried (Howard 1998, p. 149). The preference of these authors for the term 'youth' reflects the reality in many Pacific[1] societies in which social maturity may be recognised well after a person has physically matured.

In this collection, 'youth' is used rather than adolescence, while recognising that there is no widely accepted definition with the Pacific. Anthropological engagement with the category of youth in the Pacific has been mostly confined to localised studies that include some discussion of who is included in that category in both local and official definitions. The development industry, which has engaged with questions of youth potential and risk in the Pacific, as discussed later in this chapter, often tends to use 'youth' in a way that is much like adolescence: a stage in biological development, as well as one in the life course. In development discourse, 'youth' is often a subset within the broader definition of 'childhood', which includes anyone up to 18 years old, according to the UN definition in the Convention on the Rights of the Child (UNICEF n.d.). The UN definition of youth, which is an age of 15 to 24 years (United Nations n.d.), is also frequently used. Pacific governments, conversely, often have an even broader definition that extends into the 30s. In the Pacific literature, some even argue that the category of youth excludes older teenagers; in Patrick Vakaoti's (2014, p. 2) extensive survey

1 'Pacific' is of course also a contested construction, but it is taken in this book to refer to the countries that self-identify as part of the Pacific and their people, both in the islands and in the diaspora.

of young people's political participation in Fiji, he argued that '18 to 35 is preferred as a way of defining youth'. The term 'young people' is also used in highly varying ways, from broad definitions encompassing children and/or youth to those that exclude anyone under 18 and focus only on 'young' adults.

This variation is captured by Curtain and Vakaoti (2011, p. 8) in *The State of the Pacific Youth Report*:

> The age span covering youth, as a stage in the lifecycle moving from dependence to independence, varies. It can range from as young as age ten years to as old as mid-thirties, depending on the age at which some children have to start to fend for themselves and what society deems to be the end point of the transition.

Their report further notes significant variations in the age definitions of 'youth' across Pacific states. While 'the age group 15–24 years is often used', common usage in the region ranges from 12 years of age up to 34 years of age (2011, p. 8). Cameron Noble et al. (2011, p. v) agree with this but add that, in some cases, those considered youth 'might be in their 30s and 40s'.

To give a sense of the range of definitions used by Pacific governments, the Solomon Islands government defines youth as 'persons between 15 and 34 years of age, inclusive' (Solomon Islands Government 2017, p. 14). The Fijian government defined youth as 'those between the ages of 15 to 35 years of age' (Government of Fiji 2012, p. 3), but acknowledged in working documents that this definition is flexible according to community values (Government of Fiji 2012). Across the Pacific, those community values often mean that youth are understood to be those who are not yet married with children or in positions of authority. Simply being of a certain age or occupying 'adult' roles, such as being in paid employment, is not always enough to be considered fully adult.

In some parts of the Pacific, there were no pre-contact terms equating with 'youth'. Today, although the term is not consistently defined, the popular use of terms such as 'youth' to categorise groups of people 'has become a powerful index of global modernity' (Good 2012, p. 293; Chapter 2, this volume). Youth is also a category that has been the focus of increasing concern in the Pacific since at least the 1960s—and today, some of that is directed towards the sheer size of the youth population. In the introduction to their 1998 volume, Herdt and Leavitt (1998b,

p. 7) predicted that Pacific populations would get younger over time and, today, there is some alarm about the growing 'youth bulge' in Pacific populations. A youth bulge is reached when the population of people aged 15–24 years in a country exceeds 20 per cent of the total population, though this figure is 'somewhat arbitrary' (Fuller & Pitts 1990, pp. 9–10). Youth bulge theory goes further to regard such population bubbles as a security concern that is linked to an increased risk of civil unrest.

Using youth bulge theory to highlight security risks presents only one possibility for youth. Henrik Urdal, whose work on the youth bulge in the early 2000s is probably the most influential in this space, cautioned that the presence of youth bulges does not necessitate violence or unrest (Urdal 2004, p. 2). As Patrick Kaiku (2017, p. 7) noted, with reference to the youth bulge in Melanesian states: 'Where the youth bulge discourse generally depicts young people as impulsively violent and conflict-prone, it disregards youth-led initiatives that are worth knowing and supporting' (see also Kaiku 2018). Kaiku's claim captures the divergent view of youth not just in the Pacific, but globally; they can be regarded as a problem to be managed, or as having potential to make a valuable contribution to their societies. Taking the latter perspective, Rose Maebiru (2013, p. 148) observes: 'With a mean age of 21 years for most Pacific Island countries, the region has a huge resource at its disposal to address national and regional issues'.

Researching Pacific Youth

With youth now comprising a large proportion of Pacific societies (however 'youth' is defined), there is an urgent need to better understand young people's life experiences and future aspirations. However, there has been surprisingly little anthropological research focusing on Pacific youth in the years since the publication of *Adolescence in Pacific Island Societies*. Herdt and Leavitt (1998b, p. 4) claimed that their book was the first collection 'in any culture area' of 'cultural case studies of youth', and it was certainly the first for the Pacific. The edited collection *Youth and Society: Perspectives from Papua New Guinea* (O'Collins 1986) had case studies of the effects of social change across PNG, but the book edited by Herdt and Leavitt has remained the only collection with case studies on youth from across the Pacific. This is despite the fact that, as the authors highlight, there was an early surge of anthropological research into 'adolescent development' that was strongly influenced by the ethnographic research that was conducted in the Pacific by scholars such as Malinowski, Mead and Whiting in the 1920s and 1930s.

In anthropology more generally, from the 1950s to 1980s, the 'anthropological study of adolescence had been dormant, even non-existent, except for occasional ethnographic pieces scattered in monographs' (Herdt & Leavitt 1998b, p. 4). This can be mainly attributed to the decline of 'culture and personality' studies—but even since the 1990s, when child and youth studies had a revival, there has not been a significant amount of anthropological research conducted in this field in the Pacific. Instead, there has been an ongoing trickle of publications, such as Helen Lee's work on Tongan childhood (Lee 2018; Morton 1996), which also studies adolescence, as does Mary Spencer's (2015) study of the children of Chuuk, focusing on the 6–14 age group (see also Spencer, Chapter 10, this volume). Spencer (2015, p. 167) concluded that divergent views of the future existed for the people of Romonum, with some predicting that they will be 'abandoned and virtually empty' due to migration, while others hold onto hope for 'lives that are much like life today, or life with some version of on-island modernization'. In a recent update to her earlier work, Lee concluded that 'the question of how young people can negotiate both their Tongan identity and their engagement with modernity remains critical for Tonga's future' (Lee 2018). The chapters in this collection also focus on the future and provide valuable insights into the future possibilities for Pacific peoples, both in the islands and in the diaspora.

In the 2014 volume *Pacific Futures: Projects, Politics and Interests* (Rollason 2014a), it is notable that youth are scarcely mentioned, despite the volume's focus on 'the aspirations and projects of Pacific people' (Rollason 2014b, p. 1). Yet, much of Will Rollason's introductory chapter is highly relevant to youth, such as his claim that 'achieving a future that includes some measure of prosperity, dignity, self-reliance and opportunity is an object of struggle for many Pacific people in the contemporary era' (Rollason 2014b, p. 1). For young people across the Pacific, this struggle is compounded by their social positioning, which in most countries means that they are 'structurally minimised' (Craney 2018; Chapter 6, this volume). Understanding the effects of that minimisation of youth is critical when considering the future of Pacific countries.

In his introduction to *Pacific Futures,* Rollason is scathing about the 'development' literature, but this is where much of the discussion regarding Pacific youth has occurred in recent years. A significant body of published and unpublished development literature has been produced since the 1960s that is valuable for its data on youth, although it is sometimes highly problematic in its analysis of that data. Some literature has come from international bodies such as UNICEF, which produced 'The State of Pacific Youth' reports (UNICEF Pacific 2005; Curtain & Vakaoti 2011) and, in the 1990s and 2000s, commissioned a series of reports on children, youth and women (McMurray 2005; Romano 2013; Sio 2006). Numerous other organisations, such as UNDP, UNESCO, WHO, OXFAM International, the World Bank[2] and the Asian Development Bank, have at some stage focused their attention on Pacific youth, as have aid donor nations such as Australia (through AusAID, now DFAT), Aotearoa/New Zealand (NZAid) and Japan (Japan International Cooperation Agency). There are also Pacific-focused organisations that have had varying interest in youth issues, such as the Pacific Islands Forum, Foundation of the Peoples of the South Pacific International and the Pacific Community (formerly South Pacific Commission [SPC]), as well as local civil society organisations within the different Pacific countries.

What is striking about this development-focused literature is its emphasis on 'youth problems', and this has influenced the countless youth-focused reports and strategies that Pacific governments have produced over many years. While it is easy to understand why development literature disproportionately addresses issues of deficits, such a focus ignores the positive contributions that young people make to their communities. It also overlooks the resilience of young people and the joyfulness of youth. Though some chapters within this volume also focus on problems that are associated with youth, the authors acknowledge that this is a period of opportunity and that the positive potential of young people should be recognised and supported.

Reading the development literature, it is evident that the key youth problems that have been discussed since the 1960s have remained much the same—including school dropouts, youth unemployment and youth

2 It is interesting, however, that the World Bank's 'Pacific Possible' series does not include a report focusing on youth, despite claiming to look at 'what's possible for Pacific Island countries by the year 2040?' (The World Bank Group 2018). See Pacific Possible: That's What I Want (www.youtube.com/watch?v=hUmKc6_5MRM).

crime, violence and risky behaviour such as substance abuse. There has also been a significant focus on early pregnancy, mental health issues and youth suicide. 'The youth problem', as this complex situation was often characterised, was initially blamed on urban drift and the breakdown of 'tradition', but a more complex and persistent set of problems has now been identified, including:

> Poverty, education systems focused on white-collar employment skills, stagnating economies that do not provide enough employment opportunities, and rural/urban inequalities … Continuing high population growth; rapid urban expansion; political volatility; under-performing economies, now further weakened by the impact of the global economic crises; and the rising cost of food point to a future for many young Pacific Islanders that holds an increased risk of entrenchment of poverty and broadening disparities, which will cause widespread discontent. (Curtain & Vakaoti 2011, p. 5)

Since 'youth problems' were first identified, there has been an associated assumption that young people are likely to cause trouble. This has been reinforced over many years by sporadic outbreaks of civil unrest across the Pacific, such as the unrest associated with the coups in Fiji between 1987 and 2006 (Firth et al. 2009); in the Society Islands in 1995, when there was a push for independence from France (Elliston 2012); and the civil conflict in Solomon Islands between 1998 and 2003, known locally as the Tension (Kabutaulaka 2001). There have been other examples of riots and disturbances in Vanuatu in 1998 (Mitchell 2011), Tonga in 2006 (Campbell 2008), Kanaky/New Caledonia (Storey 2005) and PNG (May 2017). Despite the dire predictions of 'youth bulge' theory, these are exceptions within what are generally peaceful societies. In all the events, young people were both victims and perpetrators and they were joined by adults; these were not 'youth riots', but more general outbursts of civil unrest.

Although such large-scale events are unusual, concern about 'youth problems' persists and there is certainly evidence of ongoing, localised issues in some Pacific societies. Imelda Ambelye's study of village youth in the Central Province of PNG (Chapter 8, this volume) looks at the 'intense frustration among the youths' and blames a combination of an inadequate education system, increasing economic inequalities, weakening social structures and generational conflicts that lead youth to alcohol, drugs and other antisocial behaviour, including some cases of extreme violence. These issues have previously been linked to the existence of *raskols* in PNG—youth, typically male, who engage in unlawful behaviours such as 'serious property crime, violence and rape' (Luker & Monsell-Davis 2010, p. 81). As Vicki Luker and Michael Monsell-Davis (2010, p. 81) noted, '*Raskols* remain perhaps *the* symbol of PNG's "law and order" problems' due to their engagement in violence and other antisocial activities. They posited that rather than these behaviours being symbolic of youth and young manhood in the country, they are more reflective of a lack of education, employment and civic engagement opportunities for these young people.

The report *Urban Youth in the Pacific: Increasing Resilience and Reducing Risk for Involvement in Crime and Violence* (Noble et al. 2011) argued the need for 'youth participation in decision-making processes at the community, national and regional levels', as well as for improving the 'relevance and quality of education outcomes' to fit the demands of the job market both nationally and internationally and developing 'targeted employment opportunities and meaningful activities for young people' (2011, p. v). These 'key guiding principles for preventing youth involvement in crime and violence' were endorsed in June 2011 by the Forum Regional Security Committee (Noble et al. 2011, p. iv). Importantly, this report also noted that, as with the more dramatic outbursts of civil unrest, only some youth can be identified as exhibiting problem behaviour. Noble et al. (2011, p. 2) reported that their 'research confirmed that the majority of Pacific youth are contributing positively to society … As a significant portion of the total population, young people have a great potential as they transition to adulthood to drive economic development and contribute to society'.

Countless reports and programs that are focused on enabling youth to reach this potential have targeted either specific youth problems, such as crime and violence, or youth mental health issues (Guttenbeil-Likiliki 2009; Jourdan 2008) or youth 'development', more generally. The latter includes country-specific plans, such as the Tonga National Youth Strategy 2007–2012, and those that attempt to address the Pacific as a whole, such as the SPC's Mapping the Youth Challenge (2009) and the Pacific Youth Development Framework 2014–2023 (SPC 2015). In addition, for many years there have been calls for a more coordinated regional approach to youth issues and for each country to implement better services and support for young people.

The fact that these initiatives have resulted in so little change is deeply concerning. As Maebiru (2013, p. 148) noted, 'These "paper commitments" often lack political will, resources and capacity to realise the policy goals and targets, fuelling discontent, alienation and a sense of hopelessness among young people'. She added that 'limited available resources, weak economies and competing national and regional priorities; together with the huge challenge of promoting ownership and progressing coordination in the youth sector has hampered efforts to progress these youth commitments' (Maebiru 2013, p. 150). Daniel Evans (Chapter 4, this volume) discusses this situation in Solomon Islands, providing an insightful critique of well-meaning but underfunded interventions that often have 'negligible impact'. He shows that local politics adds another layer of complexity to engagements with youth—in this case, members of parliament who spread their largesse only to gain votes.

In their State of Pacific Youth report, Curtain and Vakaoti (2011, p. 5) concluded that 'without a major investment in young people, they may well flounder as a generation, undermining the capacity of Pacific Island countries and territories to escape aid dependence, develop economically and, in some cases, even survive as viable societies'. One of the reasons why there has not been this investment is that the limited resources that are available to Pacific governments tend not to be directed to youth issues, which is a symptom of young people's 'structural minimisation' and marginalisation. A review of the development literature that was produced in 2009 for the World Bank's Youth Engagement Strategy for the Pacific (Woo & Corea 2009) acknowledges that policy initiatives are mainly focused on addressing the symptoms rather than underlying causes. Sonya Woo and Ravi Corea recommended that young people are involved in addressing the causes rather than involving them in the 'problem stage'. Again, the issue of minimisation is relevant; while development discourse may assume that youth can be 'empowered', that they can exert their agency and be involved in this way, in reality, this can be difficult to achieve when the cultural expectation is that they are 'seen but not heard' (Craney 2018; Good 2012).

Anthropological research, including the growing body of work being produced by Pacific authors, can be invaluable to understanding this disconnection between development ideals and young people's lived experiences. A growing cohort of researchers, including some represented in this volume, are helping address the lack of Pacific literature that engages with youth. Studying areas such as online activism (Brimacombe et al. 2018), practices of contemporary citizenship (LeFevre 2013) and demonstrations of masculinity (Hawkes 2018; Marsters & Tiatia-Seath, Chapter 11, this volume), they demonstrate how understanding youth issues from youth perspectives provides a deeper understanding of social issues in the region. These texts aid in addressing a significant challenge for emerging Pacific youth researchers regarding not only the lack of focus on the causes and sociocultural factors influencing youth problems in recent decades, but also the narrow focus that much of the academic literature has taken. This volume builds on recent work that situates youth issues in broader contexts, such as Vakaoti's (2007, 2019) research into street-frequenting youth and youth political participation in Fiji, Mary Good's (2012) examination of the tensions of 'tradition' and modernity for Tongan youth, and Aidan Craney's (2018) political economic analysis of young people in Fiji and Solomon Islands. By collating research drawn from across the region that considers separate but interconnected issues, this collection provides an opportunity for a deeper understanding of how youth experience challenges of citizenship, civic engagement and personal development.

This addresses a significant gap. The lived experiences of youth have been neglected even in the international development material, which is where much of this broader focus might be anticipated, including in reviews of the literature (e.g. Woo & Corea 2009).[3] There has been some improvement in recent years, with the emerging critical development literature attempting to move away from the modernising discourse of earlier approaches that often made problematic assumptions about what people need and want and tended to ignore cultural specificities (Rollason 2014b). The post-development and recent critical development literature (e.g. Andrews et al. 2012; Esteva & Escobar 2017; Pieterse 1998) moves closer to an anthropological approach by emphasising the importance of local context, histories, ideologies and power relations, as well as more locally informed initiatives rather than one-size-fits-all approaches. It is well positioned to benefit from drawing on anthropological research to provide more culturally informed nuance to arguments about how youth can best be supported to reach their potential.

3 In their review, Woo and Corea (2009, pp. 45–48) included an Appendix, 'Selected bibliography of anthropological research on PNG', but most of the work listed is not about youth.

For example, the focus in recent development discourse regarding issues like sustainable livelihoods and youth empowerment needs to recognise the role of agency and identity, as well as the cultural aspects and social structures that shape the experiences of youth and their ability to engage with 'development' initiatives. The intersectional approach that is widely adopted in the social sciences is useful here to take into account that age intersects with several factors, such as gender, ethnicity, social status and location. There are also other important intersections that serve as a reminder that 'youth' cannot be studied in isolation. Youth are interconnected with their families and wider communities, and those who can access social media and other digital technologies can have global connections with the Pacific diaspora and beyond.

Change and Continuity in the Lives of Pacific Youth

This potential for the global connectivity of Pacific youth is a recent element of the social and cultural transformations that have occurred throughout the histories of Pacific countries. The changes that are associated with their colonial and postcolonial histories have been well documented, and some of the key changes that continue to shape those societies include the effects of indigenised forms of Christianity, formal education systems, rural to urban migration, political and economic instability and the increasingly youthful populations. More young people than ever before are living in urban and peri-urban areas in the islands, often in areas marked by poverty, precarity and disconnection from ancestral land. Pacific countries also have experienced the forces of globalisation in many ways, and Pacific peoples are mobile within and beyond Oceania in remarkably diverse ways.

Despite these changes, which were experienced within the multiplicity of Pacific cultures and histories, there remain some significant and shared elements of continuity. The lives of most children and youth still largely revolve around home, school and church and, in many Pacific nations, these contexts have not changed dramatically in recent decades. Kinship continues to play a fundamental role in organising society, including the social hierarchies, within which children and youth generally have low status. The marginalisation of youth in society can be traced to their position in these hierarchies as adults in waiting, without full recognition of their agency or capacities. While the youth studies literature now recognises young people as social actors who already engage with their worlds in many complex ways, this may not reflect how they are regarded within their own families and communities. It should be noted here, however, that this is not a situation confined to the Pacific, as young people are considered and treated as 'apprentice-citizens' (Owen 1996) in Western countries such as Australia, Aotearoa/New Zealand and the United States (US) (Bessant 2004; Harris 2006).

The tensions that were noted decades ago between 'tradition' and modernity continue to play out for Pacific people in ways that Niko Besnier (2011) described as 'modern anxieties'. Often, young people become the focus of those anxieties because their elders tend to assume that they will reject 'culture' and 'tradition' for the perceived benefits of global modernity. On closer inspection, these anxieties are often not warranted, with many Pacific young people actively and inventively seeking ways to resolve or sidestep these tradition/modernity tensions. There is a growing self-conscious pride among Pacific youth when merging traditional elements of their cultures with new forms of expression, particularly through the arts: dance, material culture and artistic expression. As Aaron Ferguson shows for Samoa (Chapter 12, this volume), this can be reflected even in the production of T-shirts and tattoos. It is also observed in the sphere of youth activism, with young people finding ways to embrace traditional concepts and values while also engaging on an international stage to urge action on issues like climate change, or to promote gender equality.

Gender has been a significant focus of both anthropological and development literature in the Pacific, and, in recent years, there has been a strong focus on gender inequality (Jolly et al. 2015; Lee 2017a) and gender violence (Biersack et al. 2016). Gender was also a strong theme throughout the conference sessions that led to this book, particularly in relation to ongoing gender inequalities and transformations in the construction of gender identity. As is clear in this collection of papers, young women continue to be excluded from positions of power in some Pacific countries and they experience inequality in many contexts.

Anthropologists have long observed that the changes of the colonial era, including the influence of Christianity, transformed the construction of masculinity to a greater extent than femininity. Within the literature on youth, there was a specific focus on the practice of male initiation in some Pacific societies, particularly in PNG (e.g. Herdt 1994). As these practices ceased, new paths to masculinity were found, some of which are now often blamed for the 'youth problems' that are so frequently noted in the development literature. Even in societies in which formal initiation ceremonies were not formerly practised, the behaviour of males is more likely perceived as problematic, whether it was as street-frequenting urban youth (Jourdan 1995) or as participants in civil unrest. Deborah Elliston used the case study of Tahitian young men who were involved in antinuclear and pro-independence activism in 1995 to argue that, like young men in many other societies, they were marginalised by 'neoliberal processes of globalization' (Elliston 2012, p. 158). She argued that 'common characteristics include young men becoming less competitive than young women in the labor market, developing elevated school-leaving rates, and becoming objects of blame in local discourses about social problems' (p. 158).

The precarity in these young people's lives echoes the experiences of youth across the globe who are trying to reconcile neoliberal promises of personal fulfilment and material abundance with the lived experience of limited opportunity—from the Occupy Movement's majority youth membership (Giroux 2013) to the youth protest leaders of the Arab Spring (Moghadam 2013). Other accounts of the construction of masculinity in the Pacific today focus on new avenues that have surfaced, notably through sport, at least for some young men (Guinness & Besnier 2016; Marsters &Tiatia-Seath, Chapter 11, this volume; Uperesa & Mountjoy 2014).

Another recurring theme in the ASAO conference sessions that led to this book was the ways in which young people in the Pacific have opportunities to engage with the world beyond their island homes. The ASAO sessions that contributed to the collection that Herdt and Leavitt published in 1998 were held in 1990, before the internet had really had influence in the Pacific (Herdt & Leavitt 1998a, p. 143). The chapters in that book do not discuss digital communication, although Lepowsky mentions 'greater access to transnational commercial media' for youth on Vanatinai in PNG (in that case, national radio and cassettes). Today, the influences of an increasingly globalised world are evident in everyday practices, such as the consumption of Filipino soap operas on pirated DVDs (Good 2013). The changes, such as the widespread use of mobile phones (Brimacombe 2017; Brimacombe et al. 2018; Foster & Horst 2018) and access to the internet in many parts of the Pacific, cannot be underestimated and have become a new source of anxiety about the dangers of modernity (Lee 2018, p. 121). Despite the vast differences in the lives of youth across the Pacific and its diaspora—such as the contrasts between the experiences of youth in urban Hawai'i and those in rural PNG—mobile phones, the internet and technological change have brought profound change. To give just one example, they have facilitated an increased civic engagement that can be observed in the proliferation of Facebook pages engaging in civic debate, including Yumi Toktok Stret in Vanuatu and the now-closed Forum Solomon Islands International (Craney 2018), or the use of hashtags on twitter when discussing civic issues, such as #TeamFiji.

Education, Employment and Economic Inequalities

In discussions about the situation of Pacific youth over many years, three of the key issues that have been continually raised are problems associated with the formal education system, high rates of youth unemployment and the ongoing effects of economic inequalities. Although none of the chapters in this collection focus specifically on education, it is a common thread and is revealed as an issue that underlies other challenges for youth, including their employment options when they leave school. In her case study of two villages in PNG, Imelda Ambelye (Chapter 8, this volume) links leaving school early with some young people's antisocial behaviour and violence.

There are differences across the Pacific regarding how highly education is valued, and literacy rates also vary significantly. Education remains problematic across the region, partly due to inadequate resourcing—which is worsened by the pressure of growing youth populations and, in some cases, similarly inadequate teacher training. There are also ongoing problems of delivering education to rural and remote communities and, within many Pacific countries, there are students who must travel some distance to school or move to a town and either attend a boarding school or live with relatives. For students who do well in school and want to continue their education, access to tertiary education is limited and, again, it often involves moving to another island or even another country. Many of the regional tertiary institutions offer only a limited range of undergraduate and postgraduate opportunities, and they do not have the capacity to enrol all students who apply.

Most young people do not pursue tertiary education and, for them, there is often a stark mismatch between the formal schooling that they receive and the employment opportunities that are available (Falgout & Levin 1992). There continues to be resistance in many Pacific nations to vocational education, as academic education has long been prized as a possible route to coveted government jobs or to professions, despite the scarcity of such jobs. As Christine McMurray (2005, p. 8; Woo & Corea 2009, p. 8) noted over a decade ago:

> Dropping out of school and high rates of unemployment are interrelated symptoms of two underlying problems: inflexible education systems geared mainly towards white-collar work and distorted economies that do not provide enough employment opportunities for young people.

The Pacific 'youth bulge' has exacerbated this situation, and Pacific governments are unable to provide employment opportunities for the ever-increasing flow of young people leaving school.

However, there are differences across the Pacific in patterns of employment and, in some cases, young people are being trained in areas with limited prospects, while certain jobs remain available and difficult to fill. In Fiji, for example, the lack of skilled workers in certain sectors has resulted in recruitment from outside the Pacific to fill vacancies in diverse occupations such as 'skilled garment cutters, pattern-makers and embroiderers, building construction managers, qualified dive instructors, beauticians, chefs and air-conditioning technicians' (Nilan et al. 2006, p. 897). In many Pacific countries, the lack of employment opportunities in the formal sector, or the mismatch between training and skills needs, increases the marginalisation of young people and can serve to extend the period of 'youth'. It can also be a 'principal contributing factor' for a young person to develop mental health problems (Guttenbeil-Likiliki 2009, p. 7), reduce the likelihood of civic engagement and even develop a sense of disenfranchisement that leads to social unrest. Curtain and Vakaoti (2011, p. 9) highlighted the potential for negative individual and societal consequences as a result of limited livelihood opportunities: 'Denial of economic and social opportunities leads to frustrated young people. The result can be a high incidence of self-harm and anti-social behaviour, including a greater risk of social conflict and violence'. Rural unemployment leads to further crowding in urban areas and places a strain on both infrastructure and the goodwill of families who end up supporting youth who migrate in search of work. In response to these issues, governments and non-government organisations have been placing a greater focus on equipping youth with skills that formal education has not provided them. This takes the form of life skills training, work-ready training, industry engagement, vocational training and entrepreneurship.

In recent years, some Pacific countries have introduced Technical and Vocational Education and Training (TVET), but this has met with mixed success due to the widely shared perception that the training is only suited to those performing poorly at school. Although opportunities certainly exist for skilled workers in Pacific countries (Tagicakiverata & Nilan 2018), vocational training is regarded negatively by both parents and young people. In Fiji, such centres are colloquially referred to as 'drop-out schools', as 'those who perform poorly in secondary school are directed to technical and vocational education' (Woo & Corea 2009, p. 9; Tagicakiverata & Nilan 2018, p. 551). A further problem is that TVET institutions are usually in urban areas, which encourages internal migration and reduces the likelihood of acquired skills being used in the rural areas. There are exceptions; for example, since 2012, Fiji has introduced outreach training through the Fiji National University, which has operated the Sustainable Livelihood Program. The aim is to provide skills training in rural communities to improve self-sufficiency and create greater economic opportunities, whether through formal or informal wage employment or microenterprise.

Entrepreneurship has also become popular with development-focused training programs, with limited success. Ferguson (Chapter 7, this volume) shows that entrepreneurship in American Samoa can be a way for young people to gain social and economic capital, but each of the three case studies he discusses are 'self-made' entrepreneurs rather than entrepreneurs as a result of development programs. Ferguson also shows that it is possible for young people to connect their business ventures with the aspects of Samoan culture and identity that they value, sidestepping the categories of 'tradition' and 'modernity' and creating their own futures.

An important cultural factor that shapes the education and employment choices of Pacific youth is the ongoing focus in Pacific societies on kinship. Many young people continue to consider helping to provide for their families their primary moral responsibility and, where employment options are limited in the home country, they may seek opportunities elsewhere, such as through the temporary labour mobility schemes that are offered by Aotearoa/New Zealand and Australia. Although these are available only to 'adults' in the Western definition of over 18 years old, many of the workers are still regarded as 'youth' in their home countries. The New Zealand Recognised Seasonal Employer scheme began in 2007 (Gibson & McKenzie 2014; Gibson et al. 2008) and the Australian Seasonal Worker Programme (SWP) commenced in 2012 after a pilot scheme that ran from 2008 to 2012 (Curtain et al. 2018; Reed et al. 2012). New schemes continue to be developed; Australia introduced the Pacific Labour Scheme in July 2018 and workers from some Pacific countries can now obtain employment for up to three years in areas such as aged care, as well as non-seasonal farm work. In September 2018, the Pacific Trades Partnership Program began a new scheme to create new short-term job opportunities in construction in Aotearoa/New Zealand to fill skills shortages there (Matangi Tonga 2018).

The current temporary labour schemes are part of a long history of labour migration, both from and within the Pacific (Connell & Corbett 2016, p. 587; Gibson & McKenzie 2014). Within that history, there are darker chapters, such as the era of 'blackbirding', in which people from countries such as Vanuatu (Mortensen 2000) were forcibly taken to work in Australia (Banivanua-Mar 2007). Parallels have already been drawn between the new labour schemes and this earlier era (Connell 2010) and, in Australia, the SWP was one form of labour that was discussed at the government's 2017 inquiry into establishing a Modern Slavery Act. There certainly are significant problems with the SWP (Ball et al. 2011; Curtain et al. 2016; Doyle & Howes 2015); however, these are unlikely to deter Pacific people seeking ways to provide for their families through the remittances that they send while working overseas for higher wages than they can earn at home (Curtain et al. 2018). Many children and youth are now growing up at a time when temporary labour migration is regarded as a method for young people to fulfil both their obligations to their families and their own ambitions to save money to start businesses, build homes and achieve the other markers of adulthood in the contemporary Pacific.

Political and Civic Engagement

As several chapters in this collection show, youth in Pacific societies tend to be expected to be obedient to their elders and to wait patiently on the sidelines to be invited into decision-making processes and institutions. Within families, schools and churches, there is often an explicit discouragement of critical thinking and young people learn that they are not expected to express their opinions, except perhaps within their own peer groups. This contributes to their 'structural minimisation' more generally in their societies (Craney 2018). In their review of literature on Pacific youth, Woo and Corea (2009, p. 23) found that 'growing marginalization of youth emerges as the most important issue'. Not surprisingly, then, political parties are unlikely to have youth representation or even to be particularly interested in youth voices. Even young people who are born into the traditional elite are unlikely to have a voice in the affairs of their country until they are socially recognised adults (Lee, Chapter 5, this volume).

Both local and international organisations have produced various reports on how to increase youth participation in civil society and how to encourage their political engagement. The World Bank's report, *Giving South Pacific Youth a Voice: Youth Development through Participation* (Jayaweera & Morioka 2008), considered six Pacific countries and focused on the marginalisation of youth, defined as those aged 15–29 years, with the aim of finding ways to increase their participation in 'the development process'.[4] The aim was also to document 'best-practice examples of youth engagement mechanisms in the Pacific' (2008, p. 8). The report identifies all-too familiar issues: education, employment, the silencing of young people's voices and the lack of social support for youth.

Youth are often not taken seriously as political subjects within their own societies; their activism is not viewed as a right and it is sometimes dismissed, sidelined or, even worse, assumed to be anarchic or even criminal behaviour that needs to be controlled. From the perspective of some adults, it becomes merged with the broader 'youth problems'. In Kanaky/New Caledonia, Tate LeFevre (2018) argued:

4 The authors are founding directors of Youth for a Sustainable Future Pacifika, which seems to be no longer active; its website, dated 2015, has had no activity for some time (orgs.tigweb.org/youth-for-a-sustainable-future-pacifika).

> Their discursive construction as ontologically and temporally 'disordered' delegitimizes urban Kanak youth as potential political actors. When urban youth engage in public protests, they are often characterized as 'delinquents' or 'thugs'. Acts of organized political resistance—such as the 2014 protests in St. Louis following an ecologically devastating chemical spill at nearby Vale Inco nickel refinery—are regularly dismissed as 'riots': ideologically empty violence committed by youths without any 'real' knowledge of Kanak culture, who refuse to respect both Kanak customary or French government authority. (See also LeFevre 2013)

Despite their marginalisation and negative perceptions of their activism, the everyday civic activities of youth in the Pacific must be considered as positive or, at the very least, neutral. Instances of youth involvement in unrest are notable precisely for their abnormality. Most young people in the Pacific, as elsewhere, spend most their time engaging in positive and socially acceptable behaviours.

In addition, some young people in Pacific countries have persisted with political engagement, as they are influenced by colonial histories, ongoing political tensions and emerging issues. Youth throughout the Pacific have been involved in increasingly politicised civil society activities in recent years, particularly in fields related to social justice—such as rights in relation to gender, sexuality and disability and issues in relation to climate change, rising sea levels and environmental degradation. Young people are often at the vanguard of change in these spaces that adults have been slow to claim and they are forcing their way into public consciousness and conversation.

There has been a proliferation of civil society organisations across the Pacific in the last decade, many of which have been established by young people. Some of these are local and often urban initiatives, such as those focusing on using the arts for activism and involving marginalised youth now seeking a voice, including LGBTIQ+[5] youth and those with disabilities. Other local organisations seek to empower females—such as the Talitha Project in Tonga, established in 2009 for young women and girls aged 10–25 years, to encourage political participation, leadership and advocacy against gender-based violence and discrimination, and

5 Lesbian, gay, bisexual, transgender, intersex, queer and others who do not identify as heterosexual and/or cisgender.

to promote reproductive rights and sexual health. There are also more 'mainstream' organisations, such as National Youth Councils in many Pacific nations that are members of the Pacific Youth Council.[6]

Young activists are becoming increasingly confident in seeking support from different funding agencies. They are more entrepreneurial in their activism, linking to global networks to a greater extent than many of the older generation of workers in non-government, civil society and faith-based organisations, who tend to stick with the well-established circuit of regional meetings and the more mainstream donors. Global connectivity is providing some Pacific youth with a means to have a voice about issues that concern them and to overcome their marginalisation within their own societies. For example, social media is used effectively by young people involved in activism (Brimacombe 2017; Finau et al. 2015) and there is now a plethora of Facebook pages that are managed by Pacific youth organisations.

Migration and the Diaspora

It is not only Pacific youth activists who are globally interconnected through social media; the spread of mobile phones and use of Facebook, Instagram and other forms of digital communication have created complex webs of connections that are accessible to many young people, even in remote areas of the Pacific and between island and diasporic populations. In addition to communication, much identity work occurs online, as it has since Pacific people first enthusiastically embraced the internet in the 1990s (Franklin 2004; Morton 1999).

As well as the work that focuses on digital communication, a significant amount of literature exists in anthropology and, more broadly, in Pacific studies on the migration of Pacific peoples and their experiences in the diaspora, particularly in Aotearoa/New Zealand, Australia and the US (e.g. Lee & Francis 2009; Spickard et al. 2002). Some of this literature focuses specifically on the experiences of young people who have spent all or most of their lives outside the Pacific—the second and now subsequent generations (e.g. Lee 2003; Schoone 2010). As in the islands, Pacific youth in the diaspora have diverse life experiences that are affected by many factors, such as where they live—which can vary from urban ghettos

6 Some existing youth councils wanted a regional youth coordinating council for the Pacific and, after a failed attempt in 1975, this was finally established in 1996 (pacificyouthcouncil.org).

to small rural towns—their family's socioeconomic status and the ethnic make-up of the local community. Pacific diaspora populations tend to build strong local communities that are often based on kinship ties and churches, but they can still experience considerable marginalisation and discrimination (Moosad, Chapter 12, this volume).

Pacific migrant communities have experienced significant intermarriage, so youth are often negotiating multi-ethnic identities (McGavin 2014)—although it is important to recognise that this can also be an issue for youth in the Pacific, as Bacalzo shows in her study of the Markham Valley in PNG (Chapter 3, this volume). Youth in the diaspora also have varying degrees of connection with their parents' homelands, and while some have strong transnational ties, others are more disconnected and may have never seen the lands of their ancestors (Lee 2017b).

Many of the youth problems that were identified in the literature on island societies also feature in the literature on Pacific youth in the diaspora. Rather than in the development literature that typically describes these problems in the islands, it is more often found in fields such as education, public health, social work and psychology (see Marsters & Tiatia-Seath, Chapter 11, this volume). Problems with education are often highlighted (see Spencer, Chapter 10, this volume, on Micronesian students), as are health issues such as mental health. In the diaspora, youth can also experience problems that are familiar to other marginalised migrant groups, such as racism, poverty and a lack of avenues for social mobility. They may even be regarded as potentially criminal and violent, leading to police harassment, encounters with the criminal justice system and negative stereotypes in the media (Irwin & Umemoto 2016).

For Marshall Islanders, youth 'problems' that are experienced in the islands are transformed in the diaspora (Carucci, Chapter 9, this volume). Larry Carucci shows that the drinking circles that had long been part of the transition to adulthood, mostly for young men, on the atolls of Ujelang and Enewetak, were regarded as transgressing Christian behaviour. However, the use of hard drugs by young men living on Majuro, Hawai'i and elsewhere in the US has created new forms of intergenerational tension, as well as increased risks of criminal charges and even deportation.

Some Pacific countries, such as Tonga and Samoa, have experienced an influx of diaspora citizens who were deported from the countries in which they grew up, many of whom fall into the broad category of 'youth' as defined within those countries—that is, between the ages of 15 and 34 (Guttenbeil-Likiliki 2009, p. 8). They have become a new source of 'youth problems' and are often blamed for the increasing rates of crime and violence (Pereira 2011). However, a study of urban youth and crime found that although deportees could be blamed for some 'increase in the sophistication of crime in island nations, the vast majority of deportees endure discrimination and a lack of support' (Noble et al. 2011, p. v).

As a trickle of young people born overseas moves into the islands, as deportees or as youth are being returned by their families to experience life in the homeland, some island-born youth leave for higher education or seek a career in elite sports. Participation in elite sports has become an ideal means of attaining social mobility for many young Pacific men—and increasingly women—although few achieve this goal. As Caleb Marsters and Jemaima Tiatia-Seath (Chapter 11, this volume) show in their work with young Pacific men playing rugby in Auckland, both the pressures of success for those who make it and the shame associated with not achieving the elite level can lead to mental health issues.[7] A much larger outflow of island-born young people is occurring due to temporary labour migration schemes and, as noted earlier, these seem likely to grow and become a significant focus of many young people's aspirations.

Conclusion

Much of the literature on Pacific youth, both academic and development-oriented reports, has focused on their problems or, to a much lesser extent, their involvement with activism or success in elite sports. The experiences of most Pacific youth, both in the islands and the diaspora, are not captured by these two extremes because they are the ordinary youth who finish school and move on with their lives, whether in wage labour, entrepreneurial activities or subsistence farming; they marry, have children of their own and make the transition into adulthood. That is to say, the overwhelming majority of Pacific youth make positive contributions to their communities.

7 In Australia, 36 per cent of National Rugby League contracts signed in 2011 were of Pasifika ethnicities (Lakisa et al. 2014), and Pasifika players make up 42 per cent of players at the professional level and over 50 per cent of junior ranks (Hawkes 2018). Nevertheless, those who manage to secure paid contracts are only a small proportion of those who attempt to reach that level.

Herdt and Leavitt (1998b, p. 5) identified that their book was being published during an important moment in Pacific history. Some 20 years later, a great deal has changed in the Pacific and the ever-growing Pacific diaspora—and yet, in that time, there has not been a similar increase in the academic literature focusing on youth. This is all the more remarkable because of the 'youth bulge' occurring in Pacific countries; with youth now being a substantial portion of Pacific populations, it is more important than ever to include them in our research. It is also another important moment in the Pacific, with geopolitical tensions rising due to China's increasing influence and Australia, Aotearoa/New Zealand and the US reconsidering their relationships with Pacific nations—all in a context of growing concern for the effects of climate change. The case studies in this book provide valuable insights into the lives of young people across the Pacific as they are being shaped by change in both local and global contexts. More of this work is needed to gain an even more comprehensive understanding of the experience of those youth—their everyday lives, their aspirations and the obstacles that they encounter. We need to know more about their diverse experiences, as they face uncertain futures.

Acknowledgements

Thanks to the anonymous reviewers who provided valuable feedback on the chapters in this volume. Thanks also to La Trobe University's Social Research Assistance Platform for funding towards copyediting, and to Peter Turner and Capstone Editing for their copyediting at different stages of the book's development. Special thanks to all the contributors to the ASAO conference sessions that inspired this collection and to the chapter authors for their patience on the long road to publication.

References

Andrews, M, Pritchett, L & Woolcock, M 2012, *Escaping capability traps through problem-driven iterative adaptation,* Center for Global Development, Washington DC.

Ball, R, Beacroft, L & Lindley, J 2011, *Australia's Pacific seasonal worker pilot scheme: Managing vulnerabilities to exploitation*, Australian Institute of Criminology, Canberra.

Banivanua-Mar, T 2007, *Violence and colonial dialogue: The Australian-Pacific indentured labor trade,* University of Hawai'i Press, Honolulu.

Besnier, N 2011, On the edge of the global: Modern anxieties in a Pacific Island nation, Stanford University Press, Stanford.

Bessant, J 2004, 'Mixed messages: Youth participation and democratic practice', *Australian Journal of Political Science,* vol. 39, no. 2, pp. 387–404.

Biersack, A 1998, 'Horticulture and hierarchy: The youthful beautification of the body in the Paiela and Porgera valleys', in Gilbert Herdt & Stephen Leavitt (eds), *Adolescence in Pacific Island societies*, University of Pittsburgh Press, Pittsburgh, pp. 71–91.

Biersack, A, Jolly, M & Macintyre, M (eds) 2016, *Gender violence & human rights: Seeking justice in Fiji, Papua New Guinea and Vanuatu,* ANU Press, Canberra, doi.org/10.22459/GVHR.12.2016

Brimacombe, T 2017, 'Pacific policy pathways: Young women online and offline', in Martha Macintyre & Ceridwen Spark (eds), *Transformations of gender in Melanesia,* ANU Press, Canberra, pp. 141–163. doi.org/10.22459/TGM.02.2017.06

Brimacombe, T, Kant, R, Finau, G, Tarai, J & Titifanue, J 2018, 'A new frontier in digital activism: An exploration of digital feminism in Fiji', *Asia and the Pacific Policy Studies*, vol. 5, pp. 508–521, doi.org/10.1002/app5.253

Campbell, I 2008, 'Across the threshold: Regime change and uncertainty in Tonga 2005–2007', *The Journal of Pacific History,* vol. 43, no. 1, pp. 95–109, doi.org/10.1080/00223340802054719

Connell, J 2010, 'From blackbirds to guestworkers in the South Pacific. Plus ça change … ?', *The Economic and Labour Relations Review*, vol. 20, no. 2, pp. 111–122, doi.org/10.1177/103530461002000208

Connell, J & Corbett, J 2016, 'Deterritorialisation: Reconceptualising development in the Pacific Islands', *Global Society,* vol. 30, no. 4, pp. 583–604.

Craney, A 2018, 'To be seen but not heard: Youth livelihoods and development in Fiji and Solomon Islands', PhD thesis, La Trobe University, Melbourne.

Curtain, R, Dornan, M, Doyle, J & Howes, S 2016, *Labour mobility: The ten billion dollar prize*, The World Bank, Canberra.

Curtain, R, Dornan, M, Howes, S & Sherrell, H 2018, 'Pacific seasonal workers: Learning from the contrasting temporary migration outcomes in Australian and New Zealand horticulture', *Asia and the Pacific Policy Studies*, vol. 5, pp. 462–480, doi.org/10.1002/app5.261

Curtain, R & Vakaoti, P 2011, *The state of Pacific Youth 2011: Opportunities and obstacles*, UNICEF Pacific, Secretariat of the Pacific Community, Suva.

Doyle, J & Howes, S 2015, 'Australia's seasonal worker program: Demand-side constraints and suggested reforms', Discussion paper, World Bank Group and The Australian National University, Sydney & Canberra.

Elliston, D 2012, 'Gendered modernities and traditions: Masculinity and nationalism in the Society Islands', in V Amit and N Dyck (eds), *Young men in uncertain times*, Berghahn, New York, pp. 133–163.

Esteva, G & Escobar, A 2017, 'Post-development @ 25: On "being stuck" and moving forward, sideways, backward and otherwise', *Third World Quarterly*, vol. 38, no. 12, pp. 2559–2572, doi.org/10.1080/01436597.2017.1334545

Falgout, S & Levin, P (eds) 1992, 'Transforming knowledge: Western schooling in the Pacific', *Anthropology and Education Quarterly*, vol. 23, no. 1, pp. 3–9.

Finau, G, Kant, R, Tarai J & Titifanue J 2015, *Social media and its impact on young men & women's political participation in Fiji*, viewed 6 September 2018, papers.ssrn.com/sol3/papers.cfm?abstract_id=2954890

Firth, S, Fraenkel, J & Lal, BV (eds) 2009, *The 2006 military takeover in Fiji: A coup to end all coups?*, ANU E Press, Canberra, doi.org/10.22459/MTF.04.2009

Foster, R & Horst, H 2018, *The moral economy of mobile phones*, ANU Press, Canberra, doi.org/10.22459/MEMP.05.2018

Franklin, M 2004, *Postcolonial politics, the internet, and everyday life: Pacific traversals online*, Routledge, London.

Fuller, G & Pitts, FR 1990, 'Youth cohorts and political unrest in South Korea', *Political Geography Quarterly*, vol. 9, no. 1, pp. 9–22.

Gibson, J & McKenzie, D 2014, 'The development impact of a best practice seasonal worker policy', *The Review of Economics and Statistics*, viewed 28 April 2014, www.mitpressjournals.org/doi/pdf/10.1162/REST_a_00383

Gibson, J, McKenzie, D & Rohorua, H 2008, 'How pro-poor is the selection of seasonal migrant workers from Tonga under New Zealand's recognised seasonal employer program?', Policy Research Working Paper, Centre for Research and Analysis of Migration, University College London, London, doi.org/10.1596/1813-9450-4698

Giroux, HA 2013, 'The Occupy Movement meets the suicidal state: Neoliberalism and the punishing of dissent', *Situations*, vol. 5, no. 1, pp. 7–34.

Good, MK 2012, 'Modern moralities, moral modernities: Ambivalence and change among youth in Tonga', PhD thesis, University of Arizona, Tucson.

Good, MK 2013, 'Filipino film lovers', *Anthropology Now,* vol. 5, no. 3, pp. 41–51.

Government of Fiji 2012, *Situational analysis of youths in Fiji 2011*, Ministry of Youth and Sports, Suva.

Guinness, D & Besnier, N 2016, 'Nation, nationalism, and sport: Fijian rugby in the local–global nexus', *Anthropological Quarterly*, vol. 89, no. 4, pp. 1109–1141, doi.org/10.1353/anq.2016.0070

Guttenbeil-Likiliki, O 2009, *Youth and mental health in Tonga: A situational analysis,* Foundation of the Peoples of the South Pacific International, Suva.

Harris, A 2006, 'Introduction: Critical perspectives on child and youth participation in Australia and New Zealand/Aotearoa', *Children, Youth and Environments,* vol. 16, no. 2, pp. 220–230.

Hawkes, G 2018, 'Indigenous masculinity in sport: The power and pitfalls of rugby league for Australia's Pacific Island diaspora', *Leisure Studies*, vol. 37, no. 3, pp. 318–330, doi.org/10.1080/02614367.2018.1435711

Herdt, G 1994, *Guardians of the flutes, volume 1: Idioms of masculinity,* University of Chicago Press, Chicago.

Herdt, G & Leavitt, S (eds) 1998a, *Adolescence in Pacific Island societies*, University of Pittsburgh Press, Pittsburgh.

Herdt G & Leavitt, S (eds) 1998b, 'Introduction: Studying adolescence in contemporary Pacific Island communities', in G Herdt & S Leavit (eds), *Adolescence in Pacific Island Societies*, University of Pittsburgh Press, Pittsburgh, pp. 3–26.

Howard, A 1998, 'Youth in Rotuma, then and now', in G Herdt & S Leavitt (eds), *Adolescence in Pacific Island societies*, University of Pittsburgh Press, Pittsburgh, pp. 148–72.

Irwin, K & Umemoto, K 2016, *Jacked up and unjust: Pacific Islander teens confront violent legacies*, University of California Press, Berkeley.

Jayaweera, S & Morioka, K 2008, *Giving South Pacific youth a voice: Youth development through participation*, International Bank for Reconstruction and Development/World Bank, viewed 6 September 2018, documents.worldbank.org/curated/en/661941468027551842/Giving-South-Pacific-youth-a-voice-youth-development-through-participation

Jolly, M, Lee, H, Lepani, K, Naupa, A & Rooney, M 2015, *Falling through the net? Gender and social protection in the Pacific*, UN Women, New York.

Jourdan, C 1995, 'Masta Liu', in V Amit-Talai & H Wulff (eds), *Youth cultures: A cross-cultural perspective*, Routledge, London.

Jourdan, C 2008, *Youth and mental health in Solomon Islands: A situational analysis,* Foundation of the Peoples of the South Pacific International, Suva.

Kabutaulaka, T 2001, *Beyond ethnicity: The political economy of the Guadalcanal Crisis in Solomon Islands*, Canberra State, Society and Governance in Melanesia Program, The Australian National University, Canberra.

Kaiku, P 2017, 'Re-thinking the youth bulge theory in Melanesia', *Contemporary PNG Studies: DWU Research Journal,* vol. 26, pp. 1–14.

Kaiku, P 2018, 'A critique of the youth bulge theory in Papua New Guinea and Melanesia', *Pacific Studies*, vol. 41, no. 3, pp. 188–198.

Lakisa, D, Adair, D & Taylor, T 2014, 'Pacific diaspora and the changing face of Australian Rugby League', *The Contemporary Pacific*, vol. 26, no. 2, pp. 347–367, doi.org/10.1353/cp.2014.0029

Lee, H 2003, *Tongans overseas: Between two shores*, University of Hawai'i Press, Honolulu.

Lee, H 2017a, 'CEDAW smokescreens: Gender politics in contemporary Tonga', *The Contemporary Pacific*, vol. 29, no. 1, pp. 66–90.

Lee, H 2017b, 'Overseas born youth in Tongan high schools: Learning the hard life', in H Lee & J Taylor (eds), *Mobilities of Return: Pacific perspectives*, ANU Press, Canberra, pp. 75–98, doi.org/10.22459/MR.12.2017.04

Lee, H 2018, 'Becoming Tongan today', in J Connell & H Lee (eds), *Change and continuity in the Pacific: Revisiting the region*, Routledge, London, pp. 118–135, doi.org/10.4324/9781315188645-8

Lee, H & Francis, S (eds) 2009, *Migration and transnationalism: Pacific perspectives*, ANU E Press, Canberra, doi.org/10.22459/MT.08.2009

LeFevre, T 2013, 'Turning niches into handles: Kanak youth, associations and the construction of an indigenous counter-public sphere', *Settler Colonial Studies*, vol. 3, no. 2, pp. 214–219, doi.org/10.1080/2201473X.2013.781933

LeFevre, T 2018, 'Moral panics and discourses of disorder: Delegitimizing the political actions of Kanak youth', Paper presented at the 2018 ASAO conference, New Orleans, LA, 31 January – 3 February.

Lepowsky, M 1998, 'Coming of age on Vanatinai: Gender, sexuality, and power', in G Herdt & S Leavitt (eds), *Adolescence in Pacific Island societies*, University of Pittsburgh Press, Pittsburgh, pp. 123–147.

Luker, V & Monsell-Davis, M 2010, 'Teasing out the tangle: *Raskols*, young men, crime and HIV', in V Luker & S Dinnen (eds), *Civic insecurity: Law, order and HIV in Papua New Guinea*, ANU E Press, Canberra, doi.org/10.22459/CI.12.2010.03

Maebiru, R 2013, 'Young people creating the future today: Youth development in the Pacific', in D Hegarty & D Tryon (eds), *Politics, development and security in Oceania*, ANU E Press, Canberra, pp. 147–151, doi.org/10.22459/PDSO.04.2013.11

Matangi Tonga 2018, *Construction job opportunities in NZ for Tongans*, Matangi Tonga, viewed 31 July 2018, matangitonga.to/2018/07/30/construction-job-opportunities-nz-tongans

May, R 2017, 'Papua New Guinea in 2016: Growing civil frustration', *Asian Survey*, vol. 57, no. 1, pp. 194–198, doi.org/10.1525/as.2017.57.1.194

McGavin, K 2014, 'Being "Nesian": Pacific Islander identity in Australia', *The Contemporary Pacific*, vol. 26, no. 1, pp. 126–154, doi.org/10.1353/cp.2014.0013

McMurray, C 2005, *Solomon Islands: A situation analysis of children, women and youth*, UNICEF Pacific Office, Suva.

Mitchell, J 2011, '"Operation Restore Public Hope": Youth and the magic of modernity in Vanuatu', *Oceania*, vol. 81, no. 1, pp. 36–50, doi.org/10.1002/j.1834-4461.2011.tb00092.x

Moghadam, VM 2013, 'What is democracy? Promises and perils of the Arab Spring', *Current Sociology*, vol. 61, no. 4, pp. 393–408.

Mortensen, R 2000, 'Slaving in Australian courts: Blackbirding cases, 1869–1871', *Journal of South Pacific Law*, vol. 4, no. 7, viewed 31 October 2018 (site discontinued), www.vanuatu.usp.ac.fj/journal_splaw/Articles/Mortenesen1.htm

Morton, H 1996, *Becoming Tongan: An ethnography of childhood*, The University of Hawai'i Press, Honolulu.

Morton, H 1999, 'Islanders in space: Tongans online', in J Connell & R King (eds), *Small worlds, global lives: Islands and migration*, Pinter, London, pp. 235–253.

Nilan, P, Cavu, P, Tagicakiverata, I & Hazelman, E 2006, 'White collar work: Career ambitions of final year school students', *International Education Journal*, vol. 7, no. 7, pp. 895–905.

Noble, C, Pereira, N & Saune, N 2011, *Urban youth in the Pacific: Increasing resilience and reducing risk for involvement in crime and violence*, United Nations Development Program Pacific Centre, Suva.

O'Collins, M 1986, *Youth and society: Perspectives from Papua New Guinea*, Department of Political and Social Change, The Australian National University, Canberra.

Owen, D 1996, 'Dilemmas and opportunities for the young active citizen', *Youth Studies Australia*, vol. 15, no. 1, pp. 20–23.

Pereira, N 2011, *Return[ed] to paradise: The deportation experience in Samoa and Tonga*, Most 2 Policy Paper No. 21, UNESCO, Paris.

Pieterse, JN 1998, 'My paradigm or yours? Alternative development, post-development, reflexive development', *Development and Change*, vol. 29, no. 2, pp. 343–373, doi.org/10.1111/1467-7660.00081

Reed, C, Southwell, A, Healy, M & Stafford, N 2012, *Final evaluation of the Pacific seasonal worker pilot scheme*, TNS for the Department of Education, Employment and Workplace Relations, Government of Australia, Hawthorn, viewed 14 July 2015, docs.employment.gov.au/system/files/doc/other/pswps_-_final_evaluation_report.pdf

Rollason, W (ed.) 2014a, *Pacific futures: Projects, politics and interests*, Berghahn, New York.

Rollason, W (ed.) 2014b, 'Introduction: Pacific futures, methodological challenges', in W Rollason (ed.), *Pacific futures: Projects, politics and interests*, Berghahn, New York, pp.1–27.

Romano, M 2013, *Kiribati Islands: A situation analysis of children, women and youth*, UNICEF, Suva.

Schoone, A 2010, 'Re-scripting life: New Zealand-born Tongan "youth-at-risk" narratives of return migration', *MAI Review*, pp. 1–11.

Sio, B 2006, *Samoa, a situation analysis of children, women and youth*, UNICEF Pacific Office, Suva.

Solomon Islands Government 2017, *Solomon Islands national youth policy 2017–2030*, Ministry of Women, Youth and Children Affairs, Honiara.

SPC 2009, *Mapping the youth challenge: The youth challenge in the Pacific Region*, Secretariat of the Pacific Community, Noumea.

SPC 2015, *Pacific youth development framework 2014–2023: A coordinated approach to youth-centred development in the Pacific*, Social Development Division of the Secretariat of the Pacific Community, Suva.

Spencer, M 2015, *Children of Chuuk lagoon: A 21st century analysis of life and learning on Romonum Island*, University of Guam Press, Mangilao, Guam.

Spickard, P, Rondilla, J & Hippolite, DW 2002, *Pacific diaspora: Island peoples in the United States and across the Pacific*, University of Hawai'i Press, Honolulu.

Storey, D 2005, 'Urban governance in Pacific Island countries: Advancing an overdue agenda', Discussion Paper 2005/7, The Australian National University, Canberra, viewed 14 July 2015, openresearch-repository.anu.edu.au/bitstream/1885/10136/1/Storey_UrbanGovernance2005.pdf

Tagicakiverata, I & Nilan, P 2018, 'Veivosaki-yaga: A culturally appropriate indigenous research method in Fiji', *International Journal of Qualitative Studies in Education*, vol. 31, no. 6, pp. 545–556.

The World Bank Group 2018, *#Pacific Possible*, The World Bank, viewed 24 September 2018, www.worldbank.org/en/who-we-are/news/campaigns/2017/pacificpossible

UNICEF n.d., *The convention on the rights of the child: Guiding principles: General requirements for all rights*, UNICEF, viewed 2 October 2018, www.unicef.org/crc/files/Guiding_Principles.pdf

UNICEF Pacific 2005, *The state of Pacific youth 2005*, United Nations Children's Fund/Secretariat of the Pacific Community, Suva.

United Nations n.d., *Department of economic and social affairs: Frequently asked questions*, United Nations, viewed 2 October 2018, www.un.org/development/desa/youth/what-we-do/faq.html

Uperesa, L & Mountjoy, T 2014, 'Global sport in the Pacific: A brief overview', *The Contemporary Pacific*, vol. 26, no. 2, pp. 263–279, doi.org/10.1353/cp.2014.0041

Urdal, H 2004, *The devil in the demographics: The effect of youth bulges on domestic armed conflict, 1950–2000*, The World Bank, Washington DC.

Vakaoti, P 2007, 'In the system but out of place: Understanding street-frequenting young people in Fiji', PhD thesis, School of Social Work and Applied Human Sciences, The University of Queensland, Queensland.

Vakaoti, P 2014, *Young people and democratic participation in Fiji*, Citizens' Constitutional Forum, Suva.

Vakaoti, P 2019, 'Young people's constitutional submissions in Fiji—opportunities and challenges', in H Cuervo & A Miranda (eds), *Youth, inequality and social change in the global south*, Springer Nature, Singapore, pp. 239–254.

Woo, S & Corea, R 2009, *Pacific youth literature review*, The International Bank for Reconstruction and Development/The World Bank, Suva.

2

Flexibility, Possibility and the Paradoxes of the Present: Tongan Youth Moving into the Future

Mary K Good

Introduction

The increasing interest in, and pressures of, seeking employment for youth in Tonga have apparently become so widespread as to be worthy of satire. In mid-November 2016, the group Facebook page 'Must Be Tongan', which regularly hosted discussions about Tongan identity and posted humorous photos and memes about Tongan life, posted a video of a short satirical job interview. In the comedic clip, an 'employer' reviews the resume of a prospective 'job seeker', given the name 'Sione Mango'.[1] Symbolic cues send up the stark differences between the two young men—the employer sits behind his shiny Mac computer wearing a close-fitting black blazer and Clark Kent, hipster-style glasses and speaking clearly yet quickly, while his interviewee sits across from him, eyes cast down in the traditional gaze of humility, with a youthful beanie pulled low on his head and slowly mumbling his answers. It seems unlikely that

1 Across the Facebook and YouTube platforms, as well as among youth I knew in Tonga, the character of 'Sione Mango' is often employed as a kind of humorous, none-too-intelligent Tongan everyman. The surname 'Mango' is considered particularly funny because of its association with the fruit, and it is not a real Tongan surname.

the poor job seeker will secure employment. The plot twists, however, when the employer says, 'Wait! Your name is Sione *Mango*? Where are you from? Who is your family?' The two young men quickly discover a distant connection between relatives. 'Well, your resume isn't so great, but you're a Mango. Come in tomorrow, we'll find you work!' The employer says, and the clip concludes.

Within just two hours of posting, this clip had been viewed over 2,700 times and had received 318 likes. One year later, it had around *80,000* views, 3,000 likes, 715 shares and 428 comments—which is perhaps even more surprising when considering that about 110,000 people live in the Pacific Island nation of Tonga, although many other people claiming Tongan heritage live in diasporic communities elsewhere.

The clip's humour relies on the apparent ubiquity of this experience and the ways that it affects youth who are currently seeking jobs. Its ability to collect likes and comments, with many laughingly narrating similar experiences, revolves around a sense of discomfort among youth in regard to the practices of relying on family connections to find employment. The comments also reveal an emerging understanding of the desirability of formal employment and the perceived stress of finding a job. It is notable that the characters in the clip are young; it would not have seemed as funny to the many Tongan commenters if the actors were older adults, because older adults often expect and rely on their familial ties to create the 'pathway', or *hala*, to success in all areas of life. This short clip encapsulates one of the paradoxes of seeking employment among the youth in Tonga with whom I work: the growing desire to find a good job based on one's individual qualifications and without the help of family connections, but the stronger moral obligation to find a job in any way possible to help one's family. For many Tongan youth, the drive for individual 'empowerment' and success is intricately entangled with notions of obligation to care for others within the circle of social relations (see Cole 2004; Cole & Cole 2007; Durham 2007).

While many people in Tonga have historically been involved in formal employment of some sort, only in the past few decades has professional waged work become increasingly important as the country moves from a primarily subsistence-based economy to a more global, capitalist-based system. At the same time, however, the path from school into the workforce is not a foregone conclusion for youth and, in fact, many families rely on at least some of their children staying out of the formal employment system to help maintain the household and their family's land for crops. Still, the growing trend towards formal employment has led to new opportunities and aspirations for young people as they move from their school years into the more uncertain and liminal status prior to full adulthood. New pressures have also accompanied these new possibilities. Tongan youth on the outer island of 'Eua felt a keen sense of obligation to find a job and to help with the mounting everyday expenses at home, but the pressure to seek employment often outstrips the jobs that are available. In my research and in discussions with aid organisations in Tonga, I found that youth reported feelings of 'stress' about finding work as well as a moral responsibility to work. Older adults highlighted this social change to me as well, noting that it seemed as if more young people wanted to work outside the traditional home-bound labour of farming, fishing or producing culturally significant handicrafts. It appears that a re-evaluation of youth is happening, moving from being defined by relative freedom from responsibility to being assessed for the value of possible paid and productive labour. Moreover, government mission statements and non-government organisation workshops project a spirit of obligation to the nation and its cultural heritage, while simultaneously espousing neoliberal visions of individually driven 'entrepreneurial' and 'proactive' youth that seem in direct competition with traditional Tongan ways (*anga faka-Tonga*). Tongan youth seeking employment, or dealing with the realities of unemployment and underemployment, present an intriguing case through which to understand the ways in which shifting roles and responsibilities on multiple levels within a local context do not always map neatly onto neoliberal notions of individual 'empowerment' and independence.

This chapter investigates the movements of youth on the island of 'Eua in Tonga as they attempt to find work and reconcile their goals and ideals with reality. In doing so, I also examine the ways in which discourses about youth and, in particular, youth unemployment become entangled with discourses of neoliberal modernity in Tonga. 'Euan youth in a variety of employment situations must all struggle to make sense of the disjuncture between their imagined possibilities for work, their sense of moral obligation to work and the actual choices that work presents.

Methods

My research on youth employment and unemployment on the island of 'Eua in Tonga grew out of a previous project focusing on how the processes of global modernity affected youths' ideas about morality and family responsibility as they engaged with new forms of digital media (Good 2012). In 2008–09, as part of my larger fieldwork, I volunteered at 'Eua High School and worked as a volunteer with the 'Eua Youth Congress, the regional branch of a nation-wide youth organisation. I also conducted participant observation with several social groups of youth across the island, participating in a range of daily life activities for young people, such as attending church youth groups, helping with chores and simply hanging out. Along with this, I conducted approximately 50 long-form interviews with students from 'Eua High School, as well as youth who had dropped out of school and those who had graduated from high school. The interviews that I conducted covered several topics, including those related to family responsibility and to youths' wishes for the future. In doing so, I collected initial observations about the employment prospects and career aspirations for young people.

Then, in 2016, I began a new research project that was specifically directed at examining unemployment, employment and entrepreneurship—topics that had begun to emerge in the conversations of my research participants and that garnered considerable attention among local media sources, government ministries and youth organisations. I discussed employment opportunities and experiences with employers and hopeful youth employees in Nuku'alofa, the nation's capital, as well as on the island of 'Eua. While on 'Eua, I conducted interviews with youth who were seeking work, as well as those in a variety of positions, including teachers, military personnel, utility operators, petrol station and grocery store attendants, and workers in the tourism industry. My previous interviews in 2008–09 were particularly interesting to revisit, with some of the same research participants who for the most part now held vastly different positions from those we had discussed. Finally, I had the opportunity to 'job shadow' a few research participants as they went about their work day. These methods allowed me to observe the ways that an increased attention to formal employment for youth had affected the lives of youth in this specific context.

A Neoliberal Monarchy in Transformation

The sociopolitical context of contemporary Tongan life provides a perspective of youth futures that emerges as intriguing and unique, even within the Pacific region. Current economic development and its social effects have led the nation of Tonga into what could be described as a 'neoliberal monarchy'.[2] Shedding light on various specific manifestations of neoliberal capitalism and its social reverberations allows us to better understand the complexities of recent economic and cultural transformations around the world, while avoiding the trap of inaccurately conceiving neoliberalism as a homogenous, and homogenising, process (Freeman 2014; Harvey 2005).

I characterise Tonga as a neoliberal monarchy because of the ways in which the nation attempts, and at times succeeds, to embrace elements of neoliberal capitalist currents that circulate around the world in a way that is distinctly influenced by its particular forms of government and cultural traditions. The privatisation and deregulation of markets, a decoupling of social services from public institutions and a shift to responsibilisation of individuals for their own financial successes have been identified as some of the standard hallmarks of neoliberalism since the late 1970s and early 1980s (Harvey 2005, p. 3; Trnka & Trundle 2017). Over the past few decades, aspects of Tonga's economy and society have followed suit. Beginning in the late 1980s, utility services, including electric power and communications (landline phones), were separated from government oversight and were privatised. Following this, changes in regulations opened the country to private multinational mobile phone companies and, later, to internet and satellite television providers. In the early 2000s, the government of King George Tupou IV began to move towards significant changes in government that would allow a greater representation of the majority of the population and other transformations (Besnier 2011; Campbell 2008). Transnational aid organisations and foreign government assistance had long been a part of the Tongan social landscape, but, particularly following the political riots of 2006, programs for youth involving employment and entrepreneurship skills proliferated. Programs

2 I wish to thank Catherine Trundle and Susanna Trnka for their help in suggesting this label for my description of Tonga's entry into a locally specific form of neoliberalism.

that were targeted at building various skills among youth reflected the discourses and central tenets of neoliberalism, which will be discussed in further detail below.

However, throughout the slow process of the development of this neoliberal, capitalist system, distinctive traits of the Tongan monarchic cultural tradition continued to hold considerable sway within mainstream discourse. Tongan people continue to uphold traditional values of respect (*faka'apa'apa*) that are rooted in a cultural and governmental system that characterises all Tongans as possible relatives and, more specifically, as siblings—thereby requiring care and generosity (Philips 2004). While popular support has seemingly grown for a more accountable and representative government, many Tongans who I know still have a sense of love and devotion towards the King and the royal family. Perhaps, most significantly, everyday social relations on the island of 'Eua still revolved around ideas of reciprocity and relations of exchange in concentric and overlapping networks of family, church affiliation and village membership that extended outward, even to island residence. Although privatisation and a gradual shift towards a capitalist economy was occurring on 'Eua and across Tonga more generally, kinship ties and other social relations of reciprocity remain critical to life. For these reasons, Tonga presents a unique case for examining the extent to which neoliberal values have affected people's lives. In particular, the growth of a neoliberal capitalist market in Tonga has motivated both the discourse regarding youth unemployment as a concept worthy of attention and the particular traits and experiences that youth have with regard to formal, waged labour.

Youth, Flexibility, Mobility and Obedience

In some notable ways, the socialisation of children throughout their years of schooling and growing up on 'Eua produces youth that mirror the qualities associated with an idealised neoliberal subject. However, paradoxically, these qualities have been cultivated in youth for certain reasons that do not necessarily coincide with those neoliberal values. Characteristics that are commonly associated with a 'neoliberal self' include flexibility and adaptability (Freeman 2014, p. 19), in which the subject becomes a collection of skills that can be added to and 'marketed' in specific ways, depending on the context (Gershon 2011, p. 539). Further, neoliberal subjects must be flexible and adaptable to new situations and demands of 'the marketplace', without any rigid reliance on the known ways of doing things, and they must be mobile enough to adapt to new places and new demands (Freeman 2014, p. 20). The neoliberal subject is ideally self-reflective and in control of himself or herself as well.

Tongan cultural notions of child development somewhat paradoxically follow similar guidelines, although they also diverge from the ideas of the neoliberal subject in important ways. Throughout childhood, the notion of unquestioning obedience to elders is reinforced both at home and at school (Morton 1996, pp. 91–96). However, a side effect of this constant emphasis on obedience (*talangofua*) that I observed among young children and youth on 'Eua was a heightened sense of flexibility and adaptability. Children learn from a young age that they do not have much control over their environments or over the expectations that adults have for them. They are simply taught to obey requests and to complete specific tasks without questioning the reasons behind them. Somewhat surprisingly, this leads to an attitude of considerable flexibility and adaptability to different situations as children grow older. As I observed youth at their jobs, it was fairly common for friends and relatives of the same age to stop by for a chat. In several instances, the young person who was working called on their friend to help with a task. Due to their socialisation involving help with whatever was requested, youth had an impressive ability to catch on to various tasks and complete them fairly quickly, with minimal supervision or instruction. It appeared that while obedience to orders might conflict with a spirit of neoliberal self-supervision and independence, the underlying flexibility and adaptability that it produced in this context helped youth become accustomed to the needs for these traits in their employment positions.

The expectations for and experiences of youth on 'Eua reflect a need for a certain type of nimble adaptability to a transforming world. However, rather than simply emphasising a flexibility in the mastering of multifaceted skills, the lived reality of these youth instead reveals a flexibility of aspirations and acceptance—making do with employment and living situations that perhaps do not take advantage of variety of skills that youth have developed. The paradox of the present for youth at this juncture in the development of Tonga's economy and its embrace of a locally particular neoliberalism is that, rather than an 'opening up' of opportunity or even a renewed emphasis on efficiency, rationality and goal-driven individualism paving the way forward, youth regard their futures as laden with new stress, competing responsibilities and ambiguous pathways that lie ahead. Youths' experiences show a mix of optimism, possibility and coming to terms with the paradoxes of the present.

Several large transnational NGOs have funded development programs that were targeted at youth, including a few entrepreneurship and small-business management workshops. These programs, as one member of a youth organisation enthusiastically explained to me, 'help everyone! They help the youth, but also women, families, the village, at home … it's good for everybody, if we can get them up and running!' As I talked to members of this organisation who had received a sizeable grant to promote organic farming among youth cooperatives, it became clear that the program was operationalised in a way that melded characteristically neoliberal discourses of youth 'empowerment', efficiency, rational decision-making and entrepreneurship with a separate discourse of relational thinking and care of others. Youth who participated in the program, according to another youth leader, would 'become their own advocates' and 'make their own pathway, have their own business'. The benefits of the program were simultaneously couched in language that made it clear that youth would be expected to share their profits to help their parents, families and extended kin. They would also share the responsibility of continuing the program by teaching others. As they learned the principles of making a business plan, keeping strict accounts and looking out for their own competitive business, emphasis was still placed on how this would help others in the youths' social worlds, extending to how to serve the economic needs of the nation as a whole.

As youth become involved in programs to develop skills or to seek employment in already-existing businesses, more youth begin to feel as if they *must* find a job, and the idea of youth as a carefree and relatively low-responsibility time of life begins to shift. The entry of youth into the developing workforce becomes spurred on by, but also sometimes thwarted by, the idea of a young person as the 'ideal worker' in Tonga. Youth are regarded as physically strong and capable of quick, energetic movement, unlike older adults who may feel both physically weaker and culturally constrained to project a sense of high-status, impassive stillness. As labourers, youth are valued for their image of obedience and their relatively low status in Tonga's highly stratified and hierarchical cultural order, meaning that few adults would have any qualms about giving them instructions. This can at times create a sense of conflict when youth are urged to make their own decisions and become 'proactive' in entrepreneurship and new work skills trainings.

Coming back to the initial opening story, another paradox of finding employment for Tongan youth revolves around the understanding of selfhood and relationality as they relate to the act of looking for work. The neoliberal discourses that dominate Tongan youth organisations and much of the education system have begun to stress the idea of empowerment and self-reliance in a way that is quite new for Tonga, in which traditional beliefs consider individuals embedded in networks of caring relatives to whom one calls on for help and is obligated to assist in turn. The idea of the 'neoliberal individual', however, focuses on one's ability to act in the interest of only oneself, without the help of, or the responsibility to, others. What has transpired, then, is that many young people espouse a desire to find work without relying on family connections for 'help' in securing a position; however, these goals often had to be abandoned, as people realised that this might be the only way that they could get work.

For example, a young woman named Malia told me the story of how she had prayed regularly for guidance in both seeking the right kind of work and then finding a job in that field. She finally had found her 'calling' in agribusiness and she knew that she could possibly have used family and church connections to help her, but she wanted to find a job 'on her own, with the skills she had learned in college'. After several months of being turned down for jobs, however, she finally told an uncle her troubles and had a secure position at a supply outlet for government agricultural works in about a week.

Dreams for the Future

As is the case in the United States, Australia and New Zealand, secondary school–aged youth in Tonga were socialised to think about their future and about what kinds of dreams they had for career aspirations. However, realistic pathways to those dreams did not always exist for Tongan children, and the idea of dreams for the future were also cast in terms of *family* responsibility and *family* conversations. The ability to have a personal dream about a career goal was often tempered by discussions that youth were involved in with other members of their family regarding what their role would be, whether to stay home to care for parents or whether to enter a particular profession for the good of the family, such as a nurse who might be able to help care for elderly family members at home. Goals also varied widely based in part on the resources of the family, or on what might be regarded as an emergent socioeconomic class position. Connections to family in diasporic communities and access to educational opportunities made a difference in the ways that youth thought about possible options for either career training or eventual employment (Lee 2003; Lee & Francis 2009).

As I discussed employment and unemployment with youth and adults in 'Eua and through my observations, it became clear that although youth feel increasing pressure to find work after they have completed their schooling, it is still not the case that a specific narrative of 'school to work transition' exists. In other words, it is not taken for granted that one will immediately find a job after secondary school, or that one will automatically enter some sort of tertiary program or even that finding a job immediately following upper-level education would be possible. Families on 'Eua still relied on young people in the family to help with the labour of farming, fishing and other self-provisioning activities—and when formal waged employment was unavailable, many youth spent their time working at home instead, altering their visions of what the future might hold.

Possibilities and Paradoxes: Three Case Studies

To show some of the ways in which opportunities for employment and pathways to work unfold for youth on 'Eua, I will employ three specific case studies of young people who I have come to know well over my long-term fieldwork. Each of their experiences shows the ways that flexibility, mobility and adaptability become critical to gaining employment on 'Eua. Moreover, their stories highlight the ways that youth, even when employed, still occupy a liminal position in Tongan culture, with considerably more responsibility and autonomy than children, but are still dependent in some ways on older adults.

Tomasi

The ways in which a sense of moral obligation to help one's family financially and how mobility and flexibility play into employment opportunities for youth are well illustrated in the story of Tomasi's path to becoming an elementary school teacher. Cheerful and always incredibly helpful to others, 21-year-old Tomasi was also an avid user of Facebook and we had kept in fairly regular contact online in the years since my last visit to 'Eua. He invited me to visit his classroom at the elementary school, which he had meticulously decorated with colourful learning charts and optimistic slogans. Tomasi seemed to enjoy his work as a schoolteacher and so I was surprised when he told me that he had not always intended to go into education. Tomasi's story lends insight into the distributed agency of career decisions for youth on 'Eua and into the many other perspectives of the possibilities and motivations for finding work.

Tomasi told me that his tight-knit family often discussed plans for the future as part of their nightly prayer time. Many families on 'Eua came together in the evening to read from the Bible, pray together and discuss important events or deliver counselling and advice (*'akonaki*) to the children. Tomasi said that he had always wanted to become a nurse and that this had been in keeping with what his family had discussed. However, at the time that he graduated from high school, the national nursing education program required all applicants be 18 years or older. Tomasi had managed to pass through his education with flying colours quickly, and so he had graduated at age 17. Rather than wait another year to apply for the nursing program, Tomasi and his family decided that he should apply to the Tonga Teachers' Training College—and he was accepted. Both nursing and teaching are considered quintessentially stable and respectable civil service positions in Tonga. Although it seemed surprising to me that Tomasi would so easily make the switch between two quite different career aspirations, he said that he became quickly happy with his decision because it would allow him to learn new skills and find a job through which he could begin to earn money for his family.

Tomasi confessed to me that he was shy and intimidated in the first year of his teacher education, being the youngest student and having come to study from 'Eua, an island whose inhabitants are often stereotyped as being less attuned to cultural standards than other Tongans. Tomasi's experience also reflected the need for adaptability to new situations, as well as flexibility and mobility. Tomasi moved from his home island of 'Eua to the main island of Tongatapu to attend the teacher training. While on Tongatapu, he said that he moved between multiple sets of relatives over the period of his training. It was fairly common for children and young adults from ʻEua to periodically visit relatives on Tongatapu or to be sent there for longer periods of time for school or work. The relatives were expected to take the children in as part of the understanding of family obligations among extended kin, yet it seemed that this could sometimes stretch social relations and food stores to near-breaking point. For Tomasi, living with extended family on Tongatapu was further complicated due to the fact that his nuclear family had converted to the Mormon faith, while many of his extended relatives remained affiliates of more mainstream Christian churches. This led to tension and disagreements between the young man and his relatives, which he said occasionally caused him to doubt whether he would be able to complete his studies. However, he finally finished the teacher training course and was delighted to discover that he was near the top of his class, which would guarantee him a teaching placement. Tomasi was able to secure a position in an elementary school on ʻEua, so he moved back into the home of his parents.

As he told me the story of his training and employment, Tomasi frequently repeated the idea that his efforts to achieve his goals were not only for himself, but for the good of his entire family. He regarded his success in the teacher training program as a reflection of his commitment to his family and as a way of showing his love for his parents. He understood this as something of a reciprocal process; in Tomasi's mind, his success and eventual employment was a way that he could return some of the love and generosity with which his parents had cared for him. Tomasi also told me that when he received his pay cheque, he immediately turned it over to his parents to contribute to the upkeep of the entire family. He highlighted that this would change when he eventually got married, for then his responsibility would shift towards providing for his own wife and children—though he was still offering help to his parents and siblings when he could.

Tomasi and I also talked about the ways that his Mormon faith had influenced his decisions to work and how it might affect his future. His faith and religious beliefs guided him during times of difficulty in his studies, Tomasi told me, and the beliefs of the Mormon Church seemed to influence his decisions to contribute his earnings to his nuclear family. As a young man in the Mormon Church, Tomasi was eligible to apply for a two-year international missionary post. Many Mormons do their mission service in their late teens or early 20s, but Tomasi delayed his missionary service for a few years to begin his career as a teacher. At the time we talked, Tomasi had decided that he would apply for a mission post soon, within the next few years, and he was unsure about whether he would return to teaching or not after his service. Although he had devoted considerable time and energy into his training to become a teacher, Tomasi told me that, following his service, other opportunities might present themselves and he might consider those—or maybe he would even apply for nursing school. Rather than committing to a career for life, as it seemed many people of older generations had done after training to be teachers or other civil service positions, Tomasi seemed more inclined to explore his options, as did many other Tongan youth with whom I spoke. Tomasi's life as a young, emerging adult had already taken a path towards the future, which involved moving for career training, work in a field that was different from his original goals and the possibility of changing careers later on—all influenced by a deeply held religious conviction.

Lesieli

When I arrived in the capital city of Tonga for research in July 2016 and met with friends at the main office of the Tonga Youth Congress, I was surprised to learn that a young woman who had been a former student in my English class at 'Eua High School had now become the office manager for the 'Eua Youth Congress branch. Lesieli, now in her early 20s, had come to this position through a roundabout series of paths, but she had become quite passionate about her work over the course of her first year with the youth organisation. The story of Lesieli's employment with the 'Eua Youth Congress highlights the ways in which new possibilities for youth employment have emerged, the adaptability of youth to new opportunities that are presented to them and some of the modes in which longstanding gender ideologies might still constrain who gets which jobs.

When I arrived on the island of 'Eua, I was able to find Lesieli and arrange an interview with her. We met in the 'Eua Youth Congress (EYC) office, in a relatively new meeting hall building that had been divided into offices with unpainted plywood partitions. The EYC offices shared the building with a Vanilla Farmers' Cooperative and, as we chatted, the smell of thousands of vanilla pods curing in the warm sun outside wafted pleasantly through the building. Despite the unfinished appearance of the building, Lesieli herself was dressed in a neat, professional skirt and blouse and her cheery smile was accented with bright pink lipstick. Lesieli's dress and mannerisms symbolically reflected how seriously she took her position as a paid office employee in contrast to the volunteers, who filtered in and out of the building in more casual attire. Later, we took a tour through the farm structures behind the office where the EYC's equipment for their organic coconut oil–pressing project was stored. Lesieli had been hired in part because of a major grant that the Tonga National Youth Congress had received to partner with a transnational aid organisation in developing new small-business opportunities related to agriculture that would specifically benefit rural women and youth. Over the course of our conversation, the program consultant from the aid organisation stopped by to review the project with Lesieli and joined our discussion.

Lesieli had graduated from 'Eua High School and then went on to study for a tertiary certificate at a vocational school in Nuku'alofa. She recounted how she had returned to 'Eua after her studies and quickly tired of 'just sitting around, doing nothing'. Few employment opportunities were to be found near her village, she said, so she spent her time helping her family with the daily household chores and visiting her friends. One day, an old schoolmate asked Lesieli to join her in volunteering for the EYC. The young woman wanted to participate in the club but was too shy to go by herself because the group was typically dominated by young men, some of whom came from other villages. Lesieli went with her friend to volunteer for a trash clean-up at one of the nearby beaches and found that she enjoyed working with the group. She continued to participate in meetings and events as a volunteer. When the project to produce coconut oil began to grow, she was offered a formal position as office manager with a small salary—and she had been working at the EYC ever since.

Lesieli enjoyed her job and discussed her passion for working with youth and helping to combat the issue of unemployment that was frequently discussed among youth organisation workers and in the mainstream Tongan media. She also seemed quite acutely aware of the ways that the process of seeking work affected young men and women differently. 'We haven't been able to get many women to participate', she said, 'because they feel ashamed/embarrassed [*mā*]. There are too many young men that work, and the women get embarrassed'. The traditional Tongan cultural value of *mā* (shame or embarrassment) is a form of moral sentiment (Mattingly 2013; Throop 2012, p. 159) inculcated in young people to show respect for elders and for upholding particular social relations within the Tongan cultural context. Particularly for young women, *mā* signals their awareness of cultural standards prohibiting young women from openly socialising with young men whom they do not know, which would be interpreted as possibly signalling romantic or sexual interest. Feelings of *mā* are often performed by young women in the appearance of shyness, in avoiding eye contact, hiding or showing physical reluctance to take part in activities, and by pulling sarongs, hoods or other clothing over their faces. More broadly, showing signs of shyness or embarrassment was often interpreted positively by older adults as a sign that young women knew the cultural values of the demure, 'pure' femininity that they were meant to uphold. However, in the case of young women seeking employment, the socialisation into this particular moral sentiment poses a paradox: showing oneself to be *mā* in the presence of strangers might reflect a certain type of respect for traditional Tongan values, yet it also prevents young people from participating in forms of interactions that are necessary for many types of employment. The moral sentiment of *mā* had kept Lesieli and her friend (as well as many other young women) away from volunteering for the EYC at first, Lesieli told me, but they had overcome their shyness and 'acted bravely', according to her, so that they could participate.

As she described her current position, Lesieli discussed the ways that it had been difficult to find young women to work in the coconut oil program because of their shyness. She also attributed some of this shyness to the types of work that the project required. The coconut oil project required participants to gather coconuts from their own farmland and to bring them into the youth centre, where they were then processed and pressed for oil. Although both men and women perform farm work on 'Eua, gender ideologies associate this kind of outdoor, dirty, physical labour with men and masculinity, whereas women's work is regarded as light, clean and located in the home (Morton 1996, pp. 100–101). Because of these longstanding ideologies, attracting young women to the coconut oil program proved to be difficult. However, Lesieli and the program consultant who chatted with us claimed that there was one thing that helped to overcome young women's reluctance and *mā* regarding the program: income. The women told me that once other young women realised that they could be paid quite well for their efforts to bring in coconuts and, sometimes, to help with processing the coconuts into oil, they became more interested and less embarrassed. Lesieli also mentioned that the organisation had done some work to promote the idea of women-only teams working together at the same time, but that this was still in development.

It was clear that Lesieli enjoyed the work that she had found with the EYC and the opportunities that it provided for socialising with other young people. In contrast to the other youth that I spoke with about employment, Lesieli did not emphasise the fact that her work helped her family through her financial contributions; however, Lesieli did mention that she was happy to be working in a way that provided youth with support. Throughout the interview, she returned to the idea of working with youth as a means of helping her community and, in a way, fulfilling her culturally understood responsibility towards assisting others (*fai fatongia, fe'tokoni'aki*).

Towards the end of our conversation, it became clear that while Lesieli enjoyed her work and hoped to continue working with youth into the future, the position itself was not totally secure. After we had talked for a while inside the office, Lesieli, the program consultant and I took a walk through the drying vanilla and into the coconut-processing sheds behind the offices. Here we saw that the processing equipment had become dusty and dirty through lack of use, covered in cobwebs and other farming equipment. The two women told me that the program had been a great success in recruiting young people to bring in coconuts, but that they were having difficulties in establishing a market base and encouraging local consumers to purchase the oil products for cooking or the soap products for personal use rather than buying the imported vegetable oil and soaps from the shops. Some of the products had been sold successfully in the local eco-lodges, but the tourism trade could not fully support the production. Lesieli and the program consultant said that the Tonga Youth Congress had been exploring export markets, but that it had yet to find a viable solution. Part of the problem, they said, was that the production volume had been too high for local markets, but that it was insufficient for export markets and that storage of products to build up a base had also proven difficult. Lesieli's job was partially funded through the grant and, if the project did not continue, her position might be eliminated. This was a fairly common issue among the young people who I talked to that had found work with non-profit organisations on 'Eua and on the main island of Tongatapu—often the work was quite satisfying and both financially and morally fulfilling for youth, but positions could be temporary or precariously dependent on continued aid funding. Lesieli remained optimistic about her future prospects but, in a typical fashion for youth on 'Eua that I had encountered before, she shrugged her shoulders and laughingly said, 'But who knows, I might go back home [to resume housework] or get married', which she saw as the effective end to her career with youth organisations.

Sita

Finally, the early employment pathways of a young woman named Sita reflect the uncertainty, mobility, flexibility and moral responsibility of Tongan youth as they move from family dependents to a role with greater perceived obligation to assist with family expenses. Sita was a 21-year-old young woman who lived with her parents and a large family of siblings, in-laws, nieces and nephews in the centre of the biggest town on 'Eua. Sita told me a bit about her employment history and the ways that she and her family worked together to make economic decisions on a sunny afternoon as she rested between her morning shift as a babysitter and her evening shift at the island's bakery. Sita had pieced together a number of different work opportunities on the island of 'Eua and had secured regular employment in a migrant work scheme abroad without significant education or special skills, reflecting the ways in which youth on 'Eua cultivate 'flexibility' and accept change as part of life. The ability of Sita and others I knew to adapt to new opportunities and work requirements as they arose was particularly remarkable for their casual acceptance of these changes, so the flexibility seemed almost commonplace rather than a new or imposed aspect of a contemporary neoliberal era.

Although Sita told me that she was never a good student and laughingly claimed that she was only interested in English so that she could watch foreign movies, she and her sisters had a fairly high degree of English fluency and practised their spoken English as often as they could with me, tourists on the island or with each other. Their older siblings, as well as their aunts and uncles living nearby, had nearly all spent some time overseas in New Zealand, Australia or the United States, and the younger sisters would often talk about the stories that their older relatives had told them about living and working abroad.

Sita had left school after failing her Form Five certificate exam three times (the maximum number of times that students were allowed to sit for the exam). Following that, she began helping one of her older sisters in her work of cleaning up the Methodist church in town and taking care of the minister's home. When her sister got married and had children of her own, Sita 'inherited' her sister's job as a housekeeper. Later, Sita found work as a babysitter, which was a relatively new type of waged work on 'Eua. Many people believed that families should be able to care for their own children or that they should rely on the help of extended kin, so paying for childcare—or being paid to care for others' children—seemed unusual at first to many people on 'Eua. Sita came across her babysitting job through a relative's co-worker. Over the years, Sita worked at many temporary jobs in housekeeping and other odd jobs that are traditionally done by young women. She told me that she felt it was important for her to find work so that she could contribute financially to her family. Sita's mother had a chronic illness and her father and brothers provided for the family by working on the farm and fishing. She saw her contributions as one of the few ways that the family could earn money apart from relying on relatives' occasional overseas remittances.

In 2015, Sita was offered the opportunity to go overseas as part of a group of women who would travel together to work as fruit-picking and packing labour in Australia. Sita discussed the opportunity with her family and they decided together that she should go. The overseas job represented both a chance to make significantly more money than she was able to in her cleaning or babysitting positions around 'Eua, and she was also excited by the idea of travelling to new places and meeting new friends. After completing a successful six-month trip, Sita returned to 'Eua and was already submitting her paperwork to go again the following year. She had made some close friends and said that she enjoyed the work, which she described as easy, if a little monotonous. Sita had also quickly found another job while back at home on 'Eua. Again, through friends of relatives, she had heard about an opening at the island's only bakery. At first, she was a little hesitant about the job because it required working at night with a small group of young men who she did not know. However, after once again discussing her options with her parents and family, she decided to give it a try. Later in the week, I visited Sita at the bakery with a friend. After she had given us a free loaf of bread to snack on, she showed us around and described the process of producing the industrial loaves. She was happy to provide for her family with her job and was especially happy about the added bonus of discounted bread, which was a rare treat for most families on the island. Sita's feelings of moral responsibility towards helping her family financially, her willingness to listen to her parents' advice and follow their suggestions about work and her industriousness in taking the positions that were available to her seemed to indicate the ways that youth on 'Eua are socialised from a young age into habits of flexibility and mobility, which are qualities prized by both Tongan adults seeking obedience as well as a neoliberal order.

Flexibility, Mobility and the Future

The case studies of Tomasi, Lesieli and Sita help to illustrate some common themes that I found throughout my interviews and observations with working youth on the island of 'Eua (Good 2012). While the entire nation of Tonga could be described as an economic system in development, the relatively rural island of 'Eua presents some interesting challenges that are specific to its own context. The people of 'Eua recognise an increasing need for cash, not only to pay the utility bills and school fees that they have become accustomed to over the years, but also to provide for new expenses, such as packaged food from the store to supplement their self-provisioning, fuel for the cars that they have grown to rely on and internet and mobile phone service. The availability of jobs has not grown at the same pace as the need for cash, which relates to the first of the common themes represented in the case studies. As in the case of Lesieli, youth on 'Eua who would like formal employment often found a lack of jobs that matched their credentials or desired goals for their professional futures. As both Lesieli and Sita did, youth on 'Eua must thus accept the jobs available to them if they wanted to work. As mentioned above, youth were often encouraged at school and by their parents and relatives to cultivate specific dreams for particular professions and visions of the future—but, in reality, they often had to settle for any position available, at least for the time being. In contrast to the experiences of young men in India, as described by Craig Jeffrey (2010a, 2010b), who decided to take additional university degrees rather than become unemployed or work in a less-desirable position, or the experiences of young men in Ethiopia who languished in a state of unemployment while waiting for a respectable job (Mains 2007), the youth who I talked with about their work and who I observed in their jobs were willing to accept a variety of positions because of the moral responsibility to contribute to the family's resources. In Tomasi's case, he was fortunate to find a position in an 'Euan school that fit with his training and amended, yet intended, goals. However, not all schoolteachers are able to find work in the place and at the level they want, and many must decide between working as a teacher in another location across Tonga or staying with their families at home. Youth on 'Eua had to maintain a level of flexibility and acceptance in securing employment if they wished to work at all.

Along with the flexibility and acceptance of types of work available, I was also struck by the ways that many youth acquired formal waged employment through relatively informal channels. Both Lesieli and Sita found jobs through social connections and did not complete formal application procedures, which highlights the paradox discussed above regarding the ambivalence that youth feel towards relying on networks for resources, including jobs. Tomasi was able to acquire his position because of his strong performance within the teacher training program, which could indicate that more established positions like those in civil service might require a more formal type of application process. However, Tomasi said that he did not need to complete interviews or additional steps to acquire his position because his class standing in the program guaranteed him employment.

Finally, the requirements for mobility and adaptability to new environments can be observed to some extent across each of these case studies, particularly for Tomasi and Sita. Tomasi's job training required him to leave his home and stay with relatives for the duration of the program, and his placement might have required further mobility. He also expects to move internationally for his mission service and was uncertain as to whether he would find a position on 'Eua when he came back. Likewise, Sita had taken jobs in several different villages across the island of 'Eua before embarking on a pattern of circular migration between Tonga and Australia to participate in seasonal labour, which could provide better wages than local employment. The youth presented here in these case studies, as well as nearly all my other research participants, also expected that they might move away from their home village and birth family eventually for marriage, work or both. The circumstances that have led youth to an increasing focus on finding employment have also led them to expectations of increased mobility and uncertainty for the future, even as they exhibit considerable adaptability to these changes.

Conclusion

In the last few decades, Tonga has self-consciously constructed itself as a globally connected nation, enacting classic neoliberal policies including the deregulation and privatisation of services that are formerly provided by the government and opening up to transnational corporations with the products and marketing budgets to establish a strong presence in the economy and in the minds of youth. The government's latest strategic development plans also emphasise 'flexibility', 'strategising for success' and 'more modern and progressive skills'—hallmarks of the neoliberal efficient and rational individual. Shifts in government on a broader scale that cede some of the powers of the monarchy to a more representative and democratic parliament also reflect social transformations that are underway. Within this context, government ministries and non-profit, non-government organisations alike have begun to produce a widely circulating discourse of youth unemployment that is accompanied by new programs and workshops that aim to reduce this 'problem'.

Young people on the outer island of 'Eua felt an increased pressure to find formal employment, but they confronted significant challenges in finding work. Focusing on job-seeking youth in a context of uneven economic development and rapidly changing discourses regarding the place of youth such as can be seen in Tonga can help to provide a finer degree of nuance in understanding the processes that are associated with the idea of neoliberalism. The case studies presented here highlight the cultural specificity of the projects of neoliberal capitalism and the ways in which social transformation does not always occur in a cohesive, homogenising way. Flexible and adaptable, yet eschewing, individualistic models of agency—and driven by perceived moral responsibility to family—the 'Euan youth who discussed their lives with me presented complex portraits of a Pacific present in which mobility and change were expected parts of life and the future seemed uncertain. For the youth on 'Eua, it seems quite likely that the future will continue to present both opportunities for new experiences and the pressures that come with new possibilities.

References

Besnier, N 2011, *On the edge of the global: Modern anxieties in a Pacific Island nation*, Stanford University Press, Palo Alto, CA, doi.org/10.1017/S00104 17515000183

Campbell, I 2008, 'Across the threshold: Regime change and uncertainty in Tonga 2005–2007', *The Journal of Pacific History*, vol. 43, no. 1, pp. 95–109, doi.org/10.1080/00223340802054719

Cole, J 2004, 'Fresh contact in Tamatave, Madagascar: Sex, money, and intergenerational transformation', *American Ethnologist*, vol. 31, no. 4, pp. 573–588, doi.org/10.1525/ae.2004.31.4.573

Cole, J & Cole, D 2007, *Generations and globalization: Youth, age, and family in the new world economy*, University of Indiana Press, Bloomington.

Durham, D 2007, 'Empowering youth: Making youth citizens in Botswana', in J Cole & D Durham (eds), *Generations and globalization: Youth, age, and family in the new world economy*, Indiana University Press, Bloomington, pp. 102–131.

Freeman, C 2014, *Entrepreneurial selves: Neoliberal respectability and the making of a Caribbean middle class*, Duke University Press, Durham.

Gershon, I 2011, 'Neoliberal agency. Special section: Keywords', *Current Anthropology*, vol. 52, no. 4, pp. 537–555, doi.org/10.1086/660866

Good, M 2012, 'Modern moralities, moral modernities: Ambivalence and change among youth in Tonga', PhD thesis, University of Arizona, Arizona.

Harvey, D 2005, *A brief history of neoliberalism*, Oxford University Press, Oxford.

Jeffrey, C 2010a, *Timepass: Youth, class, and the politics of waiting in India*, Stanford University Press, Palo Alto, CA.

Jeffrey, C 2010b, 'Timepass: Youth, class, and time among unemployed young men in India', *American Ethnologist*, vol. 37, no. 3, pp. 465–481, doi.org/10.1111/j.1548-1425.2010.01266.x

Lee, H 2003, *Tongans overseas: Between two shores*, University of Hawai'i Press, Honolulu.

Lee, H & Francis, S (eds) 2009, *Migration and transnationalism: Pacific perspectives*, ANU Press, Canberra, doi.org/10.22459/MT.08.2009

Mains, D 2007, 'Neoliberal times: Progress, boredom, and shame among young men in urban Ethiopia', *American Ethnologist*, vol. 34, no. 4, pp. 659–673, doi.org/10.1525/ae.2007.34.4.659

Mains, D 2012, *Hope is cut: Youth, unemployment and the future in urban Ethiopia*, Temple University Press, Philadelphia.

Mattingly, C 2013, 'Moral selves and moral scenes: Narrative experiments in everyday life', *Ethnos*, vol. 78, no. 3, pp. 301–327, doi.org/10.1080/00141844.2012.691523

Morton, H 1996, *Becoming Tongan: An ethnography of childhood*, University of Hawai'i Press, Honolulu.

Philips, S 2004, 'The organization of ideological diversity in discourse: Modern and neotraditional visions of the Tongan state', *American Ethnologist*, vol. 31, no. 2, pp. 231–250, doi.org/10.1525/ae.2004.31.2.231

Throop, CJ 2012, 'Moral sentiments', in D Fassin (ed.), *A companion to moral anthropology*, John Wiley & Sons, Malden, MA, pp. 150–168, doi.org/10.1002/9781118290620.ch9

Trnka, S & Trundle, C 2017, *Competing responsibilities: The ethics and politics of contemporary life,* Duke University Press, Durham, NC, doi.org/10.1215/9780822373056

3

Economic Changes and the Unequal Lives of Young People among the Wampar in Papua New Guinea

Doris Bacalzo

Introduction

The first time that I conducted fieldwork in a Wampar[1] village in Papua New Guinea (PNG) in 2009, I talked a lot with young interethnic people who spoke about their contested belonging. These were children with a father who was culturally categorised as an ethnic 'other' relative to the Wampar, and they were accordingly excluded from inheriting and accessing land of the lineage of their Wampar mother. To be born only with a Wampar mother was no longer a guarantee of incorporation into a Wampar lineage group, which is a reversal of practices in the previous generations. The older generation of the parents explained that economic conditions have changed, which prompted them to make this critical social differentiation. Seven years later, upon my return to the same village in 2016, I observed newer forms of inclusion that, to an extent, are a

1 I use the term Wampar here as the locals do when they identify and differentiate themselves from other ethnic groups in PNG. In this chapter, unless otherwise specified, I refer to the Wampar in my field site and not necessarily the whole of the Wampar-speaking and self-identifying population in Morobe province that are mostly linked by kinship and that share similarities, but also show differences that cannot be solely reduced to the particularities of their ecological and geographic circumstances.

reversal of the earlier exclusionary politics. An investigation into what happened within just a decade that so affected the lives of young people of interethnic descent among the Wampar is the focus of this chapter. I situate their experiences and the implications for their future in the current context of local engagements with competing large-scale capitalist projects.

Young people's participation in the household and local economy form aspects of their development that are thus bound to particular social relations and cultural context (Lancy 2018). Among the Wampar, kin relations are central to the organisation of social life (Beer 2006a) and to the experiences of the young: the way in which a person is categorised socially and relationally bespeaks certain political possibilities and determines the rights to inherit and access land. Claims of ownership to property such as land, and the rights and entitlements over it, are thus about social relations between people (Hann 1998). Among the Wampar, to belong to a *mpan*—the social unit defining how land is held, which is normatively, and increasingly in practice, reckoned via patrilineal descent—entails being able to exercise and enjoy crucial socioeconomic rights to the fruits of collectively and customarily held land. Young people of interethnic descent with non-Wampar fathers thus have to negotiate kin relations and other social circumstances to be able to use land as a productive resource. The experience of growing up and the constraints and possibilities for young people's future are, however, also very much inflected by rapidly changing economic conditions, as these have effects on the social relationships, including those connected to land and its use. Claims and forms of ownership over land are changing, with direct consequences to all involved, especially to those with only a tenuous claim to this form of property.

The transitions in economic life among the Wampar are progressing with increasing rapidity. Within a few years, people went from subsistence production and a more locally and directly controlled production of cash crops for the domestic market to an increasingly internationally and globally controlled capitalist economy with the entry of large-scale, internationally financed industries in the form of mining, biomass energy[2] and palm oil production. When land, as property, and its ownership has to be institutionalised in ways defined by the state, as a prerequisite

2 Biomass energy is a renewable form of energy that is sourced from organic materials, which in my field site is being developed out of wood from eucalyptus trees to generate electricity.

for engaging with these new large-scale projects, the relationships relating to land tend to change also, undergoing a revaluation that implicates membership in landowning units (Minnegal et al. 2015). These reconfigurations of economic life thus also directly implicate kin relations through the emergence of new corporate forms of ownership, leadership and the means for control over land. While lineage leaders keenly take the lead in the process of reordering relationships and in engaging with the new global capitalist projects, the young people in the background are at times more critical of the changes, as they are directly affected by the decisions that their elders made.

Focusing on young people allows me to highlight the consequences that these realignments have on the less powerful and to establish some conjectures about possibilities for the future. Young people of interethnic descent are in a particularly tenuous position—for within just a decade, they have been exposed to marked changes to the political legitimacy of their claims to membership in lineage groups, from inclusion to exclusion and then again inclusion, implicating their access to land and the benefits emanating from it. The embeddedness of young people in particular political and economic contexts thus shapes their life trajectories, with some in a better position than others. Their experience is further differentiated by the circumstances of the family and lineage of which they are a part.

In this chapter, I situate the possibilities and limits of full participation in economic life for young people of interethnic descent among the Wampar in relation to the organisation of social relationships as affected by changing economic conditions. I maintain that outcomes cannot be delinked from historical processes of social transformation, both locally and globally, because the effects of changing economic conditions and the process of encompassment (LiPuma 2001) have repercussions on the organisation of property relations. I further explore the emerging social conditions with the introduction of new forms of representational and legal collectivities in the process of corporatisation that is quickly transforming the organisation of membership and decision-making processes. Drawing on my ethnographic study among the Wampar in the Markham Valley, specifically in the village of Dzifasing, I first introduce pertinent sociocultural categories of differentiation in the life cycle among the Wampar before describing the rapidly changing economy in the field site and the repercussions that this has on young people of interethnic descent.

Growing Up in Dzifasing

Dzifasing is one of the eight Wampar villages situated on the vast plains of the Markham Valley.[3] It is about 60 km from the centre of Lae, the second largest city in PNG, which is a major hub of trade with an important seaport and airport and an expanding urban topography. In this setting, the village of Dzifasing can be classified as peri-urban. The Highlands Highway cuts through the centre of the village and is lined with shops, a gasoline station, two major marketplaces, a primary school, a small health centre (still referred to as an Aid Post) and a police station. The village has long attracted migrants from all over PNG, with migration increasing significantly since the upgrading of the highway in the 1970s. Aside from migrant workers, who eke out a living in precarious patronage relationships with some Wampar families, there are a high number of in-married male and female migrants who have settled down permanently in Dzifasing and who have established interethnic households and families. It is in this context of interethnic marriages that new social categories of identities for the offspring of such marriages emerged.[4]

Growing up in Dzifasing means going through life stages that are culturally marked. The Wampar term for a man is *ngaeng*[5] and *afi* for a woman. In the social life cycle, to be a *ngaeng* means to be cut out for assuming responsibilities, ready for marriage and having the skills and capacities for starting his own household. The female counterpart *afi* knows about cultivating and tending a garden for subsistence and maintaining the reproductive needs of her new household and the lineage that she has married into.[6]

Children are differentiated in Wampar terms based on relative age: the small and young child is called *garafu naron*, regardless of gender. When they reach puberty, terms become differentiated according to gender. Young women are referred to as *daer* and young men as *bangets*.

3 The other villages are Tararan, Gabsongkeg, Ngasawapum, Munun, Gabantsidz, Wamped and Mare.

4 For analysis of marriage patterns and changing demography in different Wampar villages see Beer (2006a), Beer and Schroedter (2014), Fischer (1975), Schulze et al. (1997) and Kramp (1999).

5 To make a distinction on the Wampar and Tok Pisin languages in this text, the former in addition to being italicised is underlined. In a multilingual environment, the mixing of language is very common. There are over 800 ethnolinguistic groups in Papua New Guinea.

6 While a woman's marriage to a man signals a transition towards her incorporation into the man's lineage, it does not mean cutting off her social ties, rights and obligations to her natal lineage.

At this stage, young men begin to build their own temporary house, the tao ntsa (bachelor's house)—or *hausboi* in Tok Pisin, the Melanesian Pidgin. A child or a young man is not yet socially accorded the term ngaeng, except for gender identification, as ngaeng also means male.[7] A socially mature man (ngaeng) and woman (afi) are capable, skilled and enculturated reproductive individuals with a sense of individual and collective identity and the comportment and rights that are implicated in their social relationships. Beside the Wampar terms, the Tok Pisin term *yangpela manmeri* (young people) or *yut* (youth) are also widely used.[8] In any case, it is the social meaning behind what it means to be culturally a ngaeng or afi and not the physiological age alone that counts.[9]

A ngaeng Wampar is a person who is ethnonymically identified as one of their own—for to be of a different ethnicity, a non-Wampar, is to be called yaner, a foreign person relative to the Wampar.[10] A child born with a non-Wampar father is referred to as ngaeng yaner naron, where the last term in this instance stands for 'child' or 'offspring'. Children with Wampar fathers are then called ngaeng Wampar naron. It is common to hear the terms in a mix of Pidgin and Wampar—*pikinini bilong* ngaeng Wampar (child or children of a Wampar father) and *pikinini bilong* ngaeng yaner (child or children of a non-Wampar father).

The Wampar differentiate and identify relationships by referring to one's mpan and sagaseg. The mpan refers to the collectivity of all the descendants of a named ancestor (from which the mpan takes its name) and thus can be regarded as an extended family or lineage. The term sagaseg refers to more encompassing named groupings, akin to the concept of a 'clan', which among the Wampar remains an instrumental concept in the process of adapting in the changing social, economic and political situations. Men

7 While the term ngaeng is a social marker for gender and life stages differentiation, it also simply means a 'person'.

8 The local usage of the term *yut* is rather fluid and its meaning is not bound by the age-based definition that is used by the PNG government, which ranges between 12 and 25 years old (Noble et al. 2011). It is also not unusual that unmarried and married women and men in their 30s continue to lead and participate in local youth programs.

9 Older parent generations, as those in their 50s and 60s, criticise how younger generations today are marrying too young, to mean that they are not yet culturally fit to start their own households. It does not seem unusual to find some married couples, even in their late 20s, who eat with and remain part of their parents' household, usually the husband's, for more than a year.

10 This term is mostly used for other New Guineans (Beer 2006b). The Melanesian Pidgin term, 'white man' is still widely used for foreign nationals who can be further specified based on their known country or international region of origin, such as 'Kongkong' for all those perceived to be from China. The nomenclatures are elaborated through contexts of contact and interactions—and thus keep evolving.

who are lineage leaders and who are at the forefront of such engagements are referred to as *ngaeng faring*, which is the Wampar rendering of the commonly used Tok Pisin term, *big man.*[11] The first-born son usually gains this status, but it is not necessarily exclusive to him, as other brothers can have the same recognition through their active role as spokespersons for their lineage.[12] The term *faring* is also socially associated with someone, male or female, who would already have grandchildren, the descendants of whom are vital in the social reproduction of the lineage. While women would also be referred to as *afi faring* in this same vein, they are normatively not the lineage leaders in the context of representation, especially with outside groups and with their engagement with the state and companies. However, there are outspoken and respected women who are equally heard during family and lineage meetings. There is a case of a lineage that has no sons in which the daughters stand up for their lineage. Locals recognise these daughters as the proper lineage representatives during community meetings, even if their participation in male-dominated fora is limited.[13]

In the next sections, I describe the experience of young people with a non-Wampar father and explore how recent developments and the transition from a subsistence and small cash crop economy to the entry of large-scale and international capitalist projects are effecting changes on the young people's social position and forms of incorporation and economic participation.

11 For an understanding of the Melanesian 'big man' concept, see Roscoe (2000, 2012). See also Godelier and Strathern (1991) for a clarification and elaboration of the 'big men' and 'great men' contrast in different social contexts in Melanesia. In the precolonial period, Wampar male warriors who gained prestige in their leadership during warfare are referred to as *gar a weran*.

12 The distribution of the role, as a spokesperson, is not unusual and again manifests in the current context of engagement with large-scale capitalist projects, when other brothers share the duties and responsibilities of representation and negotiations. When this happens, it is usually a mutually recognised and agreed process between the brothers.

13 On the reconfiguration of gender relations and emerging inequalities among the Wampar in the postcolonial and recent context of large-scale capitalist projects, see Beer (2018).

Economic Changes and the Effects on Social Relationships

In 2009, a local government official from Dzifasing spoke of the Markham Valley as the 'fruit bowl' of PNG.[14] The valley has considerable areas of fertile soil. Locals already sell a range of mostly indigenous varieties of cooking and sweet bananas, papaya, mango, pineapple and coconuts in their self-managed marketplaces along the highway or at the city market in Lae. Women collect these products from their gardens, where they plant several crops. These gardens are usually established on the land either of their natal or their spouse's lineages and are typically in or near secondary forests, hidden from sight if one only drives along the highway through a grassland savannah.

Before 2007, the Markham Valley had been one of the main production areas for betel nut (*buai*), a mild stimulant and an essential commodity in PNG.[15] Betel nut palms were planted either as pure betel palm orchards, usually on land belonging to one's lineage, or were then interspersed in subsistence gardens. Subsistence gardens were established in grassland or secondary forest, often not too far from one's house, even if the forest or grassland did not belong to one's lineage. Since betel nut palms have a longer productive lifespan than vegetables and some bananas,[16] the garden plot then over time is transformed into a betel nut palm orchard. People said that everybody had enough land to use for planting betel nut palms. Usufruct rights were accorded to anyone who expended labour in clearing a garden in the grassland. This right could then be transferred down the generations, and descendants of *ngaeng yaner* fathers could thus continue to use old garden sites of their fathers. While there is a difference regarding the size and location of landholdings between lineages, planting betel nut palms did not require a vast area, as they could be planted in one's backyard or in vegetable and banana garden plots.

14 The whole of the Markham Valley, touted for its fertile plains, is increasingly known in the national and international scene of business, development and media world as the 'food bowl' of PNG. See, for example, the recent report of the Oxford Business Group (2016).

15 See Sharp (2016) for a description of the betel nut trade in PNG.

16 While most bananas need to be replanted from suckers to remain productive, the Wampar also have some varieties of bananas called *oriats* and *mayamas* that produce fruit for about 15–20 years from the same underground stem.

Wampar thus had a quick and straightforward way of generating a relatively significant cash income, by selling the harvested nuts to bulk buyers mostly from the Highlands. Some men were also more actively involved in the betel nut trade as middlemen between Watut and Wampar producers and Highland buyers. Women and men alike would travel to other towns, even to the capital Port Moresby, to sell their betel nut there. People reminisce about the 1990s and the early 2000s as their *taim bilong buai,* the time when the betel nut economy was flourishing, and they always had enough cash at hand by their local standards. It was also the time that approximates what I qualify as a more 'egalitarian' local economy and inclusive social relations. Young and old people attest to how women and men, girls and boys, ngaeng Wampar as well as the ngaeng yaner among them, all could participate in the production and marketing of betel nut. Accordingly, the difference in how much money one generated at that time did not lie in how much land one's own family or lineage claimed, but on how much land one was able to *access* to plant as many betel nut palms as possible. Industriousness is a trait that locals also link to through the act of accessing available land and planting betel nut palms.

Hardworking and industrious men and women are referred to as ngaeng a gom and afi gom, respectively.[17] To be so is a desirable trait and, together with the virtue of generosity, this makes up a ngaeng or afi ngarubingin, a good person. A selfish person, in contrast, is called a ngaeng a mut-eran (literally, a person who stinks). Anyone, regardless of descent, is measured in the same terms. A non-Wampar father and his children are thus not different when it comes to the acquisition of such traits. During the time of the betel nut economy, they were neither constrained from accessing land for subsistence nor were they prevented from participating in the production and marketing of betel nut.

In 2007, an unknown pest completely devastated the betel nut orchards, rendering the palms unable to produce flowers and nuts—the trunks became brittle and often the top crown was blown off by wind, killing the palm outright. This catastrophe forced a rapid economic transition. Families had to turn back to their other garden crops to sell in local markets, while those who had available and accessible land focused on

17 Gom is a Wampar term commonly heard to refer to productive work and to a subsistence garden, which traditionally and still today is an important site for their sustenance and source of food contribution for exchange rituals and contemporary feasts in church, school and political events. See Lütkes (1999) for notions of work and economic life in Tararan, another Wampar village.

planting cacao trees and expanding their cattle herds. In contrast to betel nut production, both cacao and especially cattle require much larger tracts of land.[18] Lineage leaders began to fence land that they claimed for their lineage and, with that, disputes about boundaries and rightful ownership increased. Along with new disputes, old and dormant land cases were resurrected, reaching the attention of land mediators and the village courts.

The shift to cacao plantations and the intensification of cattle herding also linked the local economic life to the vagaries of the global market. Betel nut, being an only locally traded commodity, had its price swings, but these were seasonal and correlated to locally easily recognisable differences in supply. With cacao, if there is a bad harvest, the price on the global market could still be exceptionally low. The competitive international market similarly affects cattle farming for beef consumption and live export. Cacao plantations and cattle ranches also require a much larger work input, placing higher demands upon female and younger male labour. Gender relations are also affected, as women formerly had a dominant position in the sale of betel nuts, whereas the sale of cattle or cacao is mainly in the hands of men.

This economic downturn and the higher pressure on available land led to a preoccupation in social differentiation on who has rights to access land and who does not, and who can stay and reside on Wampar territory and who will have to leave. It was a differentiation drawn along the lines of ethnicity, descent and gender that directly affected children of *ngaeng yaner* (Bacalzo 2012). At the end of the betel nut economy, community meetings were held to discuss 'rules' to secure land for the Wampar and even to banish *ngaeng yaner* and their families from their proclaimed Wampar territory. However, the rules did not become an official law at the level of the local government.[19] The decision was left to the lineage leaders to discern for themselves regarding how they would apply the rules. Arguments for the exclusion of the *ngaeng yaner* living among them not only as settlers, but also those who were in-married men, and their sons and daughters—as *pikinini bilong ngaeng yaner*—were frequently heard. The rule, which in the words of a local government official served as a 'guide', was applied

18 See Bacalzo (2012) for the effects of the shift to cacao and the intensification of cattle herding on local social relations.

19 Papua New Guinea has three levels of government: national government, provincial government and local-level government.

variably and to different degrees. However, outright forms of exclusion existed, as in the case of a court battle between a Wampar lineage leader and a male descendant of a *ngaeng yaner* with a Wampar mother. The former wanted to prevent the latter from continuously using a piece of land that forms part of a larger area that he wanted to convert into a cattle range. The latter defended his customary right to continue the use of that piece of land that his parents had previously cleared for gardens. It is on this land that he had planted cacao that was interspersed in their subsistence garden.

Large-Scale Projects and Reorganising Collectivities

With the arrival of large-scale capitalist projects in the last few years, the formalisation of land ownership became urgent and the process of corporatising landowning units accelerated. Many different new corporate and business entities have since then been established in Dzifasing. The first project that drew local attention is a gold and copper mining project at Wafi-Golpu, which in 2009 was already inching towards feasibility. An application for a mining licence was eventually lodged in 2016. The proposed Wafi-Golpu mine is a joint venture between an Australian mining company, Newcrest, and a South African one, Harmony Gold—and together they plan to establish a world-class underground copper and gold mine that is about 30 km south of Dzifasing, upstream along the Watut River. There had been ongoing exploratory drilling for minerals in the area since the late 1970s, without much direct influence on the constitution of social groups in Dzifasing. Groups in other Wampar villages on the southern side of the Markham River have been much more invested in the endeavour to claim ownership of the area where the drilling was occurring. In several legal battles, it was argued that Wafi-Golpu constitutes the ancestral homeland of all Wampar people.

When a Special Land Titles Commission was established in 2008 to determine the customary ownership of the mine site and hearings commenced in September 2009, this also had repercussions in Dzifasing. Several *mpan* and *sagaseg* started to form Incorporated Land Groups (ILG) in preparation for being recognised as 'customary landowners' as stipulated by the state law, and being able to benefit from royalties and spin-off businesses from the mining activities. *Sagaseg*-based group meetings began to be held, primarily to raise funds for the costs of registration, which entails administrative, mapping and legal service expenses. It was a time of speculations, questions, imaginations, expectations and accommodations, but also of confrontations (Bacalzo et al. 2014), as locals, led by few but influential and competing *ngaeng faring*, began to organise themselves in relation to ideas of opportunities and problems. A new landowner association was formed with the intent to defend the interest in the mine in the name of all Wampar. This landowner association has been involved in costly court battles with other landowner associations from neighbouring non-Wampar groups over the ownership of the mining area, and they opened the membership to anybody living in the affected communities, provided that they paid an initial membership fee.

With the prospect of the development and construction of the mine and associated mining infrastructure, lineages in Dzifasing also started to prepare to benefit from potential spin-off businesses. A mining company in PNG usually has to engage companies that are established by 'landowners' to provide necessary support services, and so people started to register business names and companies to be ready once the mine started offering contracts. There was thus a proliferation of new businesses that locals first only registered on paper, without undertaking any particular business activities.

The other two companies that started to engage landholding lineages in Dzifasing were PNG Biomass, a subsidiary of the oil and gas giant Oil Search, which is in the process of planting over 16,000 ha of eucalyptus trees to fuel two 15 MW wood-fired power plants; and New Britain Palm Oil, a long-established oil palm company that intends to plant oil palm on at least 5,000 ha to establish a new oil mill in the area. Both companies are entering into long-term lease agreements with the landholding lineages and are actively competing against each other to secure land for their business projects. The leasing of land for eucalyptus and oil palm plantations is accomplished through ILGs, which means that the local landholding lineages must coordinate among themselves to form new ILGs on the 'clan' level. The two companies are aiding the landholding lineages in registering their ILGs and in surveying the land that the latter are willing to lease to the companies. Through the Voluntary Customary Land Registration process, a title to customary land can be issued to the ILG. Afterwards, the titled land can then be subleased to the companies.

PNG Biomass also created a local Business Group for the participating landholding lineages that will eventually assume the day-to-day running of the plantations.

One of the prerequisites for registering an ILG is providing a list of all members of the landholding unit. The actual writing down of names of lineage members means that lineage elders now had to make a conscious decision regarding who to incorporate and, in the case of children of interethnic descent, in what terms to include them. The changing configuration of lineage membership, to either narrow or broaden the base, is not an unusual process. As Kirsch (2011, p. 93) points out, it is characteristic of kinship that kinship relations are 'always subject to telescoping and collapse for various purposes'. In this new context of corporate forms of organisation, however, the registration and listing of membership now entail legally recognised shared rights of ownership and, presumably, control of land.

The ILG law also stipulates that an ILG needs a 'management committee' of six to 10 members, with a chairperson, deputy chairperson, secretary, treasurer and at least two female representatives. The law also prescribes the collective decision-making that will have to be supported by documented proceedings. Registering a business entity with the Investment Promotion Authority (IPA)[20] also requires setting up a management committee and a dispute settlement authority for the Business Groups—and, for a company, the appointment of directors, a secretary and the acquiring of shareholders. All this leads to the formalisation and hierarchisation of leadership that transforms the earlier, more egalitarian, fluid and situational form of leadership.

The intricacy of registering and managing businesses and ILGs requires certain levels of skills and knowledge. For lineage groups, having members who have reached secondary or tertiary education and who have strategic work experience becomes an advantage. Young people of interethnic descent are often favourably positioned in these endeavours, as some of them have achieved an above-average education. I demonstrate this in the three case studies of young people that follow and I describe how the opportunities and limitations that they face are shaped by the

20 The IPA is the PNG government agency that is 'mandated … [to] administers key PNG business laws' (Investment Promotion Authority 2018).

particularities of the Wampar lineages in which they are embedded. I focus on three brother–sister sets for illustration, although each case has additional siblings.

Case Studies

Greg and Betty[21] are examples of a son and daughter of a *ngaeng yaner* and a Wampar mother. Throughout the transition from the betel nut economy to the recent entry of large-scale capitalist projects, they fared better than most other young people of interethnic descent, as far as their experience of being included in their Wampar mother's lineage was concerned. The threat that they experienced during the height of the discursive exclusionary politics was benign and not immediate, although the overall local political climate was tense. At that time, Greg and Betty, as with their other cohorts in similar circumstances, were discursively challenging notions of who and what is 'Wampar', for they understood the rights that are attached to belonging. Greg stated:

> I consider myself as a Wampar, though my father is not from Wampar … Because I was born in a village called Dzifasing … to a local Wampar woman who is married to someone from outside Wampar … I speak the Wampar language fluently and I understand the cultures and traditions of the Wampar very well.

Betty similarly expressed this notion and emphasised her connection to the place: 'I have been brought up in Wampar'.[22] Their father is from an island province, had a tertiary education and was professionally working in the Markham Valley when he met and then married a Wampar woman.[23]

In 2009, Greg was in the upper secondary school and he acknowledged that he was well integrated into his mother's lineage, as he had good relations with his maternal uncles who were the lineage leaders. Betty was in the lower secondary school and kept herself busy in school when not helping with work in the garden or marketing her produce. Their Wampar mother's lineage has an undisputed claim to a medium-sized area

21 Names in this article are pseudonyms. Since missionisation at the turn of the twentieth century, the Wampar began to use Christian or biblical names and, since then, increasingly Anglo and Anglicised names.

22 It is not unusual to hear locals speak of 'Wampar' as an ethnic identity and in reference to a place.

23 See Beer (2006b) for marriage patterns among the Wampar, including hypo- and hypergamous marriages.

of land[24] and there was no conflict over land within their lineage. Greg was allowed by his maternal uncles to plant some cacao trees, which is unusual for a young man of his age who has a non-Wampar father. At this time, the exclusionary 'rule' limited the planting of permanent cash crops, such as cacao, only to descendants of Wampar fathers. Greg recognised that his and his siblings' situation was potentially tenuous, for, in the long run, they would be dependent on their male cousins with Wampar fathers for allowing them to continue being able to make a living and reside in Dzifasing.

Lineage leaders expressed their good impressions of Greg, his siblings and their non-Wampar father, as their comportment approximated the ideal behaviour for kin. They were *ngaeng* and *afi gom*: hardworking, focused on studying and performing the fundamental obligation of caring for the needs of their own nuclear family *and* their wider Wampar kin. When they were just born, their maternal uncles ensured that they would grow up in Dzifasing with them; this would be better than at their father's place of origin, which they assessed had a poorer infrastructure and fewer educational and job opportunities to offer. It was still a time of economic prosperity, with the booming betel nut economy. After the betel nut pest, however, Betty's future became tied to her choice of marriage partner due to the exclusionary 'rule' that ensued. Unlike her mother, who remained in Dzifasing after marrying a *ngaeng yaner*, she was made to understand that if she marries a *ngaeng yaner*, she would have to leave. If she wanted to remain in Dzifasing, she would have to marry a *ngaeng Wampar* (or remain unmarried).

In 2016, when I met Greg again, he had already earned a degree in tropical agriculture from a PNG university, but he has not yet found any secure employment. His mother's lineage has decided to lease 100 ha of their land to the oil palm company and had started to form an ILG. Their ILG comprised his mother's lineage and another lineage within the same *sagaseg*, and they used the name of everybody's common ancestor (Greg's great-great-great-grandfather) as the registered name for this ILG. Greg's father, mother and siblings were also listed as members of this ILG. They were among the first to receive a National ID card, one of the new preconditions to be registered on a family list in an ILG. His father,

24 The area is around 400 ha, which is neither small nor excessively large relative to other landholdings. Single-named pieces of land in the ownership of lineages can be as large as 2,000 ha, or as small as only a few hectares.

with experience working on oil palm plantations, is an asset for palm oil production. Greg and Betty were given official titles in the management committee of their ILG. Greg, with his degree in agriculture and tertiary education, was tapped for his skills and knowledge and was made the secretary of the ILG. Betty, who had already reached secondary school, was appointed as one of the two mandatory female representatives. She and Greg are actively participating in the administrative side of the business. When I asked them how they got to this new role, they said, 'We are only helping. We let our elders decide'. They continue to acknowledge that it is their maternal uncles, the lineage leaders, who make the decisions regarding engagements with the company and the state and the disposition of responsibilities. In return, their lineage leaders acknowledge the importance of having highly skilled and better-educated members of their lineage and continue to speak highly of Greg and Betty for their comportment and contributions.

Another example of siblings, Robert and Lani also benefit from the currently inclusive trend. Their situation back in 2009 was much less favourable than that of Greg and Betty. Robert was unable to plant cacao trees on his Wampar mother's lineage land. He then thought that his future would lie elsewhere, not in Dzifasing. In contrast to Greg, Robert did not feel comfortable in Dzifasing, being aware of land disputes that his mother's lineage has with other lineages, and of the tensions between his father and his maternal uncles about helping each other out—especially in regard to sharing financial burdens, such as school fees and the costs of court battles over land. Robert's father, Francis, reached secondary school, but since he moved to Dzifasing at the height of the betel nut economy, there was no need for him to find a job. Even during that time, though, he was pushing his children to have as much schooling as possible. Robert was finishing the last year of high school in 2009 and considered making a living at his father's place of origin, where he would have ancestral rights to the land. Robert had spent a few years growing up and going to school there and had good and amicable relationships with his paternal uncles, some of whom ran small businesses. In 2009, his Wampar lineage, along with other lineages of the same *sagaseg*, also began preparing for an ILG registration—but they did not push through with it, as amendments to the ILG law changed the process. While Robert was listed as a member of this old ILG plan, his sister Lani was not. As she is a daughter, the rationale was that she would be marrying out anyway.

In 2016, the situation had considerably changed for Robert and Lani. Robert had finished high school and had wanted to take tertiary level courses, but his family did not have the money to support his higher education. In the meantime, he had been helping his maternal uncles complete the registration forms to establish a building construction and maintenance company for their lineage in expectation of competing for contracts from the mining company. His maternal uncles made him one of the four directors of the company and appointed him as treasurer, as he is the only one in their small lineage with a completed higher secondary education. One of his maternal uncles said that they would not know how to run a business properly and are thus lucky to have Robert and his father as their relatives. Some of Robert's paternal uncles had experience in running businesses and had encouraged Robert's Wampar lineage to register a company in preparation for the mining to start. They also promised that they would come and assist them by imparting some of their business knowledge.

Their Wampar lineage has not yet entered into palm oil or biomass production agreements, as their land claims are all disputed. They are involved in an ongoing court battle over a piece of land on which another lineage had already started to plant eucalyptus trees for the biomass project. These unsettled land claims have thus far also prevented them from forming an ILG, as it would be too costly to pay both court costs and registration costs for an ILG without the help of the companies. Should they eventually be in a broader *sagaseg*-based ILG, or form one of their own, they plan to register all the family members, including Robert's father. For the time being, Robert and Lani are included as members in an ILG that their maternal grandmother's lineage is forming. Their inclusion here shows the flexibility of kin group membership that is not restricted in unilineal terms, as it can also be extended bilaterally. The lineage leaders in that group planned to engage with the oil palm company, but they later shifted to biomass. In either case, they are aware of the problematic land situation of Robert and Lani's mother's patrilineage, so they wanted to extend them the future benefits from the land lease and royalty payments.

Another case is that of Linda and Oscar. Their father is from the Sepik and he has extensive consulting experience after working at the Department of Agriculture, as well as considerable input in advising their lineage business projects. In 2016, Linda was in secondary school and, as she was performing academically well, could thus potentially reach the tertiary level of schooling. She understood through the example of her father and her brother that having a higher education and being highly skilled would be valuable in their ongoing lineage projects. Oscar, her older brother, had acquired computer skills and was continuing to educate himself by taking courses in business schools whenever they could afford it. Back in 2009, Linda was still in elementary school and was not yet fully aware of the ramifications of the exclusionary politics that affect children with non-Wampar fathers. Oscar had already dropped out of school, after having married his high school sweetheart when he was just 18 years old. Oscar was ensuring that he stayed on good terms not only with his maternal uncles but also with his male cousins who potentially would be lineage leaders when their time comes. Through his computer skills, he helped his Wampar lineage with the paperwork for their ongoing court battles and business plans.

In 2016, I discovered that his Wampar lineage was one of the first to plant eucalyptus trees for the biomass energy project on quite a large piece of undisputed land. They had started to form an ILG on the *sagaseg* level, encompassing lineages in other Wampar villages long before other groups in Dzifasing and before the biomass or oil palm company became active. They received a title for their land in November 2016—the first and only ILG to do so in Dzifasing as of 2018. They also started their own business company ahead of others. Compared to the lineage groups mentioned above, many lineage leaders in this group have considerable work experience and some have college degrees. Oscar has cousins who also attained or are pursuing tertiary education. They also have much larger areas of undisputed land compared to the Wampar lineages of Greg and Robert. Cash income from the biomass plantations was, according to the lineage leaders, spent to cover the expenses of the ILG leaders in processing the surveying and titling of their land and the costs entailed while attending court cases—but there had already been a sense of disgruntlement felt by some members, including the younger generation, regarding the distribution of money. Some young people, including Oscar, voiced their apprehension regarding how the lineage leaders made decisions and complained about not being heard enough. They fear that their lineage leaders are becoming 'yes men', that they too eagerly accept the terms of the companies without negotiating for the best interest of the lineage and the future generation.

In their ILG, Oscar was listed with the second name that was taken from his maternal grandfather, not his non-Wampar father (which is the more frequent practice). Naming practices among the Wampar that extend to the context of interethnic marriages exhibit flexibility of affiliation, as it is a social site for balancing relationships on both sides of a married couple who keep and strengthen their respective kin ties through the naming of the children (Bacalzo 2015). Oscar being given his mother's father's name as his second name thus emphasises his link to his mother's lineage, signifying his maternal uncles' claim that he rightfully belongs to their lineage.

Conclusion

Young people of interethnic descent in Dzifasing have grown up in a rapidly changing economic environment. Most, particularly those with non-Wampar fathers, thus gained an understanding of what it is like to be excluded, and they challenged this exclusion. They have come to understand the importance of belonging to a kin group and to belong to their Wampar mother's lineage. It is here that their rights and limits to accessing land and benefits are socially taking shape—from the time when economic life revolved around the betel nut and subsistence gardens, to the end of the betel nut economy, to the corporatisation of ownership of customary land through ILGs and to the structuring of businesses that are directly linked to global capital. Local kin groups that are situated at the interface of these changing economic conditions and that are in entanglements with increasingly encompassing capitalist relations of production evaluate their social position in relation to one another and with the incoming new regime of collectivities, especially with the companies that intend to use their land. In doing so, they also define the membership of their respective lineages and make decisions about extending economic and social rights to descendants of non-Wampar fathers. Social and economic participation for these young people is thus a continuing process of negotiations—not just through time as they reach a certain age, but also as economic conditions change and power relations are recast in the reconfigured organisation of kinship and property relations.

Relations of production among the Wampar have been shifting from mostly subsistence and domestic market production—in which young people were able to directly participate—to relations that involve mechanisms far removed from their previous life world. They must apprehend these new mechanisms that are structured in the organisation and dispensation of land and the expected benefits, the access to cash among them. Young people, differentiated by age, gender and especially by having a *ngaeng yaner* father, are in a tenuous position. Previously, the primary site of struggle was access to land for subsistence and small-scale cash crop production, based on the difference in ethnicity and descent and extended to gender—which are notions that they are familiar with and that they are able to negotiate in cultural terms through the relationships in which they are embedded. With large tracts of land that are now allocated for plantations, the limits for subsistence and small-scale cash crop production are becoming more defined. With this transformation, the struggle is complicated by issues regarding the distribution of financial and other forms of expected and imagined benefits, as well as the decisions about usage and dispensation of available and remaining land.

In a much more competitive environment that is buoyed by the entry of several large-scale projects, lineage leaders come to see the value of the young people's current and potential contributions of their labour, skills and knowledge. Such views make it advantageous for young people of interethnic descent who now formally became members of their Wampar lineage, with some holding key management and administrative positions. Their negotiations for meaningful 'incorporation', however, are compounded by the new and still less familiar terms of engagement under a new form of 'corporate governance'. For what is a corporate group now, when it is still largely kinship based but also having to operate by the demands and imperatives of international business corporations? With the codification of leadership positions, legal representation and collective organisations, how conflict over power position, decisions and distribution of benefits within a lineage will unfold under this new structure of governance could yet again potentially place young people of interethnic descent in a contentious position, in this generation and in the future. Leadership not in administrative matters but in decision-making for the lineage remains the key position of power, which is primarily reserved for male descendants of a *ngaeng Wampar*. The turn to ILG and corporate business entities further makes the social groups' collective unit and their relationship to land governable by the state and, by extension, by the corporations that bring in values, ideas and structures of social organisation to accumulate wealth, including the concentration of the legal capacity to the ILG.[25] The entrenchment of hierarchical relations

25 See the case of a PNG National Court decision in favour of the ILG against a clan in *Morris v. Panfilo* [2017] PGNC 278; N6976. It is a sample case in which an ILG gains legal recognition against an individual representing a clan.

could potentially limit the manner and terms of negotiations, especially for those not in a position of power. One of the effects of the entry of large-scale, capital-intensive projects is that there is not only a proliferation of new collective entities, but that lineage leaders are increasingly taking the immediate recourse to settle disputes in state courts, which is a costly process that syphons off the lineages' cash income and creates conflict in the way that money is distributed.

It is thus with caution that I have described here the positive side of how young people are becoming incorporated in lineage groups in this new context of corporate control and ownership of land. After all, they remain potentially vulnerable to exclusionary politics and continue to depend on the goodwill of their elders and lineage leaders. They also need to cultivate good relationships with their Wampar male cousins, who are the future lineage leaders. The possibilities and constraints for the future of young people with contentious descent are thus mediated by the fluidity of the local structures of relationships, such as the deployment of kinship practices in a culture of inclusive and reciprocal sociality, and conversely by the interpolation of a static ordering and disembedded social relationships that are increasingly taking shape with the corporatisation of economic life. It would not be in favour for young people of interethnic descent if they are regarded, once again, as competitors who only desire the money. They thus have to walk a thin line between engaging and helping and staying in the background. Such considerations underlie the disposition of the young people who experience the effects of changing economic conditions. It is understandable when Greg and Betty made it clear that they are merely helping, as usual, and not making the decisions.

Acknowledgements

I thank Bettina Beer, Willem Church, Donald Gardner, Helen Lee and Tobias Schwoerer for their helpful comments on the earlier versions and drafts of this paper. Research in PNG, in 2009 and 2010, and subsequently in 2016 and 2017, was made possible through the collaborative Wampar projects led by Bettina Beer, with the support of the Swiss National Science Foundation. I am deeply grateful to the young women and men and their families in Dzifasing for welcoming me into their homes and for helping me gain insights about their situation and ways of living.

References

Bacalzo, D 2012, 'Transformations in kinship, land rights and social boundaries among the Wampar in Papua New Guinea and the generative agency of children of interethnic marriages', *Childhood*, vol. 19, no. 3, pp. 332–345, doi.org/10.1177/0907568212444740

Bacalzo, D 2015, 'Names as a means of inclusion and transformation: Naming and transcultural kinship among the Wampar, Papua New Guinea', *Pacific Studies*, vol. 39, nos 1–2, pp. 108–125.

Bacalzo, D, Beer, B & Schwoerer, T 2014, 'Mining narratives, the revival of "clans" and other changes in Wampar social imaginaries: A case study from Papua New Guinea', *Le Journal de la Société des Océanistes*, nos 138–139, pp. 63–76, doi.org/10.4000/jso.7128

Beer, B 2006a, 'Interethnic marriages: Changing rules and shifting boundaries among the Wampar in Papua New Guinea', in B Waldis & R Byron (eds), *Migration and marriage: Heterogamy and homogamy in a changing world*, LIT, Münster, pp. 20–39.

Beer, B 2006b, 'Stonhet and yelotop: Body images, physical markers and definitions of ethnic boundaries in Papua New Guinea', *Anthropological Forum*, vol. 16, no. 2, pp. 105–122, doi.org/10.1080/00664670600768284

Beer, B 2018, 'Gender and inequality in a postcolonial context of large-scale capitalist projects in the Markham Valley, Papua New Guinea', *The Australian Journal of Anthropology*, vol. 29, no. 3, pp. 348–364, doi.org/10.1111/taja.12298

Beer, B & Schroedter, J 2014, 'Social reproduction and ethnic boundaries: Marriage patterns through time and space among the Wampar, Papua New Guinea', *Sociologus*, vol. 64, no. 1, pp. 1–28, doi.org/10.3790/soc.64.1.1

Fischer, H 1975, *Gabsongkeg '71: Verwandtschaft, Siedlung und Landbesitz in einem Dorf in Neuguinea*, Renner, München.

Godelier, M & Strathern, M (eds) 1991, *Big men and great men: Personifications of power in Melanesia*, Cambridge University Press, Cambridge.

Hann, CM 1998, 'Introduction: The embeddedness of property', in CM Hann (ed.), *Property relations: Renewing the anthropological tradition*, Cambridge University Press, New York, pp. 1–47.

Investment Promotion Authority 2018, *Business registration, regulation and certification*, Investment Promotion Authority, viewed 19 August 2018, www.ipa.gov.pg/business-registration-regulation-and-certification/

Kirsch, S 2011, 'Science, property, and kinship in repatriation debates', *Museum Anthropology*, vol. 34, no. 2, pp. 91–96, doi.org/10.1111/j.1548-1379.2011.01110.x

Kramp, R 1999, *Familienplanung in Gabensis. Fertilitätswandel aus ethnographischer Sicht*, Reimer, Berlin.

Lancy, D 2018, *Anthropological perspectives on children as helpers, workers, artisans, and laborers,* Macmillan, New York, doi.org/10.1057/978-1-137-53351-7

LiPuma, E 2001, *Encompassing others: The magic of modernity in Melanesia,* University of Michigan Press, Ann Arbor.

Lütkes, C 1999, *Gom: Arbeit und ihre Bedeutung bei den Wampar im Dorf Tararan, Papua-Neuguinea,* Waxmann, Münster.

Minnegal, M, Lefort, S & Dwyer, PD 2015, 'Reshaping the social: A comparison of Fasu and Kubo-Febi approaches to incorporating land groups', *The Asia Pacific Journal of Anthropology*, vol. 16, no. 5, pp. 496–513, doi.org/10.1080/14442213.2015.1085078

Morris v. Panfilo [2017] PGNC 278; N6976.

Noble, C, Pereira, N & Saune, N 2011, *Urban youth in the Pacific: Increasing resilience and reducing risk for involvement in crime and violence*, UNDP Pacific Centre, PIFS, Suva.

Oxford Business Group 2016, *The report: Papua New Guinea 2016*, Oxford Business Group, viewed 19 August 2018, oxfordbusinessgroup.com/papua-new-guinea-2016

Roscoe, P 2000, 'New Guinea leadership as ethnographic analogy: A critical review', *Journal of Archaeological Method and Theory*, vol. 7, no. 2, pp. 79–126, doi.org/10.1023/A:1009512726844

Roscoe, P 2012, 'Before elites: The political capacities of big men', in T Kienlin & A Zimmerman (ed.), *Before elites: Alternatives to hierarchical systems in modelling social formations*, Rudolph Habelt, Bonn, pp. 41–54.

Schulze, W, Fischer, H & Lang, H 1997, *Geburt und Tod: Ethnodemographische Probleme, Methoden und Ergebnisse*, Reimer, Berlin.

Sharp, T, 2016, 'Trade's value: Relational transactions in the Papua New Guinea betel nut trade', *Oceania*, vol. 86, no. 1, pp. 75–91, doi.org/10.1002/ocea.5116

4

'Things Still Fall Apart': A Political Economy Analysis of State–Youth Engagement in Honiara, Solomon Islands

Daniel Evans

Introduction

With the assistance of outsiders (donors, non-government organisations (NGOs) and their external consultants), a steady stream of state-endorsed, youth-related policies and activities have populated the urban landscape in Solomon Islands. These efforts have coincided with, and have been shaped by, the growth of the capital, Honiara, and an attendant increase in what are now universal storylines surrounding male urban youth in the country: idleness, criminality, alcohol and drug consumption, violence and, more recently, security. It is through the prism of these various pronouncements and interventions that we can glean one version of how the Solomon Islands' state, and its outsider partners, have considered the status of urban male youth and how they have responded to them as a collective. In assessing this approach, this chapter adopts a political economy framing to understand state–youth engagement.

The proceeding discussion commences with a historical overview detailing how the state and outsiders have engaged with young urbanites in Solomon Islands. This analysis of official statements and media reporting shows that a 'youth as a problem' narrative (Wyn & White 1997, pp. 21–25) is far from new, being portended in parliamentary debates in the early 1960s and evolving into a now commonly invoked youth-related trope. It documents a history of activities in this space that were spearheaded by non-state actors, particularly 'outsiders', as defined. A feature of pre-independence debates (pre-1978) was a perennial concern with urban youth returning 'home' (i.e. the village). Also documented is the evolution of state-endorsed youth policies from the inaugural version in 1980.

Turning directly to issues of political economy, an outline of archetypal state and outsider engagement relating to youth in Solomon Islands is critiqued. This discussion initially highlights the thinness of the state and the limited resources that public officers working in this space have at their disposal. It is argued that this position contributes to low-risk, non-transformative interventions and to a form of co-production: an over-reliance on outsiders—largely international donors and NGOs who apply globally orthodox methods of youth engagement. Standard iterations of their approach are presented. The second half of the chapter is concerned with documenting how outsiders, in the form of a number of international NGOs, and the state, in the form of members of parliament (MPs), are encountered by male youth residents in two urban field sites of Honiara: Burns Creek and White River. Following John Cox (2009), these entry points provide helpful contrasts between efforts for youth development that endeavour to incorporate 'active citizenship' (NGOs) and those that are based largely on 'passive clientelism' (MPs).

While it is acknowledged that 'youth' has a fluid, relational meaning in Solomon Islands, this chapter generally follows the official definition. Most of the young men quoted were aged between 18 and 34 years at the time that they were interviewed,[1] although a broader demographic of males was spoken to, some of who were mature, married men.

1 Youth in Solomon Islands are defined as 'persons between 15 and 34 years of age, inclusive' (MWYCFA 2017, p. 14). Prior to 2017, youth were those aged 14 to 29, inclusive (MWYCFA 2010, p. 4).

A Note on Framing and Methodology

This chapter draws on traditional elements of political economy analysis (see DFID 2009; Fritz et al. 2014; Menocal et al. 2018), albeit confined to the issue of youth and telescoping between the national and the local. It seeks to broadly document and understand the relationships between actors in the youth development sphere who possess political and economic power. This involves moving beyond bald assessments of institutional responses and engaging with those political, economic, social and cultural drivers that influence youth development in Solomon Islands. The discussion presented is particularly concerned with how underlying incentives and constraints have shaped policies and activities (with a focus on youth-related 'projects'); who are the 'winners' and 'losers'; and, through the use of examples involving NGOs and MPs, what the implications are for the interventions detailed: why did things end up the way that they did (Menocal et al. 2018, p. 1)? This chapter touches on the political economy of the outsider development industry itself, including the way it represents its activities, the language it employs and the infusion of its approaches into the 'everyday' of Solomon Islands.

This chapter draws on interviews and observations that encompass a period of fieldwork from May to December 2016 and intermittently throughout 2017 and 2018.[2] This was conducted in Burns Creek, a peri-urban community located around 8 km to Honiara's east (population approximately 5,000) and White River, a more established urban community located around 4 km to the west of the city centre (population approximately 6,000–7,000[3]). Both are popularly, although perhaps erroneously in the case of White River, referred to as 'settlements'.

Differences characterise the two field sites. Most Burns Creek residents are of a Baegu or Lau-Baelelea background, language areas of north Malaita. Malaita is the most populous province of Solomon Islands. A degree of subterranean enmity characterises the relationship between these

2 Conducted as part of the author's PhD research focusing on male youth interactions with, and views of, the Solomon Islands state and its institutions. This entailed around 130 interviews with young male residents in the two field sites, as well as with government officials and others. Pseudonyms are used throughout this chapter. All interviews were conducted in Pijin and were then translated into English.

3 At the last census (2009), Honiara's Ngossi ward, where White River is located, had a population of 10,062 (SIG 2013, p. 5).

two language groupings,[4] which has a bearing on youth interactions, as discussed below. Many Burns Creek residents are squatters, in the sense that they do not hold legal titles to the land on which they reside. White River is a mixed community, with the main ethnic groupings being Malaitan, Renbel, Temotuan and Gilbertese. Most of the land is registered and, unlike Burns Creek, residents generally have access to state-provided services, including water, electricity and sanitation.

Historical Overview of Interventions in the Urban Youth Field

In the public sphere, the emergence of urban youth as a topic of national discussion in Solomon Islands occurred in the 1960s—a time when Honiara was still in its infancy.[5] The dominant theme of the first parliamentary debate on this subject can be summarised by the chosen tagline: 'the youth problem in the B.S.I.P [British Solomon Islands Protectorate]' (BSIP 1964). This provides an insight for how the topic of young Solomon Islanders was being shaped in public discourse. Its mover, Dr John Kere, argued that 'this problem' (the youth problem) had not yet arisen in the Protectorate, but that the tenor of the discussion was one of impending trouble. In a prophetic portrait of youth migration to the fledgling capital, he argued:

> There is a drift of the youth away from the village life into towns like Honiara and Gizo because it is attracting the youth with its entertainment and life in the town. The village life is dull for the youth and he tries to get away from the council work, and the work of the Churches. The youth is trying to get away from all this work to a much easier life. (BSIP 1964, p. 146)

The next parliamentary foray into the subject of youth occurred almost a decade later (BSIP 1973a, p. 328). In the intervening period, although Honiara had transformed—from a sleepy town of around 6,700 people in late 1965 to what was becoming, by Melanesian standards, a fully-fledged metropolis of some 11,200 people in 1970 (BSIP 1972, p. 11)—the discourse relating to youth had not. Young people had, however,

4 See Harold Ross (1978, pp. 122–123), who details historical mistrust and antagonisms between Baegu and Lau groupings.

5 Honiara become the capital of Solomon Islands in the mid-1940s, utilising remnant Second World War infrastructure that was left by the departing American forces (see Moore [forthcoming]).

graduated from being a budding problem. The country needed 'to take careful note of the crosscurrents which threatened to cause it to founder on the rocks of unrest' (BSIP 1973b, p. 4). The 1973 adjournment debate was replete with now common motifs: there was 'worry at the number of juvenile delinquents in towns' (BSIP 1973a, p. 4), youth had lost respect for their 'elders' (1973a, p. 4) and they were 'restless' (1973a, p. 332). Ultimately, there was 'no answer yet to the problem' of youth (BSIP 1973b, p. 4), although one issue had been firmly resolved: the Rubicon of 'youth as a problem' had been crossed with a hand-wringing narrative now entrenched in the public consciousness.

A moral dichotomy is evident in the media representations of young people in the 1960s. The most commonly reported topic was church youth group happenings: the timing of get-togethers and the activities of various denominations. These reports were interspersed and, to some extent, contradicted by articles on youth-related criminality and social disturbances, particularly public drinking. A recurring youth-related concern registered in parliamentary debates in the lead-up to independence was the utility of a 'white-collar' education as opposed to vocational and technical training, particularly in agriculture (the latter championed by first chief minister and former prime minister, Solomon Mamaloni; see Chevalier [forthcoming]).

While pre-independence governments had provided financial support to youth associations through their social welfare division, little evidence of structured engagement can be found until the late 1960s and the first half of the 1970s, with the establishment of the Honiara-based community centre in 1969[6] and the emergence of the first significant youth-related initiative in the capital in 1975: the Masta Liu Project.[7] Both received a portion of government funding—although they were notably initiated and managed by outsiders.

The Masta Liu Project was aimed at 'young people who come to Honiara and cannot find work' (The Solomons News Drum 1976, p. 3). Following a standard model of youth engagement (see Evans 2016), a concurrent

6 The Honiara Community Centre, operated by the Solomon Islands Christian Association, was largely directed towards 'young, single men' (BSIP 1969). Its early incarnation included a youth club, short courses and sporting activities.

7 Masta liu incorporates the English word 'master' combined with 'liu', derived from north Malaita (To'abaita language area) meaning to walk around aimlessly. It is typically used to describe unemployed youth who roam Honiara's streets (see Frazer 1985; Jourdan 1995; Palmer 1979).

focus on soft skills (personal development such as punctuality and reliability) and technical skills (carpentry, agriculture and electrical work) was featured.[8] This was done with the hope that young men would return to their village homes, where they could use their newly acquired abilities to help 'their own' (The Solomons News Drum 1977, p. 5). The project appealed to what was then a nascent but now common theme: that of unemployed urban males. The project coordinator encapsulated this position: '[I]t is really keeping the boys off the streets preventing social problems caused by unemployed gangs' (1977, p. 5).

Government efforts to develop a youth policy emerged shortly after independence. The first policy was released following a White Paper on the topic in 1980. It was accompanied by the most extensive parliamentary debate on the status of youth to that date. As with subsequent iterations, the policy was largely concerned with matters related to education, livelihood and youth participation in 'cultural, political and spiritual development' (National Parliament 1980, para. 2.1). An annual government grant to a newly instituted National Youth Congress was provided, as was the establishment of a National Youth Training Centre at Aruligo, west of Honiara.[9]

Following the inaugural youth policy, further iterations were produced in 2000, 2010 and 2017.[10] 'Guiding principles' for youth development were released in 1988. In addition, urban youth policies directed towards Honiara-based youth were drafted by the Honiara City Council in 2006 and 2011.

Since the end of a period of civil conflict that stretched from 1998 to 2003, a parade of youth-related interventions of varying degrees of reach, duration and effectiveness has also been performed by outsiders

8 The project largely involved the provision of a small wage and equipment to carry out agricultural work (Palmer 1979), although it included animal husbandry, carpentry, electrical work and odd jobs for private individuals and companies (The Solomons News Drum 1977, p. 5; interview with Charles Fox, National Youth Congress).

9 This fell into disrepair during the civil conflict of 1998 to 2003. An effort to build a youth centre in Honiara in the 1990s ('the Rainbow Project' funded by the British High Commission) failed to eventuate (interview with Charles Fox, National Youth Congress). In 1994 the 'Commonwealth Youth Program South Pacific Centre', funded by the Solomon Islands government, was established in Honiara (Scales 2003, p. 46), but it was discontinued in March 2014.

10 The 2010 policy was accompanied by a series of provincial youth policies. In late 2017, a triumvirate of documents were produced: a 'National Youth Policy 2017–2030'; a 'Strategic Framework for Youth Development and Empowerment'; and a 'National Youth Employment and Entrepreneurship Strategy'. The first two documents were released in August 2018.

in Honiara with state consent, a number of which are touched on below. Similar to the pre-independence position, the provision of small grants to youth groups has remained the state's preferred modality for its modest recurrent funding of youth activities (see footnote 12).

State Thinness and the Role of Outsiders

Official youth programming in Solomon Islands has since independence seen a focus on outputs over outcomes and 'process turned into product' (Yanguas 2018, p. 11). Workshops, meetings and policy development—including a never-ending need to 'consult'—have become ends unto themselves. Despite the steady stream of policies documented above, official youth-related objectives have more often than not been left unrealised. The 1998–2003 conflict stymied efforts in all areas of government service provision at the start of the new millennium, but it was the issues that were frankly outlined in the 2010 Youth Policy that better explained this inertia. Youth were identified as a 'low priority for governments from 2000–2008', with there being 'no real sense of ownership' of initiatives (MWYCFA 2010, p. 3). Similar concerns were repeated in the 2017 policy (MWYCFA 2017, p. 12), with implementation 'found wanting'.

Within the Solomon Islands' bureaucratic state, relatively innocuous foundations help account for the current position of state–youth engagement: a thinness of the state (an inability to project its authority and provide services across the country) together with a failure to dedicate the resources needed to fulfil its plans and policies.[11] My discussions with, and observations of, public servants working in the sphere of child and youth development and, to a lesser extent, the related areas of health and education underscored the miniscule resources that they had at hand, as well as the over-reach of plans. Allocations invariably decreased as the distance from Honiara increased. I was repeatedly told that beyond meeting recurrent costs, particularly payroll, there was little left over for policy implementation. This is not uncommon in the developing world. In an analysis that rings true of the Solomon Islands experience, Thomas

11 This argument is premised on an assumption that policy statements in Solomon Islands represent an agreed and intended course of action—a proposition not without contention.

(2015, p. 76–88) documents how globally poor governments 'govern less', with 'the size of the gap and its implications [being] underappreciated' (2015, p. 77).

Historical budget allocations for youth-related activities in Solomon Islands show that they are negligible on a per capita basis, particularly in relation to rich liberal democracies—a position that has seemingly always been the case.[12] This helps explain the lack of ownership that is documented in the 2010 youth policy and it contributes to the otherwise publicly minded state officials giving up any hope of making a difference—they simply do what they can or do nothing at all. As Luis Eslava and Lina Buchely (2019) highlight in the security and development context, I would contend that the prospect of interventions succeeding in the youth field in Solomon Islands are 'very small'. In discussing urban Colombia, they argue that a key reason for this is macroeconomic in nature. While not to suggest that money is the sole solution, the same, somewhat banal but infrequently acknowledged, explanation can be proffered for Solomon Islands. In the absence of improvements to a raft of economic indicators and thus the budget bottom line, the prospect of consequential, encompassing change in the state–youth relationship seems remote.

This situation has numerous consequences. The constraints described contribute to an over-reliance on outsiders in a form of co-production. Co-production, as used here, refers to a variety of actors who provide input for the provision of public goods and/or services, though it is not citizen co-production that marks the Solomon Islands' experience (Ostram 1996; see also Mitlin & Bartlett 2018). Rather, a variety of outsiders have played the most significant role in the delivery of youth-related services, undertaking traditional state responsibilities. Contemporary and historical youth-related efforts in the country have been heavily influenced by international and domestic NGOs, regional organisations and bilateral and multilateral donors, including the multilateral banks and the 'UN system'. It is not possible to assess the political economy dynamics

12 In 1973, parliamentarians lamented the miniscule budget allocation for youth—SBD$2,000 (approximately US$250 on October 2018 rates)—being made available by means of grants to youth groups (BSIP 1973b, p. 4). The struggle to raise funds for the Honiara Community Centre (see footnote 6) was a recurring feature of media reporting from 1968 to 1972. In 2018, the recurrent budget allocation for 'youth development' was estimated at around SBD$2.5 million (approximately US$312,500). The most sizeable portion, SBD$690,000 (approximately US$86,250), was allocated to the 'national youth grant' (SIG 2018, p. 444).

of state–youth engagement in Solomon Islands without broaching the role that this group has played. Their resources invariably outweigh those that the state has at its disposal.

The dominance of outsider engagement has one tangible outcome that is relevant to the following discussion. Owing in part to the diverse and unique position that youth are observed to occupy—ranging somewhere on a spectrum from delinquents in the making to future leaders—outsider-supported interventions are overlayed by standard global development agendas that are considered ripe for youth consumption. Fashioned in New York, Washington DC or Brussels, and often couched in the language of 'rights', these norms are premised on transitory—and often cyclical—development paradigms. The suite of contemporary efforts includes good governance and anti-corruption; gender and economic empowerment (or 'livelihoods'); climate change, resilience and disaster–risk management; and peace building and security. During my period in Honiara, I witnessed all these agendas play out in one form or another. Rather than being '"on the edge" of global discourses about rights', as Sue Farran (2016, p. 401) has stated in relation to the Pacific Islands, I would argue that Solomon Islands, and its neighbours, are the ground zero of these efforts.

The situation in Solomon Islands also means that low-cost, narrow and discrete interventions are more often than not favoured. In a mimicry of the jargon of the new economy, today's engagements in the youth field often strive to apply 'innovation' (the prefix 'social' sometimes added), to be 'flexible', to encourage 'entrepreneurship' or to foster 'experimentation' (during my fieldwork, one outsider held a youth peace-building innovation summit in Honiara and another was involved in 'pre-accelerator innovation training' for youth). These initiatives—often premised on goals of 'building capacity', 'empowering', 'mentoring' and 'enhancing leadership'—seek to foster individual or group behavioural change and/or more fully integrate youth, or pockets of youth (often 'the vulnerable'), into society. Irrespective of the slew of standard descriptors that are applied, they are frequently based on weak or non-existent evidence,[13] they pay little heed to contextual variation and the results are invariably limited. Positive individual cases can be pointed to, but foundational, encompassing change is absent.

13 On the lack of nuance in contemporary youth entrepreneurship discussions in the African context, see Irwin et al. (2018, p. 11). Similarly, for a critique of 'youth entrepreneurship' in Africa, see Dolan and Rajak (2016).

Outsiders in Action: Standard Models of Youth Engagement

Operating under the constraints of funding cycles, foreign procurement guidelines and financial instructions, and monitoring and evaluation frameworks (i.e. the 'project modality'), outsider-supported youth interventions play out in a largely predictable form in Solomon Islands. As occurs elsewhere (see Ferguson 1994, p. 259), a menu of standard form engagements are employed, some better categorised as 'inputs'. Three will now be presented.

The first iteration—conducted by the state and outsiders—as well as being the most popular in Solomon Islands (fitting a geographically diverse, disconnected country), can be broadly tagged under the 'awareness' and, to a lesser extent, the 'training' schema. In addition to being standalone activities, these are often inputs to the other initiatives that are discussed here.

Awareness often involves international and/or domestic workshops, conferences and training sessions (variously framed as 'summits', 'forums', 'retreats', 'outreach' or 'dialogue'). Such efforts can be cynically regarded as an effective means by which to get 'money out of the door'. Awareness is applied equally in rural and urban communities throughout Solomon Islands—so much so that it has evolved into a verb: 'awareness' is something that is done to citizens across the country. An over-emphasis on awareness and training is a source of criticism that is evident in the two field sites. Accompanying this is a risk of perceived moralising on behalf of those advocating a specific agenda: a view that introduced practices are superior to extant norms. This is matched by a broader frustration that outsiders (of all persuasions pursuing varying agendas) will visit a community for a short period of time, impart messages and/or collect information and leave without any subsequent follow-up or any tangible benefit.

During my fieldwork, I experienced the apathy of 'awareness raising' by attending a stultifying evening presentation at the Burns Creek playing field by police and the international NGO World Vision on new family violence legislation. With the help of a makeshift projector and a sound system, the intricacies of the law—section by section—were detailed to around 20 attendees sitting in the dark. Nearby, in the light afforded by a row of parked cars, children played and youth socialised, oblivious to the messaging.

I observed 'awareness' to have a negligible effect in terms of the subject matter presented, especially that of seeking to champion behavioural change. Many of my young interlocutors ignored requests to attend events. These frustrations were articulately summarised by Junior, aged 27, a resident of White River:

> Most people who come and do awareness, the way they present it is out of date. There has to be a different way to do awareness. If I were to say 'there is an awareness being held in the playing field right now', it will be empty. Why? Because everyone knows it's just the same old approach … If it was a business, the way they are doing sales and promotions is boring. If it was presented on paper, I would just skip it and turn to another page.

The concerns expressed here are not new. In the early 1980s, criticisms regarding 'grass root consultations' in rural Solomon Islands were recorded by Joan Herlihy (1981, p. 276–277). Simon Foale (2002) presented a more recent critique by dissecting a long-term conservation project in Western Province, Solomon Islands. He documented tensions regarding what beneficiaries ('partner communities') saw as an over-emphasis on 'awareness and information' campaigns over concrete 'development' (2002, pp. 50–51). My own encounters of 'awareness' shared closer parallels with those that were documented by Anna-Karina Hermkens (2013, para. 45) concerning Solomon Islands: '[m]any of my interlocutors are tired of having to do another workshop, or attend another meeting that will improve their leadership skills, bring awareness about their rights, etcetera'.

The final two forms of youth-related intervention can potentially involve more material outcomes, or, at the least, involve youth as direct beneficiaries. The first are, as Farran (2016, p. 407) argued, 'very much slanted towards acceptable Pacific activities such as sport, culture, scouting and ministry [church]'. While the popularity of scouting has diminished in Solomon Islands, it was a variety of NGO-supported activities that centred on these other pursuits that were most visible in the field sites, as outlined below. A further version of this form of assistance is the provision of small grants that are awarded on a competitive basis to groups who are commonly involved in undertaking these activities, often youth groups.

The last form of engagement, usually of a more sizeable nature, is in the livelihood sphere. Such undertakings, of the ilk of the 1970s Masta Liu project discussed, were the largest youth-related projects that I encountered in Honiara, both by measure of funding and by participation. Two projects of this nature were being implemented: Youth at Work was instigated and supported by the Secretariat of the Pacific Community, and the Rapid Employment Project was funded by the World Bank.[14] A further, smaller livelihood program, going by the officious title Honiara Youth Development, Employment and Small Enterprise Project, was also being executed by World Vision when I was conducting research in the two field sites.

Outsiders on the Inside: Clarification, Inclusion and Exclusion

Continuing the political economy framing, the rest of this chapter follows Stuart Corbridge et al. (2005, p. 7) and inverts the lens that has been applied thus far: instead of 'looking at the ways in which the state might see its citizens', it is interested in the way the state is viewed by urban male youth. State and outsider-supported projects can play out in Honiara in vastly different ways from that which is envisaged in design documents, strategies or 'log-frames', having 'unintended consequences' (McDougall 2005, p. 96). Often community–outsider mismatches lie in axiomatic rationales with conflicting worldviews being evident. While much of the Melanesia-related literature in this space has focused on Western approaches to environmental conservation (see Filer & Sekhran 1998; Foale 2002; McDougall 2005, 2016; West 2006), it is also evident in youth and child-related programming. The key flashpoints in this domain are equally foundational concerns related to 'rights'. A Western human rights discourse in Solomon Islands (the lens adopted by almost all international NGOs and donors operating in the country) is, in the main, contested and opposed by the public—most commonly on the basis that it is regarded as contrary to what are perceived indigenous norms, which are sometimes equated with the Pijin term *kastom*.

14 This project was not exclusively targeted at youth, as it sought to have 50 per cent youth participation, defined as those aged between 16 and 29. A new phase of this project, using the acronym CAUSE, commenced in 2018.

However, resistance to the standard form project modality that is employed by outsiders (and that is internalised by the Solomon Islands' bureaucratic state) extends beyond a repudiation of rights. Such are the misgivings regarding outsiders' motivations and actions—forged by decades of encounter and anecdote—that almost all proposed interventions in the familial and social arena are subject to suspicion and contestation. 'Project' has become a dirty word across the archipelago.

The initial site for analysis is the modus operandi of youth engagement. Debra McDougall (2005, p. 81), in the context of analysing property rights and indigenous land tenure in Solomon Islands, talks of efforts to 'transform complex, crosscutting, localized relationships into rights that are commensurable, predictable, and knowable to outsiders'. The dominant concern of this approach is legal clarification seeking to encourage economic development and make Solomon Islands 'safe for capitalism' (2005, p. 83). Just as McDougall described Ranongganss'[15] desire to elucidate property rights in a foreign form, now divorced from any form of external influence, a preoccupation with clarification—documenting and ordering—was evident among portions of my young urban informants. In practice, this translated to a focus on a variety of administrative tasks: forming groups capable of being officially recognised and producing an array of written documents to demonstrate competence and order. This too, at its core, had an economic imperative, an underlying goal to make engagement by and with outsiders easy by facilitating the transfer of resources in a safe and predictable form.

In the ultimate form of 'institutional transfer' (Larmour 2005, p. 2), clarification is concerned with the appropriation of the language, aspirations and ethos of 'development'. Terms such as 'awareness', 'sustainability' and 'capacity building' were spoken by a segment of my young informants, seemingly absorbed into Pijin. In describing the most frequent requests for assistance by youth groups, a staff member at the Youth Division of the Honiara City Council said that the main priority of 'every' youth group (18 were active) was assistance with 'building the capacity of their executive'. This translated into help with, inter alia, understanding roles, writing minutes, public speaking and managing finances.

15 Residents of Ranongga, a small mountainous island in the Western Solomon Islands (McDougall 2005, p. 81).

While there were advantages to the form of engagement described, particularly for outsiders, there were potential downsides. This was demonstrated during my research with the international NGO Oxfam while implementing a small grant program for Honiara-based youth groups.[16] Their entry point was those youth groups who were affiliated with the Youth Division. In line with the political economy dynamics that were discussed, the project's fiduciary requirements undoubtedly contributed to this, allowing Oxfam to readily access an assemblage of youth who, owing to a proven ability to organise, were less likely to squander resources. Those closely associated with the project stressed the principal funder's desire to support groups that were 'sustainable'. This approach exemplifies a tension that I observed in forms of outsider youth engagement linked to legal clarification—the risk-averse modalities of outsiders often pare involvement. Owing to this methodology, outsiders and state agencies frequently engage with a narrow cohort, arguably those youth with the least-demonstrated need. Depending on the nature of the activity, beneficiaries are often far from marginal, being those that understand how the 'system' works: they are connected, urbane, educated, possess the confidence to engage and have some appreciation for what outsiders seek. This is a small assemblage of youth in Solomon Islands. It excludes most of my interlocutors in the backblocks of Burns Creek or White River who were oblivious to the opportunities available or how to unlock them—this is to say nothing of parochial social and class rivalries among segments of youth in Honiara, which can also stymie involvement. The flaws of this approach were not lost on some. When I asked Peter, a 30-year-old resident of Burns Creek, what the main problems were that young people in his community faced, he stated: 'They [the collective of outsiders] always forget the perpetrators [marginal youth]. They don't involve them in the activities that happen in the community'.

The outlined approach also exemplifies the supply-side nature of youth engagement. All significant youth-related activities that I came across involved outsiders taking the lead. While state agencies had often been conferred the title of 'implementing partners', 'implementing agencies' or simply 'partners', in truth, I saw little evidence of state implementation, agency or, indeed, partnership. This is not necessarily a criticism of such a practice, with co-production of this nature often a legitimate development praxis, especially in the face of state ambivalence

16 This went by the Pijin title, *Statim Faia* ('start a fire').

or incapacity. There was, however, little open acknowledgement of this reality, thought for how it could be surpassed and concern that it had become omnipresent and representing 'business as usual'.

The approach detailed allows outsiders to act with the imprimatur of the state, lending their involvement the legitimacy that is required, while essentially implementing projects unilaterally. This too can be partly explained by the political economy dynamics that are discussed. Outsider funds are highly ring fenced. None of the youth-related initiatives that I came across involved outsiders financing initiatives through Solomon Islands government systems. This was explicable. A public servant working in the youth arena lamented, 'No one likes to give money [direct to government] because it is mismanaged'.

Getting Burned in Burns Creek: NGO Youth Engagement in an Urban Community

The forms of outsider engagement that I observed in the field sites entailed a degree of youth organisation, but not of the same magnitude as described above. This, together with the fact that there were no direct fiduciary responsibilities imposed on youth participants, helped ensure broader involvement. These were the in situ activities most frequently performed by international NGOs, with target locations chosen owing to their perceived vulnerability. They most commonly involved activities such as sporting events or talent competitions. Conducted with the assistance of community contacts, these public occasions presented an opportunity to 'raise awareness' of any number of issues. The other forms of NGO engagement that I documented were forays into the realms of crime prevention and livelihood.

While having a somewhat ordinary appearance, outsider-devised and implemented activities in the field sites were, more than other interventions I encountered, sites of divisiveness, competition and, at times, violence. It is not possible to insulate projects in Solomon Islands from an amalgam of correlates that can conspire to frustrate, including pre-existing contests. They can become very visible arenas for acting out disputes. My observation was that the word 'project' had become synonymous with personal benefit and 'gaming the system'. Outsiders actively contributed to this situation, the modalities employed often being a direct cause of contest, as can be observed in the following examples.

Burns Creek was labelled by various informants as a 'red mark' place—a dangerous and insecure environment regarded by some as off limits. This had various repercussions. One was that it had attracted the attention of outsiders. During the time that I resided in Burns Creek and, to a lesser extent, White River, casual conversations revealed all manner of defunct NGO-led endeavours; a plethora of project detritus littering both sites, including manufactured committees and youth groups; and abandoned project infrastructure. Burns Creek appeared as the epicentre of these efforts, with post-conflict security concerns and flooding in 2014 having attracted major NGOs operating in Honiara. Its young, 'vulnerable' population was particularly predisposed to outsider assistance. This included youth-specific interventions involving the local arms of international NGOs Save the Children and World Vision. At the time of my research, only World Vision remained active in the area.

World Vision's engagement in Burns Creek was part of an Honiara-based, five-community initiative, with places chosen because of their perceived 'marginality' (a common label, although one I never saw defined; see Auerswald et al. 2017). John, a former contract employee of World Vision, said that the choice of Burns Creek as a 'target' site was due to it being a 'low place', with the idea being to 'lift the youths'.

World Vision's key undertaking in Burns Creek was part of a larger gender-based violence project. It included marshalling resident youth on a periodic basis to participate in sporting and singing competitions. The *raison d'être*, however, was not recreational activities per se, but the social messaging that was imparted on the sidelines, delivered with the goal of behavioural change. On paper, the project's objective was to use 'faith-based messaging to address community attitudes about gender and gender-based violence' (Wu & Kilby 2015, p. 4).[17] For those male youth with who I spoke in Burns Creek, this was in many respects one of the least important by-products, and relevant messaging was quickly forgotten. Few of the young participants could provide details of what awareness sessions canvassed, and they showed little interest talking about it. An informal roadside discussion with a group of five young male residents in mid-2018, over a year since World Vision's last awareness

17 The undertaking described here was World Visions' Communities for Hope project. It involved the adoption of World Vision International's Channels for Hope endeavour, an initiative that commenced in Africa. An 'end of project outcome evaluation' incorporating Solomon Islands (Meyer & Nikulainen 2018, p. 41) observed that youth involvement in the project had not been 'systematic nor … strategic'.

effort, was demonstrative. Asking what these awareness activities had involved was met with silence and blank stares until one of the boys provided a one-word response: 'violence'.

While the activities of World Vision were welcomed, unintended consequences conspired to frustrate efforts. This had nothing to do with the project's objectives. Instead, it had everything to do with the undercurrents running deep within Burns Creek. In part, these spoke to broader intra-Malaitan relations and the modalities by which youth grievances are frequently aired in Honiara, both of which have deep historical dimensions.

The most overt act of disaffection under the auspices of the World Vision project occurred following a soccer game that occurred in Burns Creek in 2015. The losing team, comprised of Baegu-language speakers, was angered with what they believed were unfair refereeing decisions. Their opponents consisted of boys who had a Lau-Baelelea background, as did the offending referee. In what is a common motif in male sporting contests in Solomon Islands, linked to masculinity and perceptions of *wantokism*,[18] the end of the game saw the losing team's anger spill over, resulting in the destruction of the soccer net and rocks being pelted at a World Vision bus, shattering its windscreen.

This was not the first time that an NGO vehicle had been targeted in Burns Creek. Peter, a 27-year-old resident of Burns Creek, detailed an incident that happened a few years earlier, invoking the familiar 'red mark' tag:

> Save the Children put a red mark on Burns Creek. One incident happened here. They [Baegu-speaking boys] stopped a Save the Children vehicle … They took the keys from the driver, demanded money and took things from inside. After that, Save the Children called the chairmen of the [youth] groups in the Burns Creek area. We went down to [their office]. They told us that Burns Creek was a red mark area and that they wouldn't be coming back.

Save the Children had a particularly fractious relationship with Burns Creek, eclipsing the problems that other NGOs had faced. At the time of my fieldwork, they no longer worked in the community. The episode

18 Relationships of mutual obligation and support, most commonly between those who speak the same language.

described above was not an opportunistic act of criminal conduct, but part of a pattern of destructive behaviour that was targeted at the organisation. Various buildings that they had constructed in the community were destroyed. A youth centre was the subject of arson. A community hall—described to me by a group of boys as a 'crime prevention centre'—had been dismantled and its materials looted, with only a concrete slab remaining. A third building—the remnants of a youth livelihoods project—sat forlornly idle, essentially co-opted by a neighbouring resident.

At the time of my research, some three years after their decision to pull out from Burns Creek, Save the Children's engagement remained a sore point. They had earned the facetious title of 'Save the Big Man', a title reflective of a belief that their involvement in the community was only benefiting one or two leaders. If this was the case, a Baegu leader that I spoke with who had been involved in the NGO's endeavours relayed little sense of benefit, or gratitude, explaining that they were 'banned':

> Because they made a lot of promises but did nothing. They told lies. I was chairman twice,[19] for about four years. Nothing happened. I don't really know what they were doing too. They would just come and visit, sing [makes clapping noise with hands] and that was it. I think if they really wanted their project to work, they would have someone come and stay in the community all the time. Have an office here. That's the way to do it. But they would aimlessly hang around and then go back to their office.

This portrait was an exaggeration designed to denigrate Save the Children. Nevertheless, it was demonstrative of a fracturing of trust, with portions of the Baegu community deliberately targeting the organisation and the default position becoming one of contestation. The Baegu youth that I spoke with shrugged their shoulders when I quizzed them on this, explaining that maybe 'community leaders' did not cooperate with the NGO. The underlying, unspoken trigger for the breakdown was, however, directly related to the political economy of youth engagement. In a theme that I was to hear occasionally, it was apparent that the Save the Children's failure to pay community members ('leaders') involved in the project was the underlying cause of angst. A 29-year-old Baegu youth, related to the leader quoted, explained:

19 The project being referred to was named 'Children and Youth in Conflict with the Law', which was implemented with donor funding from 2006 to 2013. The reference to 'chairman' is likely a reference to chairing a 'Crime Prevention Committee' that was established under the project.

> [B]ecause our view is … it doesn't matter even if you do small work, you must pay … So, when they [Save the Children] came here and some people did work, but they weren't paid, that's what some people didn't like.

It is a position discussed by Cox (2009, p. 975), who decries NGO–beneficiary negotiations in Solomon Islands around money, particularly in which arguments 'hamper the implementation of projects which, after all, are intended for the common benefit'. Exacerbating this situation for Save the Children was that those they failed to renumerate could muster a cohort of youth. The consequences of the breakdown of trust were clear: with the imprimatur of various 'leaders', young Baegu men performed acts of violence and sabotage against the NGO. According to others, the leader I spoke with was a key instigator of this, being the main beneficiary of the timber and iron roofing from the ransacked crime prevention centre. As an ultimate irony, a project premised on preventing crime had become a cause of community crime and conflict.

Acknowledgement of the situation was conveyed by a staff member of Save the Children who had been involved in the project. Like various youth that I spoke with, she laid responsibility for the breakdown on the shoulders of 'leadership', explaining that they were failing their youth and that they were not interested in developing their community. An initial flaw in this view was a belief that there was a coherent and legitimate cadre of leaders in Burns Creek. There was a false hope in the convening powers of various individuals who were not universally acknowledged or respected. A further mistake was a belief that NGO activities should not cost anything—that altruism should be welcomed, which is a compounded position when overlayed by a view of communities as essentially homogenous and always eager for assistance. These erroneous perceptions, not limited to Save the Children, rested on a failure to appreciate complex communal power dynamics. They helped to explain why the NGOs' projects were ultimately unsuccessful. Her assessment was also accompanied by a standard characterisation of Burns Creek youth as 'aggressive'.

A myriad of additional concerns regarding outsider engagement were relayed to me while in Burns Creek. Some believed that NGO staff were dishonest. A 30-year-old resident told me: 'The community facilitators aren't honest. They mislead because they don't have the heart for the community. They act for their own interest.' Relatedly, there was a perception that NGO staff and/or putative beneficiaries would misappropriate project assets: 'How did the project breakdown? I don't know, I think they [project beneficiaries] most have eaten [misappropriated] the money' (interview with Sam, a 42-year-old Burns Creek resident). Robert, a 26-year-old male, commented on the strictures imposed by outsiders' time-constrained engagement: 'Save the Children don't work in Burns Creek now. They must have gone to some other place. That's how NGOs work.' Finally, I recorded frustration that was felt when dealing with the wash-up of expired projects. Trevor, a public official, summarised this: 'These projects kick off for two years … and then they're all gone … donors pull them out and take their money. So, we are left with the problems. The beneficiaries are cross with us.'

'The Honourables': MP Youth Engagement in Two Urban Communities

If the approaches adopted by international NGOs can be critiqued for failing to deliver on a number of fronts, the simplicity of youth engagement as practised by urban MPs, arguably the most visible embodiment of the state in the field sites (see also Tucker 2017, pp. 138–139), stood in stark contrast. An initial point needs to be made about the status of MPs in Solomon Islands. Among many youths with who I spoke, MPs were not considered part of a collective. Generally, there were low levels of understanding regarding the prescribed roles of MPs and the manner in which the parliamentary system worked.

The straightforward transactional nature of the MP–constituent relationship in Solomon Islands—as documented elsewhere (Batley 2015; Cox 2009; Fraenkel 2011; Hiriasia 2016; Hou 2016; Tucker 2017; Wood 2014)—played out true to form in Burns Creek and White River. Textbook clientelism took place with unconditional cash handouts being received by those youth with whom I interacted.[20] Sponsoring of a variety of youth-related activities was also featured. Among many informants,

20 This was funded by MPs' constituency development funds: public funds allocated to individual MPs for their discretionary use (Wiltshire & Batley 2018, p. 1). As at 2018, the amount allocated to each MP 'hovers somewhere between SBD8 and 10 million (USD1–1.3 million) per annum' (2018, p. 1).

leadership was largely measured by these forms of largesse, together with an MP's willingness to engage with young people. These attributes overlapped, helping to shape youth voting intentions.

The visibility of MPs in the two field sites was a common topic of discussion. This was particularly so in Burns Creek, which is situated in Central Guadalcanal constituency, but being where the MP for Lau-Baelelea constituency (located in north Malaita) resided, his house was a visible landmark in the community. The presence of MPs in Burns Creek and White River, as well as the distinctive styles of politicking employed, speak to distinct state–youth engagement in the two sites as well as to other contextual variations.

Place of residence, or even birth, often bore little resemblance to the constituency in which my informants exercised their franchise. In Burns Creek, most of the people I interviewed voted 'at home' in Malaita. The most popular candidate among my Burns Creek, Lau-Baelelea–speaking informants was an MP from the northern region of Malaita. The standard quantum that he was said to have provided individual youth in return for their vote in the 2014 national election was SBD$2,000 (US$250).[21]

The incumbent MP for East Honiara constituency, bordering Burns Creek, was Douglas Ete. He drew mixed reactions among resident youth. He had no relatives living in the community, perhaps not surprising, given his mixed Malaitan/Guadalcanal heritage and, in 2010, less than a handful of his campaign managers were located there.[22] By most accounts, Ete had received few votes from Burns Creek in 2014, though this was not possible to quantify. He reciprocated by doing little there beyond reportedly providing direct cash payments to supporters, including youth. Early in his campaigning, Ete had endeavoured to build a health clinic in the community. A flagship of his election campaign in 2010, some eight years later, the shell of the incomplete clinic had become a symbol of how political rivalries can conspire to block development. Various resident youth that I spoke with had played a pivotal role in frustrating Ete's ambitions to complete the building, spreading rumours that the clinic was not his idea and that he had not contributed financially to the project.

21 Six informants stated that they had received this amount from the MP following his election.

22 In the 2010 election, Ete had about 400 people who were campaign managers (representatives for Ete in their communities, helping to marshal voters). Only four or five of these were in Burns Creek—a very low share of the overall number (personal communication, Terence Wood).

When discussing what voters in his constituency sought in the context of the 2010 election, Ete had told another researcher, 'it depends … [f]or the Burns Creek area, what you do for them [directly]' (Wood 2014, p. 159). This was demonstrated in my discussions with various Burns Creek men who had voted for Ete in 2014 and who told me that they had received monetary handouts in the weeks prior to our interviews, well after the campaign and election. Some had received one-off payments of several hundred dollars, while others had visited Ete's house regularly to request smaller sums. Brian, aged 27, described his last interaction with the MP a few days before we spoke: 'I went direct to him and I asked … "sshhh… Honourable. I'm hungry. There's nothing [to eat] at my house". He said, "Oh, here is $100 [US$12.50] son"'.

I observed benefits in the form of cash payments or in the provision of other items to be a normalised course of action, which was tolerated and expected by many youth of Burns Creek. These allocations were openly discussed, a perennial concern being to 'pick the winner' come election time to benefit throughout his or her term in office. Among various interlocutors, there was a belief that this 'top-up'[23] or 'bus fare' mindset was ingrained in voters' psyche with a dependency mentality that was now an entrenched feature of Solomon Islands politics. It was perceived as being highly unfair and a potential spark of future unrest.

Many of the young men I spoke with were also acutely aware of their marginal position relative to their senior peers when it came to interactions with MPs. Clayton, a Burns Creek resident aged 19 years old, told me how he was given $2,000 (US$250) after voting for a particular Malaitan MP in 2014:

> After I took the $2,000, I went and saw him again. I asked him [for assistance] and he gave me $350 [US$43.75]. This was only last week. I said to myself, 'eh, I need to go and check him for any money to buy betelnut or food' … With some leaders, us small men [youth] ask [for money] but it's hard for them to give it to us. They don't like to talk with us small men. But our [ballot] paper is the same as big men. If someone does [talk to us], it makes us boys happy.

23 A ubiquitous term in Solomon Islands referencing the purchase of mobile phone credit.

Emmanuel, aged 22, voted for a different Malaitan MP and had not received any benefit: 'Twice in a row I have voted for you, but you still forget me … My [ballot] paper is the same paper as all of the big men. But you give everyone a project … at least try and help me once'. He went on to describe how youth are treated when seeking an MP's assistance:

> You know what it's like in Solomon Islands. Honourables are treated like a God. So, it's hard for him to be free [to meet]. He's busy all the time in meetings, so us kids keep away. Sometimes we go past: 'Eh, you kids go away. Us big men are sitting down here.' That's the kind of experience we have.

The Constituency Development Officer (CDO)[24] of the MP for East Honiara provided his thoughts:

> They [youth] think that they are small. Low self-esteem is one issue they have. They think if they come to the Honourable, Project Officer or CDO, then they won't regard them as true people or as genuine about their request.

Politics played out somewhat differently in White River, in line with important contextual variations. None of the youth that I spoke to had received money from the incumbent MP for the West Honiara constituency, Namson Tran.[25] Instead, I observed Tran to be the first port-of-call among those seeking funding for one-off recreational activities. This appeared to be the MP's preferred modality of youth largesse. Tran's CDO explained that the MP no longer provided unconditional cash handouts, having ceased doing so in 2015.[26]

Tran was not a visible presence in White River and he did not allow constituents to visit his house, which was not located in the community. He did, however, sponsor several youth-related activities. During my time in White River, the MP had given SBD$10,000 (approximately US$1,250) to a male hip hop dance group, assisting them to travel overseas. Being home to a sizeable Renbel population[27]—with a strong

24 A public servant responsible for managing government funds for the constituency (Wood 2014, p. 173).

25 There are likely a number of reasons for this. Many of my interlocutors resided in Namoruka, an area of White River where, anecdotally, Tran did not receive a great deal of support. Similar to Burns Creek, many White River youth did not vote in the West Honiara constituency. Anecdotally, West Honiara also saw a large number of non-resident voters cast their vote there.

26 A position disputed by a number of informants.

27 Those hailing from the Polynesian outliers of Rennell or Bellona islands.

affinity for sport—he had also provided funds for rugby tournaments; his generosity was lauded. Similarly, while I resided in White River, he provided trucks to three schools.

While adopting modalities of assistance more straightforward than the NGOs that I encountered, contest and violence were also a feature of the youth–MP relationship. The physical violence that youth directed at MPs or 'the government' was a topic of discussion among my interlocutors. It also visibly played out during my time in Honiara. The mildest examples of this that I came across were the threats made by those youth who had sought assistance from MPs being rebuffed. Emmanuel, aged 22, having twice had his request for assistance rejected, had warned his MP's driver not to venture past his residence (the inference being that he would damage his vehicle should he do so). Brian, aged 27, adopted a facetious tone, laughing as he told me that because he had not received the support that he expected from his MP, he should 'shoot [throw rocks at]' his 'blue three-tonne [truck]'.

Direct violence and destruction featured in the youth–MP relationship. During my fieldwork, an incident occurred in another well-known Honiara settlement in the east, Gilbert Camp.[28] According to newspaper reports, this involved an unnamed government MP who was driving his family to church on a Sunday morning. His vehicle was 'punched' and 'youths threatened him and his family members' (Solomon Star News 2016, p. 1). The precise nature of the threat or the rationale behind it were not disclosed, with simplistic references to marijuana and *kwaso*[29] consumption used to explain away the incident.

The Gilbert Camp episode paralleled an occurrence in Burns Creek some years prior, the ructions of which remained ongoing. Many of my young informants recounted the targeting of the MP for Lau-Baelelea. This involved boys from Baegu partaking in the well-versed act of throwing rocks at the MP's vehicle. This incident had a complex backstory, with several violent confrontations having occurred. However, the underlying motivations spoke to the already detailed enmity between Baegu and Lau-Baelelea youth and the partisan political rivalries that saw Baegu speakers supporting a political opponent of the MP.

28 For a detailed, albeit dated, portrait of Gilbert Camp, see Stritecky (2001) and, for a more recent engagement, see Maggio (2018).

29 A homemade, distilled alcohol.

Conclusion

Political and economic incentives and constraints have shaped state-implemented and/or endorsed approaches to urban youth development in Solomon Islands. From the first forays in this area in the 1960s to its present-day guise, a continuity has been evident. Outsiders have dominated, acting with the consent of the state, but rarely as equal partners. Superiorly resourced, they have adopted a consistent methodology that is premised largely on the 'project modality'—an approach internalised by the Solomon Islands state. After around 50 years of effort, this has not observed an encompassing change in the youth field, nor, arguably, has it improved 'leadership'.

It is easy to point to a lack of contextual appreciation when critiquing outsider approaches to youth engagement in Solomon Islands. While it is difficult to deny that aspects of context had been underplayed in the examples presented above, the approaches that were discussed point to a dilemma. In engaging with state bureaucratic actors who work in the youth field, outsiders invariably narrow the cohort of young people that they can reach. In venturing into 'the field', irrespective of levels of contextual knowledge, they risk exposing themselves to a low-trust environment, with communities having experienced decades of problematic or unsatisfactory encounters.

MPs who have benefited from significant increases in discretionary funds at their disposal (Batley 2015) have mainly practised a direct form of youth engagement in Solomon Islands, premised on a hope of reciprocity come election time. It is difficult to assess the extent to which this particularistic approach of MPs has shaped the expectations of young people towards outsiders. There can be little doubt that the provision of direct benefits has not made the latter's job any easier, helping to entrench a handout model based on clientelism.

A number of observations can be made about the approach of outsiders and MPs as described in this chapter. First, it is the collective of MPs that should regulate, and guide, outsiders. There is little evidence of this in urban Solomon Islands. Instead, the two neither cooperate nor compete, being driven by different incentives. By no means can it be said that the Burns Creek interventions, unlike 'development projects' elsewhere, operated as a 'machine for reinforcing and expanding the exercise of bureaucratic state power' (Ferguson 1994, p. 255). Rather, the state was completely absent.

Second, and related to the first point, part of the reason for the problems that outsider-supported youth initiatives encountered was a lack of local ownership and/or a local champion. The Burns Creek NGO-initiated youth projects were left floating, with little evidence of local support. The incumbent MP for East Honiara, who, like all MPs in Solomon Islands, practised a localised form of politicking, clearly saw no political advantages in cooperating with outsider-led endeavours, nor did outsiders involve him.

Third, when MPs strive to move beyond direct, personal benefits and to implement 'projects', such as establishing a health clinic, they quickly see themselves facing the same issues that outsiders do, albeit overlayed with overt political considerations. Both MPs and outsiders respond to similar temporal pressures: the four-year electoral cycle and the two- to three-year project timeline. When faced with obstacles, the fall-back position of MPs becomes the provision of 'cargo' or the engaging of the sponsorship of one-off activities, just as outsiders are prone to favour standard form, input-based, sequestered 'projects'. The result for both actors is the same: little evidence of broad-based youth development (or, indeed, community development) and a risk of communal conflict.

It has been argued that the position towards youth development described in this chapter is understandable when applying a political economy lens. Efforts to address the status quo lie, initially, in appreciating the interwoven political, economic, social and cultural drivers that are discussed. Even then, interventions in this area that adhere to the project modality come with a high probability of 'failure'.[30] Above all, the elemental question of how to best undertake youth development in urban Solomon Islands needs to be revisited if anything beyond transitory, non-transformational change is to occur.

30 Acknowledging that, even in failure, there may be positive, often invisible, 'side effects' (Ferguson 1994, pp. 251–256).

Acknowledgements

I am indebted to those young men of Burns Creek and White River who so generously shared their stories, as well as to Honiara-based public officials and NGO staff. Thank you also to the Solomon Islands Ministry of Education and Human Resources Development and Guadalcanal Provincial Administration for permission to conduct this research. Gratitude is extended to John Van Den Akker who carefully proofread an earlier version of this chapter. For their sage advice on content, I wish to thank Terrence Wood, Joanne Spratt, Michael Goddard and Helen Lee. Finally, appreciation is extended to Clive Moore for his monumental work in digitising and generously sharing historical documents that were used in the preparation of this chapter.

References

Auerswald, C, Piatt, A & Mirzazadeh, A 2017, 'Research with disadvantaged, vulnerable and/or marginalized adolescents', *Innocenti Research Brief 2016–06*, UNICEF Office of Research, Florence.

Batley, J 2015, 'Constituency development funds in Solomon Islands: State of play', *SSGM In Brief 2015/67*, The Australian National University, Canberra.

British Solomon Islands Protectorate (BSIP) 1964, *Legislative council debates*, fourth session, second meeting of the Legislative Council, 10 June 1964, p. 145.

BSIP 1969, 'Community centre opened', news sheet, 30 June 1969, p. 5.

BSIP 1972, *British Solomon Islands: Report for the year 1970*, Her Majesty's Stationary Office, London.

BSIP 1973a, *Governing council debates*, 10th meeting of the Governing Council, 20 July 1973, p. 328.

BSIP 1973b, 'Govco 2nd session 1973 continued', news sheet, 14 December 1973, p. 4.

Chevalier, C (forthcoming), *Understanding Solo: A biography of Solomon Mamaloni*.

Corbridge, S, William, G, Srivastava, M & Véron, R 2005, *Seeing the state: Governance and governmentality in India*, Cambridge University Press, New York, doi.org/10.1017/CBO9780511492211

Cox, J 2009, 'Active citizenship or passive clientelism? Accountability and development in Solomon Islands', *Development in Practice*, vol. 19, no. 8, pp. 964–980, doi.org/10.1080/09614520903220784

Department for International Development (DFID) 2009, 'Political economy analysis how to note', *DFID Practice Paper July 2009*, DFID, London.

Dolan, C & Rajak, D 2016, 'Remaking Africa's informal economies: Youth, entrepreneurship and the promise of inclusion at the bottom of the pyramid', *Journal of Development Studies*, vol. 52, no. 4, pp. 514–529, doi.org/10.1080/00220388.2015.1126249

Eslava, L & Buchely, L 2019, 'Security and development in question: A story about petty crime, the petty state and its petty law', *Revista de Estudios Sociales*, no. 67, pp. 40–55, doi.org/10.7440/res67.2019.04

Evans, D 2016, 'Hard work: Youth employment programming in Honiara, Solomon Islands', *SSGM Discussion Paper 2016/7*, The Australian National University, Canberra.

Farran, S 2016, 'At the edges and on the margins: Hearing the voices of young people in South Pacific island countries', *The Round Table: The Commonwealth Journal of International Affairs*, vol. 105, no. 4, pp. 401–414.

Ferguson, J 1994, *The anti-politics machine: 'Development', depoliticization, and bureaucratic power in Lesotho*, University of Minnesota Press, Minneapolis.

Filer, C & Sekhran, N 1998, 'Loggers, donors and resource owners', *Policy that works for forests and people series no. 2: Papua New Guinea*, National Research Institute, Port Moresby.

Foale, S 2002, 'Where's our development? Landowner aspirations and environmentalist agendas in Western Solomon Islands', *Asia Pacific Journal of Anthropology*, vol. 2, no. 2, pp. 44–67, doi.org/10.1080/14442210110001706105

Fraenkel, J 2011, 'The atrophied state: A supply-side perspective on politician "slush funds" in Western Melanesia', in R Duncan (ed.), *The political economy of economic reform in the Pacific*, Asian Development Bank, Mandaluyong City.

Frazer, I 1985, 'Man long taon: Migration and differentiation amongst the To'ambaita, Solomon Islands', PhD thesis, The Australian National University, Canberra.

Fritz, V, Levy, B & Ort, R (eds) 2014, *Problem-driven political economy analysis: The World Bank's experience*, The World Bank, Washington DC, doi.org/10.1596/978-1-4648-0121-1

Herlihy, J 1981, 'Always we are last: A study of planning, development and disadvantage in Melanesia', PhD thesis, The Australian National University, Canberra.

Hermkens, A 2013, '"Raits blong mere?" Framing human rights and gender relations in Solomon Islands', *Intersections: Gender and sexuality in Asia and the Pacific*, no. 33, viewed 9 September 2015, intersections.anu.edu.au/issue33/hermkens.htm

Hiriasia, T 2016, 'Kin and gifts: Understanding the kin-based politics of Solomon Islands—the case of East AreAre', *SSGM Discussion Paper 2016/4*, The Australian National University, Canberra.

Hou, R 2016, 'A day in the life of a member of Parliament in Solomon Islands', *SSGM Discussion Paper 2016/2*, The Australian National University, Canberra.

Irwin, S, Mader, P & Flynn, J 2018, 'How youth-specific is Africa's youth employment challenge?', *K4D Emerging Issues Report*, Institute of Development Studies, Brighton.

Jourdan, C 1995, 'Masta liu', in V Amit-Talai & H Wulff (eds), *Youth cultures: A cross-cultural perspective*, Routledge, London.

Larmour, P 2005, *Foreign flowers: Institutional transfer and good governance in the Pacific Islands*, University of Hawai'i Press, Honolulu.

Maggio, R 2018, 'According to Kastom and according to law: "Good life" and "good death" in Gilbert Camp, Solomon Islands', in C Gregory & J Altman (eds), *The quest for the good life in precarious times: Ethnographic perspectives on the domestic moral economy*, ANU Press, Canberra, doi.org/10.22459/qglpt.03.2018.04

McDougall, D 2005, 'The unintended consequences of clarification: Development, disputing, and the dynamics of community in Ranongga, Solomon Islands', *Ethnohistory*, vol. 52, no. 1, pp. 81–109, doi.org/10.1215/00141801-52-1-81

McDougall, D 2016, *Engaging with strangers: Love and violence in the rural Solomon Islands*, Berghahn Books, New York and Oxford.

Menocal, A, Cassidy, M, Swift, S, Jacobstein, D, Rothblum, C & Tservil, I 2018, *Thinking and working politically through applied political economy analysis: A guide for practitioners*, USAID, Washington DC.

Meyer, A & Nikulainen, N 2018, *Evaluation report: PTL reducing gender based violence project*, Finnish Overseas Consultants Ltd, Helsinki.

Ministry of Women, Youth, Children and Family Affairs (MWYCFA) 2010, *Solomon Islands national youth policy, 2010–2015*, The Ministry, Honiara.

Mitlin, D & Bartlett, S 2018, 'Editorial: Co-production—key ideas', *Environment & Urbanization*, vol. 30, no. 2, pp. 355–366, doi.org/10.1177/0956247818791931

Moore, C (forthcoming), *Honiara: The village city, urban social space in Solomon Islands, 1942–2018.*

MWYCFA 2017, *Solomon Islands national youth policy, 2017–2030*, The Ministry, Honiara.

National Parliament (Solomon Islands) 1980, *Solomon Islands youth policy*, National Parliament Paper No. 2/1980.

Ostram, E 1996, 'Crossing the great divide: Coproduction, synergy, and development', *World Development*, vol. 24, no. 6, pp. 1073–1087, doi.org/10.1016/0305-750X(96)00023-X

Palmer, P 1979, 'Masta liu farmers', in P Larmour & B Waita (eds), *Land in Solomon Islands*, Institute of Pacific Studies, Suva.

Ross, H 1978, 'Baegu markets, areal integration, and economic efficiency in Malaita, Solomon Islands', *Ethnology*, vol. 17, no. 2, pp. 119–138, doi.org/10.2307/3773139

Scales, I 2003, *Youth in Solomon Islands: A participatory study of issues, needs and priorities, final report*, Hassall and Associates, Canberra.

Solomon Islands Government (SIG) 2013, *Report on 2009 population & housing census, Honiara*, Solomon Islands National Statistics Office, Honiara.

SIG, 2018, *2018 recurrent budget*, Ministry of Finance and Treasury, Honiara.

Solomon Star News 2016, 'MP threatened: Leaders must be protected, a leader's plea', 13 September 2016, p. 1.

Stritecky, J 2001, 'Looking through a moral lens: Morality, violence and empathy in Solomon Islands', PhD thesis, University of Iowa, Iowa.

The Solomons News Drum 1976, 'Master lius move in on the potato market', 12 November 1976, p. 3.

The Solomons News Drum 1977, 'Meet the masta-lius: Youth of all trades', 26 August 1977, p. 5.

Thomas, MA 2015, *Govern like us: US expectations of poor countries*, Columbia University Press, New York.

Tucker, A 2017, 'Incorporating the archipelago: The imposition and acculturation of the Solomon Islands state', PhD thesis, UC San Diego, San Diego.

West, P 2006, *Conservation is our government now: The politics of ecology in Papua New Guinea*, Duke University Press, North Carolina.

Wiltshire, C & Batley, J 2018, *Department of Pacific Affairs in brief 2018/4*, The Australian National University, Canberra.

Wood, T 2014, 'Ties that unbind? Ethnic identity, social rules and electoral politics in Solomon Islands', PhD thesis, The Australian National University, Canberra.

Wu, J & Kilby, P 2015, *Evaluation of Honiara community vision for change project*, The Australian National University, Canberra.

Wyn, J & White, R 1997, *Rethinking youth*, Sage, Sydney.

Yanguas, P 2018, *Why we lie about aid: Development and the messy politics of change*, Zed Books, London.

5

The New Nobility: Tonga's Young Traditional Leaders

Helen Lee

Introduction

The Kingdom of Tonga's progress towards democracy has been slow and, although the country has had as prime minister a 'commoner' and long-time pro-democracy activist, there is still widespread uncertainty about Tonga's political future. The King has retained important executive powers and all aspects of Tongan society are still influenced by the hierarchical ordering of the monarchy, nobility and commoners (*tu'a*). In the context of significant political tensions, an unusual initiative has been occurring quietly in the background since 2012: the formalisation of a group of the children of royal and noble families by a Tongan civil society organisation which is intent on changing, at least to some extent, leadership in Tonga. This chapter examines this group of 'young traditional leaders', asking whether it constitutes a potentially radical development in Tonga's sociopolitical context or whether it simply serves to shore up the power and privilege of the country's traditional elite.

Political Change in Tonga

Members of the royal and noble lineages in Tonga exemplify what has been described as 'indigenous modernity' (Hogan & Singh 2018). They embody 'tradition' and 'culture', but they are also members of a powerful elite in modern Tonga, and many engage in capitalist enterprises and other aspects of modernity both within and beyond Tonga. Their claims to embody tradition lie in the close connections between the current hierarchical structure and those of Tonga before European contact; although there was no 'king' then, the current royal and noble lines can be traced back to the pre-contact ranking system (Bott 1981; James 1992). Tonga's 1875 Constitution established the royal dynasty that still rules today and appointed some of the former chiefs to noble titles, which are inherited through a system of patrilineal primogeniture. The Constitution also put all of Tonga's land under the control of the royal family and nobles, dividing the country into estates (*tofi'a*) on which commoners have the right to lease allotments of land. The *kau nōpele*, the holders of the 33 noble titles, vary in their birth rank in relation to the royal family and thus in their power (James 1997, p. 56), but they all exercise considerable authority and privilege in their interactions with commoners, even those who are part of Tonga's 'educated elite' (James 2003).

As well as retaining their crucial role as estate holders, the nobles are also deeply embedded within Tonga's social structure, which centres on kinship ties and the concept of *ha'a*, or lineage. This further supports their ongoing power in society as traditional authorities within that structure; they are regarded as the heads of *kāinga*—the extended kinship groups that live on their estates (Marcus 1977, 1980). The traditional elite also symbolise the pride that Tongans have in retaining their independence throughout the colonial period.

There has been a pro-democracy movement in Tonga since the 1980s that has influenced changes that have reduced the political power of the nobles (James 1994; Lawson 1994). There was a 'momentous decision' in 2010 to amend the Constitution of Tonga to shift most of the monarch's executive powers to an elected cabinet (Powles 2014a, p. 1). Tonga's parliament was dominated by nobles until these constitutional reforms also led to a shift in power to elected 'people's representatives', with nobles retaining only nine of the 26 seats (Powles 2014b).[1] In the elections of November 2010, the people of Tonga had more power to choose their leaders than ever

1 Until the reforms of 2010, nobles held an equal number of seats in government as those held by ministers who were elected by the people. Today, certain positions in government can only be held by nobles: the minister of lands, speaker of the house and deputy speaker of the house.

before. The outcome of the subsequent election, in November 2014, was a commoner prime minister, 'Akilisi Pohiva, one of the most outspoken and dedicated pro-democracy campaigners.

During this period of political change, there were sporadic outbreaks of civil unrest in Tonga, from the first street marches in the mid-1980s to the six-week public servants' strike of 2005, and riots in 2006 that destroyed many buildings in Nuku'alofa. More recently, there have been a growing number of scandals involving members of the nobility, from possession of firearms to allegations of involvement in drug running. This has led to increasingly strident criticisms of the traditional elite, publicly by academics (Brown Pulu 2011, 2012), journalists (Moala 2002) and pro-democracy activists, and more privately by many commoners who resent being called on by nobles for services and even money and who regard them as disconnected from their people.

However, ideas upholding the importance of respect and obedience to traditional authority are still deeply entrenched in Tonga. It is still the case that political change is 'readily characterized in terms of tradition versus democracy' (Lawson 1994, p. 113), with many Tongans still unsure of how democracy can work alongside a royal family and the nobility. Even those who support democratic reform, who are well educated and do not 'need' the nobles (and may privately be critical of them), typically defer to their authority and observe the requisite protocols in their presence. As Kerry James (1997, p. 70) concluded of Tonga's nobility:

> If the abuses of power can be halted, the Tongan people will be glad to continue to honour those they believe should lead the nation … [they] do not want to replace their unique system; they only want to be able to trust and respect it.

In the context of calls for democratic reform in the 1990s, Epeli Hau'ofa (1994, pp. 426–427) argued:

> Although the aristocracy will always be few in number, Tonga will continue to need them far more than their social and economic contributions to our progress. Like their ancestors, they serve the nation in ways that no one else can; and therein I believe lies their great and continuing importance.

It does seem highly unlikely that Tonga's royal and noble families will lose their places in Tonga's hierarchical society in the foreseeable future, but further change does seem inevitable. As Guy Powles (2013, p. 15) observed:

> Another potential crisis may be triggered by threats to abolish the nobles' electorate and throw open all seats in the Assembly to popular vote—where nobles would stand as ordinary candidates. Such a move could encourage the nobles to insist on constitutional privileges that protect them—thus testing the Constitution further.

The head of a prominent civil society organisation in Tonga commented to me that people consider political change 'unfinished business' and that the nobles are 'seeing the walls cracking!' In August 2017, King Tupou VI dissolved the parliament, a sign that he was uneasy with the extent of democratic reform in his country (Fraenkel 2017). In snap elections in November 2017, most of the ministers, including 'Akilisi Pohiva, regained their seats and, eventually, Pohiva was returned as prime minister (Tora 2018).

Young Traditional Leaders

The changing roles of traditional leaders have long been of interest to scholars of the Pacific. As the editors of the volume *Chiefs Today* argued:

> Far from premodern relics, the chiefs of modern Pacific states increasingly figure in the rhetoric and reality of national political development … the renewed significance of chiefs, and the debates and disagreements that surround them, emerge from a collision of discourses of identity and power circulating in the Pacific today … the status and power of the chief have become public issues in the context of national political change and development. (Lindstrom & White 1997, pp. 3–4)

More than 20 years later, these issues continue to be discussed, but surprisingly little has been written about what is done to prepare younger members of chiefly families to take on either titles or supporting roles in the context of political and social change. For example, for the Cook Islands, Arno Pascht (2014, p. 168) considered the political futures of traditional title holders and described how they draw on the past 'as an important basis of chiefly authority and legitimacy', while also aiming to ensure that they continue to have 'political influence and power'. However, he only discusses the existing title holders, not those who will take on those roles in the future. Similarly, a collection of papers on chiefs in Fiji (Pauwels 2015) does not address how younger generations of traditional elites are learning about their roles.[2]

For Tonga, most discussions about the pro-democracy movement and political change have focused primarily on the monarchy, portraying the nobility as part of the privileged strata of Tongan society without considering in any depth the implications for nobles and their families of the democratic reforms. Perhaps this lack of attention to the younger generation is partly due to the assumption that chiefly titles are 'ascribed' rather than achieved and that the roles and responsibilities—and privileges—are simply passed on through the generations. However, as this case study of Tonga shows, it is important to consider not only how the roles of traditional leaders are changing, but also how their children are affected by change, as this can potentially shape the future of their country. Epeli Hau'ofa (1994, p. 426) observed of Tonga: 'Like everything else, the aristocracy is changing, and there are signs of reinvigoration in its ranks'. The younger generations, he noted, were better educated than their parents and grandparents and were working in both the public and private sectors using their tertiary qualifications. He also commented that 'they seem to be more egalitarian in their attitudes than their forebears and may even be more favourably disposed toward an open and democratic system than their elders have understandably been' (1994, p. 426).

As with commoner Tongans, members of the royal and noble families of Tonga are now scattered across the diaspora and have been since the late 1960s, when waves of Tongan migration to New Zealand, Australia and the US began. All three of King Tupou VI's children were born in New Zealand and spent many of their formative years in Australia. Even when noble families are based in Tonga, their children are often educated overseas and only visit Tonga occasionally. Many people I have interviewed in Tonga, across different ranks, expressed serious concerns about the current cohort of youth from noble families. A common theme was their 'disconnection' from the communities on their families' estates and with Tongan culture and society more broadly. Those who have spent much of their lives overseas have poor Tongan language skills, and I was

2 The collection includes one paper on Micronesia (Petersen 2015), which also focuses only on the role of chiefs, not on how future leaders learn about that role (see Feinberg 2018).

told that their knowledge of cultural matters may be so limited that some do not even know to which *ha'a* they belong. Some have never been to their family's estate, especially estates on the outer islands, where the local people may never have met the family of their noble.[3] As well as being away from Tonga at times, their lack of knowledge was also attributed to a lack of good role models, with some people claiming that parents are not explicitly teaching their children the roles and responsibilities associated with their rank.[4]

Overall, there was agreement that many of these young people lack confidence and feel confused and uncertain about possible changes to the roles and position of the nobility in Tongan society. This is not helped by their sheltered and overprotected existence when in Tonga, in which they grow accustomed to a life of privilege and special treatment. They tend to stay at home much of the time, especially females, as the strict protocols around commoners' interactions with nobility can prevent them from simply mingling with other young people. Poor Tongan language skills also make it more difficult to interact with villagers. The expressions commoners used to describe noble youth is revealing: they are 'in a bubble', 'way over there', 'in their own little world' and 'in a tightly guarded space'. This lack of connection of youth from noble families with the wider community is regarded as adding to people's increasing lack of trust in the nobility.

These future leaders' 'disconnection' and their experience of living overseas also leads to concerns within the nobility that their youth are becoming too independent, that they are struggling with the restrictions on their behaviour and that they are questioning practices such as arranged marriages. It is widely believed that they are facing significant challenges in relation to the expectations placed on them for future leadership: 'privileged but struggling' was how one commoner interviewee described them.

3 In some cases when the noble dies while still relatively young, the people on his estate may not have met his son before he inherits the title.

4 Lack of direct instruction is a common feature of Tongan socialisation, as children are expected to learn primarily by observation (Morton 1996). However, the children of nobles who spend a lot of time overseas have less opportunity for such observation.

Establishment of 'the Namoa'

It is in this context of concerns for the younger generation of noble and royal families that efforts have been made to bring them together and to provide a form of training, which is strongly influenced by a focus on developmental leadership. This was facilitated through the Pacific Leadership Program (PLP), based in Fiji and funded by the Australian government, which helped to establish several leadership coalitions in the Pacific from 2008. In Tonga, the coalition was the Tonga National Leadership Development Forum (TNLDF), which operated from 2010 through the Civil Society Forum of Tonga, an umbrella body for civil society organisations. TNLDF has as its patron Princess Angelika Lātūfuipeka Tuku'aho, daughter of King Tupou VI,[5] and its board members include several nobles and representatives from all sectors of Tongan society.[6]

One of the key activities of the TNLDF was their development of a national leadership code ('the Code') through extensive public consultations throughout the whole archipelago; it was launched in December 2013. It is a set of 14 leadership principles and it has shaped the work of TNLDF in its attempts to influence leadership in Tonga, at a time when Tonga is at a critical juncture, with significant political reforms already and the potential for more change in future. To a great extent, the Code reinforces what Tongans now regard as 'traditional' values; although there are some standard leadership values such as accountability and transparency, the first principle is to live a religious life, followed by *'ofa* (love, generosity and compassion), then respect, humility and other

5 The Princess exemplifies the experiences of many young traditional leaders, having spent significant periods outside Tonga. She attended Queen Sālote College in Tonga and lived with King Tupou V when her parents moved to Australia while her father studied. She spent time in Switzerland after high school, then went to university in Canberra in 2010. In 2012, she became the High Commissioner to Tonga and remains based in Canberra. Born in 1983, she has only recently moved out of the category of 'youth', as defined in Tonga (15–34).

6 Between 2014 and 2017, I worked as a consultant for the PLP, looking at the work of the TNLDF. I was given ethics approval by La Trobe University (#E16-028) to draw on that work for my research. In addition to participant observation during TNLDF activities, I conducted formal interviews with the Princess, members of the TNLDF board, the TNLDF working committee, members of the Namoa (see below), village youth group leaders and other village youth, leaders of other civil society organisations and other contacts that I have in Tonga from my research with Tongans since the late 1980s.

values that are defined explicitly in relation to Tongan social norms.[7] The Code shifts the emphasis of the role of leaders from privilege and power to responsibilities, framed within the context of the ideals of what traditional, pre-contact leadership entailed in Tonga. The TNLDF very proudly regard the Code as uniquely Tongan and it has been endorsed by the King and Queen, government ministers and church leaders, with many Tongans signing a pledge to uphold the Code.

At a TNLDF meeting in Ha'apai 2012, the board discussed how to encourage Tonga's nobles to accept the Code and decided to start with the younger generation. They formed the Young Tongan Traditional Leaders (YTTL) group and held the first meeting in December 2012 at Vakaloa resort on Tongatapu, facilitated by TNLDF. Only a small proportion of the funding received from the PLP was directed to this group, which is financed primarily by Princess Lātūfuipeka and the parents of its members. In a detailed review of the work of PLP in the Pacific, in the 'country scan' for Tonga discussing the local effects of PLP, there is no mention of this group (Barbara & Haley 2014), although it was a crucial aspect of their activities from the perspective of the TNLDF. The TNLDF operate on the assumption that in the foreseeable future, the nobility will continue to play an important role as traditional leaders in Tonga, so the aim is to influence future leaders as part of the TNLDF's broader agenda of shaping developmental leadership in Tonga.[8]

As well as being a means to encourage Tonga's future leaders to adopt the Code, TNLDF perceived a need for the younger generation to be a more cohesive group and to learn more about Tongan culture, society and their own families' histories so they would be prepared for the roles that they would assume as adults. As one board member described it, these young people 'have extremely few positive role models'. There had been some cases of nobles dying at a young age and their sons inheriting the title without fully understanding the role; TNLDF wanted to ensure that, in the future, young people were more prepared, whether to take on a title or to carry out the many other roles associated with being a member of the

7 The 14 leadership principles (*makatu'unga*), as translated by TNLDF, are: *mo'ui faka-e-'otua* (live a religious life); *'ofa* (love); *faitotonu* (honesty); *faka'apa'apa* (respect); *mamahi'ime'a* (commitment/loyalty); *tauhi vaha'a* (maintain relationship); *vahevahe taau* (equality); *fa'a kataki* (patience/endurance); *tali ui* (accountability); *falala'anga* (trustworthy); *mo'ui visone* (visionary); *loto to* (humility); and *mo'ui lelei fakaesino* (healthy).

8 TNLDF is involved in a range of other projects, including developing Tonga's Green Growth strategy, school leadership programs and local governance initiatives.

traditional elite. At the same time, TNLDF wanted these young people to be aware of change in Tonga and to consider their place in the context of that change.

In 2015, the group changed their name from YTTL to *Namoa 'o e taki Lelei*, after Princess Lātūfuipeka asked King Tupou V for his approval. As she explained on the group's Facebook site:

> The term 'Namoa' is the very FIRST premastication (pre-chewing) that is given to a baby by his/her mother/mother figure which in Tonga is a piece of baked coconut. It is believed that the behavior of a person when older is determined from the 'Namoa' that he/she received when still an infant. 'Taki Lelei' is good leader (20 January 2015).

Although the acronym NOETL was initially adopted for the group, members and the TNLDF board quickly referred to it as simply 'the Namoa'—the term that is also used in this chapter.

Membership of the Namoa

Initially, the intention was to include only the heirs to the noble titles, but the Namoa has expanded to include the younger generation of the royal family and any children from noble families, including members from noble–commoner marriages. It also includes children from the families of *matāpule ma'u tofi'a* (ceremonial attendants holding hereditary estates) and others who are linked by blood to the King, as they could all play important leadership roles in Tonga in the future. Members are invited to join the group by Princess Lātūfuipeka and, once they register as members, they are expected to attend meetings or to send a representative. There are over 100 members, although only some are in Tonga at any given time, as many either live overseas or are away studying or travelling. December seems to be the most active time for the group, when members return to Tonga to spend Christmas with their families. Membership of the Namoa has continued to grow and, in 2017, it expanded to include the children of *tauhifonua* (minor chiefs who care for estates when the title-holding noble is absent). Not all potential members have joined the group; some are not interested and others are part of the Royal Guard and travel with the King, so they do not get involved with the group's activities.

The ages of members range from very young children to young adults, and this presents a challenge when organising activities. The younger children are primarily included in social events, but otherwise all members from about the age of 10 are involved in activities such as meetings and community work, as discussed below. In Tonga, the official category of 'youth' extends to 35 years old, so there is a significant span of ages within the Namoa. Another challenge is the respect (*faka'apa'apa*) relationship between brothers and sisters (broadly defined to include cousins), which precludes them from interacting closely. However, Tongans are used to managing that issue.

The group aims to come together two or three times a year, and this is when activities organised by TNLDF often occur. Each of these meetings is hosted by members of a particular *ha'a* as a deliberate attempt to encourage identification with what one member referred to as 'blood lines, bound together with the common aspirations along those tribe lines'. The Namoa has an executive committee but the group is primarily run by a subcommittee of mostly lower-ranking female members based in Tonga, which meets twice a month to plan ongoing activities. The executive committee has had problems with members leaving Tonga for long periods, tensions between members competing to claim higher rank and with the lack of organisational skills of committee members, but TNLDF board members assert that simply getting committee members from rival *ha'a* to work together has been a considerable achievement.

In 2017, the executive committee was headed by Prince 'Ata (son of King Tupou VI) as president of the Namoa, and his two deputies were nobles' sons, Lord Vaha'i and Hon. Tevita 'Unga Ma'afu. Prince 'Ata also became a TNLDF board member and its vice-chair, and the secretary of the Namoa committee, Volasinga 'Ahio Salatielu, has also joined the board. They were welcomed by other board members who want them to be aware of the issues that TNLDF addresses. In addition, they have the opportunity to observe the interactions of the nobles with other board members, as a model of traditional leaders working in a coalition with other Tongans.

The Namoa's Vision and Mission

Through their work with the TNLDF, the Namoa have developed a vision statement: 'To give life to Tongan Culture through collaboration, leadership, working together and strengthening ties with the people, land and the environment as a response to change with the influence of custodians'. Their mission statement is that 'Young Tongan Traditional

Leaders aim to make a positive difference and create value with and for Tonga'.[9] One of the group's aims is to thus influence the behaviour of future leaders through the National Leadership Code and the activities of the group, to be more in line with the ideal roles of nobility, including those of 'service' and reciprocity.

In a document dated 23 May 2014, the objectives of the group are listed as '5–10 year short-term goals' and '10–20 year long-term goals', with an ambitious list of possible activities, primarily in regard to historical knowledge such as reviving 'old Tongan sports' and promoting Tongan dance and music, as well reviving traditions such as tattoo (*tatau*) and reconnecting 'with relatives from times of Tongan empire'. The goals also involve social issues, including supporting various civil society groups, focusing on health, education and the environment and even involvement in restorative justice and developing 'a village system to restore order and justice and to help deportees on a village level'.

In an interview in June 2014 on The Whatitdo, a website described as an 'Urban island review media platform for Pacific Islanders in sports and entertainment and social community awareness', Princess Lātūfuipeka explained:

> We hope to make a difference in leading by example for our people at the village level as that is where our authority lies. To name a few, as young leaders we want to be able to work together as a Ha'a and as Custodians of the land to improve the lives of the people who are under our responsibilities through: promoting a healthy lifestyle by having health talks and fitness programs; encouraging tree planting and cleaning up (*fakama'a kolo*) to deal with environmental concerns; support disable people through volunteer work; revive traditional Tongan sports, dances (*faiva*) and preserving village landmarks (*mātanga fakakolo*); documentation of village history.

9 The vision and mission statement are taken from the document 'YTTL goals final' provided by TNLDF, which appears to have been created by Princess Lātūfuipeka in May 2014. In the workbook distributed to members at a meeting in July 2014, the vision is stated simply as 'give life, value and be proud of our Tongan culture and responsibilities' and the mission is listed as:

- custodian of culture
- traditional responsibilities
- political responsibilities
- community leadership.

As well as emphasising both the 'authority' and 'responsibilities' of the group, the Princess reveals her broad ambitions. She has further plans to expand its scope—for example, to extend its activities throughout the archipelago, as well as to make connections with traditional leaders in Fiji and Samoa and with Tonga's diasporic communities. In her interview, she continued: 'Leading today ought to be responsive to the changes of time such as identity and cultural crises, climate change, and the transfer of knowledge to name a few'. The Princess's views were echoed by a noble, not part of TNLDF, who described the Namoa as partly about reviving Tongan culture that is perceived to be declining and, in doing so, reviving the role of the nobility and royal family as leaders. He talked about:

> how we can evolve that and amend it to make it relevant, and how we have to deal in the future as leaders, while maintaining that which makes it unique. Maintaining the best things and adapting so that we don't become irrelevant in future.

One of the nobles on the TNLDF board described the Namoa as a 'long-term investment in the future of the country'.

Managing Protocol, Building Trust

Before describing the activities of the Namoa, it is important to note that it has been extremely challenging for the TNLDF to work with these young traditional leaders. As an independent body, TNLDF has the advantage of not being regarded by Tonga's elite as jostling for power, but its position is delicate because, in the Tongan context, it is difficult for the youth to be regarded as working with a 'commoner' civil society organisation to receive mentoring and advice. The members of the TNLDF working with the group, primarily a 'working committee' of commoners, have had to slowly build their trust and confidence. They also have to deal with the protocols surrounding Princess Lātūfuipeka, which makes it difficult for them to talk explicitly or directly with her about the messages that they hope are being conveyed to the members of the Namoa about leadership. However, the leaders of TNLDF, including the nobles on the board, have opportunities to do this when meeting separately with the Princess.

One of the commoner board members observed that the TNLDF needed to be discreet because it was important to gain the trust of the noble families. She said that those families could lose face if the work of the TNLDF with their children was known, because: 'To be seen as needing support is not easy for them'. For this reason, there has been little publicity of the activities of the Namoa, although Princess Lātūfuipeka mentioned them in her Christmas message on television in the early stages of the group's development and subsequently in various interviews on social media. Another board member explained that it was important that the information came from the Princess, because if others involved with the TNLDF took that initiative, Tongans would regard them as wanting to raise their own social status or they would assume they were in it for their own advantage. There was also concern that, as the nobility was such a 'tightly guarded space', publicity would 'bring their barriers down' and the TNLDF would lose access to the Namoa.

Despite the concerns about the effects of publicity, there has been a gradual increase in Tongans' awareness of the Namoa. Since 2016, some members of the Namoa have been involved with the TNLDF's media and advocacy program, joining TV and radio panel discussions on the experience of Namoa members and how the Code and the Namoa activities have influenced them in relation to leadership. In 2016 and 2017, my interviews with representatives from other youth groups in Tonga revealed that they knew little about the Namoa, but they all expressed interest in connecting with them and in finding ways to address the significant obstacle of protocols that restrict interactions between noble and commoner youth.

There are also clear indications that the TNLDF has managed to gain the trust of the Namoa members' families. Initially, many adults from those families did not support the group and were not convinced that it would make any difference either to the young people involved or to Tongan society. In addition, the parents' generation was focused on the longstanding rivalries between noble families. Gradually, they have increased their support and many now encourage their children to take part in the activities. Another group that had to be won over included the 'nannies' of these young people: the 'ladies in waiting' who accompany them when in public and who tend to be overprotective of their charges. According to members of the TNLDF's working committee, during the early events organised for the Namoa, the 'nannies' and/or parents would be present and members would seek their approval to join in activities. As trust in the TNLDF grew, the nannies and parents began dropping the children and youth at Namoa activities or waiting outside rather than watching their every move.

'Training' the Namoa

The activities organised for the Namoa have changed significantly over time. Initially, they held events that reflected their privileged status: beach parties, dinners at Tonga's best restaurants and day trips to the small islands near Tongatapu that have tourist resorts. They held events such as a games day for the children, in which they could simply have fun and get to know each other. Previously, these young people tended to only see each other a few times a year at functions, during which they sat and watched proceedings rather than interact with each other. As they became more comfortable with each other, the TNLDF introduced some formal workshops, or 'training', and the first included a discussion that was facilitated by Princess Lātūfuipeka on the importance of earning respect rather than expecting it. The TNLDF surveyed members in 2013 to discover what they were interested in learning about and, consequently, workshops and activities have been developed around two key themes: Tongan history and culture, and current social issues.

Training has included Tongan language, such as public speaking and the three registers of language for commoners, nobles and the royal family, and key Tongan values. Facilitators and guest speakers from a range of organisations, government departments, the church and judiciary have been involved in the workshops, which have been organised mainly by the one paid staff member of the TNLDF, Mr Manitasi Leger. A workshop held in 2015 acknowledged the challenges that the Namoa members face, including having to speak at events in Tonga, balancing traditional obligations with personal and social obligations and even being nervous and lacking confidence. The Leadership Code is a strong focus throughout the workshops, and a noble's wife, whose children are Namoa members, proudly said they know the Code by heart.

As well as formal 'training', the Namoa are encouraged to apply their learning through their community work. As part of the focus on history, members have developed projects in which they visit people in the villages on their family's estate to learn about the history of the area and of their *ha'a*.[10] This has been limited to some villages on Tongatapu, but the

10 Some of the Namoa talked enthusiastically about wanting to collect and document all the historical data collected by the Namoa members and even about making documentaries, but, given the lack of funding, this seems unlikely to occur.

group aims to extend this activity throughout the Kingdom.[11] In some of these villages, the Namoa have designed storyboards for roadside signs to display aspects of local history, and, at their meetings, the members tell each other what they have learned about their village, *ha'a*, local place names, and so on. They are asked to report on what involvement they have had with their *kāinga* and community. As well as responding to the survey of members' interests, the TNLDF board saw this focus on history as a way for these young people to understand their role and position in Tongan society.

Preparation for the coronation of Tupou VI in July 2015 saw a surge in activities involving members of the Namoa working in some of the villages on Tongatapu, primarily to research historical information, but to also ensure that the villages were cleaned and decorated for the event. This included rubbish collection, in which Princess Lātūfuipeka herself participated. These village clean-ups were followed by 'inspections' (*a'ahi*) in which some of the Namoa would visit a village and observe what had been achieved. The coronation itself also involved some of the Namoa, who the King appointed as liaison officers to assist VIP guests. A TNLDF working committee member observed that while those young people had been 'born to be served', they were now helping others and willingly being involved in a range of activities.

After the coronation, the focus shifted to issues relevant to the community, such as climate change, the environment, livelihood issues and a range of other topics. TNLDF wanted to ensure that the training activities aligned with national planning, such as Tonga's Sustainable Development Framework, and to internationally recognised development aims, such as the United Nation's Sustainable Development Goals. The Namoa began planning some of their own activities and events, rather than these being driven solely by TNLDF—but the TNLDF continued to offer monthly workshops for Namoa members who were in Tonga, which aimed to build their capacity as leaders. The workshops emphasise group work and discussion and encourage the members to feel more comfortable interacting with each other and with public speaking.

11 A long-term aim is to link to Tongan youth groups overseas and encourage them to visit the country to learn its history, with organised tours, homestays and so on.

It is inevitable that the focus of the workshops on the roles that these young people play as members of the nobility to some extent reinforces their view of themselves as members of the elite in Tongan society. However, the TNLDF's aim is to consistently challenge them to consider what that means in terms of their responsibilities in the context of political reform and the changing social, political and economic environment of Tonga. There has also been emphasis on their responsibilities to the physical environment, with a focus on the effects of climate change. The workshops aim to lay the groundwork for a new generation of traditional leaders who are focused more on their responsibilities than on the privileges that come with their birthright. Yet there has been little explicit discussion of how nobles' roles in the political arena could or should change in future, and no discussion of contentious issues such as land reform. The focus is squarely on their traditional roles and how they can best uphold them in the current context.[12]

Another topic that has not received much focus in the workshops is gender, although the TNLDF is proud that the Namoa has provided opportunities for young women to be involved in the committee. The Princess herself admitted that the women 'run the show' and that they are more involved with organising Namoa activities. The Namoa's involvement with village youth has also included females and they participate in workshop activities such as building confidence in public speaking. Yet there has been no attempt to address the fundamental gender inequalities of everyday life in Tonga, and there has been a reinforcement of what I have called elsewhere the myth of female privilege (Lee 2017). Perhaps not surprisingly, there has been no discussion of whether women could or should hold noble titles.

Community Chapters

The work of Namoa members in villages led to the formation of 'community chapters' in some villages, in which members work closely with the young people of the village. Together, they carry out projects such installing a water tank for a poor family or building a ramp for a disabled man to access his home. TNLDF organises these projects, liaising between the Namoa and village youth, so the Namoa can observe for themselves

12 One of the nobles, a government minister not on the TNLDF board was enthusiastic about this 'training' and said that he would like to see the Namoa formalised and incorporated, to run a formal academy for the children of the traditional elite.

the extent of poverty in Tonga—all the while aiming to inspire them to want to address the growing inequalities. The chapters also give the young nobles 'a platform for them to exercise leadership', as a TNLDF board member explained, again with the aim of seeing leadership as involving responsibilities. Another aim is to increase acceptance of youth leadership within the village; some elderly villagers have opposed youth involvement in community chapters, as for them it challenges their ideas of appropriate social roles. By encouraging youth leadership within villages, TNLDF hopes to inspire village youth to be more proactively involved with their community rather than simply waiting to carry out elders' instructions.

One of these community chapters was established in Pea village, on the King's estate, and it organised a week-long celebration in January 2015. Princess Lātūfuipeka was very involved and helped the community chapter to organise an array of activities, such as a sports day, various competitions and production of signboards using the historical information that the youth collected from the elders of the village. The King and Queen toured the village during the week and people dressed as they did in ancient Tonga. A community chapter youth leader said that the event had helped give youth a sense of pride in the history of their village and that they had been able to feel a sense of ownership in the process of planning the week's activities. He also explained that the village youth who had been involved were motivated by wider concerns regarding youth unemployment, school dropouts and problems with alcohol consumption and associated violence.

The events that I observed that brought together village youth and the Namoa were a fascinating mixture of traditional protocol and informality. One was a tree planting ceremony held on Sia Ko Veiongo, a small hill near the royal palace in Nuku'alofa, where the very early stages of what was planned as a tourist attraction had been constructed. The top of the hill had been landscaped and the event was to plant heilala trees, which can only be planted by members of the royal family. A structure had been erected to provide shade for the special guest, Princess Lātūfuipeka, who was seated on an ornate chair placed on layers of woven pandanus mats, with tables on either side of her holding flower arrangements, a fine china teapot and cup, and a tiered cake stand with small cakes. Children and youth from Kolomotu'a, a village that has now merged with the urban sprawl of Nuku'alofa, were present, as were members of the Namoa. While the village youth stayed on the fringes, the younger children sat in front of the Princess, on the ground, as did a leading member of TNLDF who made a speech welcoming her. A village youth leader gave an emotional speech, followed by a speech by a member of the Namoa, then a song by the children and youth. Despite the formality and observance of protocol, the Princess was wearing casual clothes—a T-shirt and black pants, a straw hat and runners—and, after the speeches and singing, she used a shovel to move some dirt around one of the heilala trees, to symbolically plant it, then spent some time joking with the village youth and posing for photographs with them.

Another event was an 'inspection' in the Hihifo (Western) district of Tongatapu that was organised in June 2016, following work that was undertaken by members of the Namoa and community chapters in 12 villages to research the history of the villages and identify culturally significant sites that need restoration work. To prepare for the event, the son of the village noble made all the arrangements that usually would have been done by his father or the 'talking chief'. The son, a member of the Namoa, did this through his work with youth leaders in the village; thus, it became a direct exercise in leadership training for both noble and commoner youth. The usual presentations that would be involved in a royal visit to a village were pared back to a token gift, to ensure that the visit was not a burden for the village. One TNLDF board member claimed that through activities like this, they were 'shaking the whole structure but in a way that's acceptable' to both nobles and commoners.

The Hihifo visit began in the village of Kala'au, with great excitement; women danced and clowned in the street and the villagers gathered to watch. Princess Lātūfuipeka and Prince Ata arrived—breaking protocol by attending without the 'talking chiefs' who would normally accompany them—and, with other members of the Namoa and representatives from the village, they took their places in the village hall while villagers cheered outside. The token gift of kava root and sugar cane was presented by a young man of the village, followed by speeches and a hymn, then two members of the Namoa (male and female) introduced themselves and explained which *ha'a* they were from. Afterwards, a procession of vehicles with the Princess, the Namoa, the TNLDF representatives and villagers drove through the Hihifo district using their car horns to announce their presence and express their excitement. They finished their journey at the large town hall in Kolovai village, where there were more speeches, including the Princess speaking proudly about the Namoa and their work with village youth. After the meeting, food that had been gifted by villagers during the visit was divided up and given to people to take home.

The Princess and the Namoa

Although facilitated by the PLP through the TNLDF, the Namoa are also strongly influenced by their patron, Princess Lātūfuipeka, who has often spoken out about the responsibilities of leadership. In a speech that she gave at the Australian Professional Pacific Women Symposium in August 2014,[13] she reflected:

> Leadership does not materialize because you gain a specific position, a pay grade or a level of seniority or popularity. Instead, leadership is about the choice you make to influence and the freedom to accept personal responsibilities.

She talked about 'positive change' and working 'collaboratively with community leaders', emphasising that Tonga's National Leadership Code enables communities 'to hold their leaders accountable'. The Princess spoke of the Namoa as 'a lifelong dream of mine' and recited its vision and mission. In another interview, on The Whatitdo (2014), she says of the Namoa:

> We are inspired by participative leadership which necessitates that leadership is practiced through involvements and commitments at the village level. I believe that a better Tonga is built through participatory commitments beginning at the basic levels of our society.

One of the TNLDF board members observed that the Princess's role with the Namoa has not been easy, as she has to negotiate 'a social minefield' in the relationships between noble families. Given the competition and rivalry between *ha'a,* she sees it is as 'a miracle' that their children are able to meet together as the Namoa. She explained that during the early meetings facilitated by TNLDF, the youth were uncomfortable with each other because of that rivalry, adding: 'It's all about power and authority'. From her perspective, getting the young people comfortable with each other is an important step: 'You can't measure the impact of their conversations'. Another board member claimed that there has also been an effect on the parents' generation, with nobles collaborating more, especially within their *ha'a*. However, the TNLDF are also realistic and acknowledge that

13 www.youtube.com/watch?v=HRHL_YGX3HQ.

rivalry between nobles is likely to continue. Even within the Namoa, there are political struggles in which members use their relative closeness to the Princess, and thus to the King, as a way to seek power within the group.

Another important role that Princess Lātūfuipeka has played for the Namoa has been through the Facebook page that she established, assisted by her cousin who uploads her posts and Manitasi Leger from TNLDF who also adds content.[14] She also set up a private Facebook page for the Namoa committee members. The main page began in August 2013, with a picture from 2012 of some Namoa members at their first meeting, at the Vakaloa beach resort. By 2015, long posts started appearing that focused on Tongan history, legends and tradition, primarily about Tongan royalty and nobility. These were particularly frequent when the Namoa was focused on collecting histories in their villages and when the content was often of an idealised past, emphasising the role of nobles in redistribution and service.[15] The posts trailed off after late 2015 and began again in late 2017, with posts by TNLDF about the final PLP event, after its funding was ended, until mid-2018 when posts stopped, suggesting that the Princess now uses one or more of the closed groups and that TNLDF is no longer contributing. Namoa members also use email, phones, Skype and other social media that enable them to stay in touch, despite being geographically scattered for much of the time.

Transforming Tongan Traditional Leadership?

The involvement of PLP, via TNLDF, in the Namoa could be viewed as a form of neo-colonialism. Having a program funded by a foreign government overseeing a training program for young traditional leaders has unsettling echoes of the training for the elite in the colonies before foreign powers withdrew. Tonga had escaped that process to a large extent, as it was never formally colonised, and Tongans' pride in their independence has become an integral part of their identity. Even with TNLDF, this resistance to external influence has been obvious, as they have engaged in

14 www.facebook.com/Namoa-o-e-Taki-Lelei-218694194955558/.

15 There are now other Facebook pages, such as the closed groups 'Royal Tongan Dynasties/Nobles Forum' with 5,263 members; 'Royal Tongan Dynasties Forum' with 20,501 members; and 'The Kingdom of Tonga: Royal Dynasties', with 10,817 members, indicating many Tongans' ongoing fascination with their traditional leaders.

activities that the PLP did not consider valuable, including all the time and effort spent on developing the National Leadership Code (Barbara & Haley 2014, p. 34). If this was a neo-colonial attempt to manipulate leadership in Tonga, it has been largely ineffective.

Within Tonga, some of those who know of the Namoa consider it simply reinforcing the existing power structures, with the young members learning to take their privileged position for granted. I was told that the group is 'elitist and conservative' and that the members 'are not learning anything new'. Even a PLP staff member described it as an 'elite social club'. An unintentional consequence of forming the Namoa has been to further shore up the nobility; bringing the young people together has enabled some to find marriage partners. A TNLDF board member commented that this was causing 'dramas', as mothers vied to push their daughters towards partners as high ranking as possible. However, the wife of a noble commented that the Namoa was making things easier for everyone by helping ensure that 'nobles marry nobles', as there was growing concern among Tonga's elite about the increasing number of marriages to commoners as young people resisted arranged marriages.

Despite claims of elitism, the TNLDF board members view the Namoa as one of the coalition's greatest achievements. They argue that because many of the Namoa were so disconnected from Tongan language and culture, some of them would have been unable to function in their traditional roles once they reached adulthood, without the training TNLDF provided. Further, they believe that their training gives Namoa members the opportunity to think critically about their future roles in the context of social, cultural, economic and political changes in Tonga. They hope that this will prevent future leaders from abusing the privileges and power of their position and make them more likely to be involved in addressing the very serious problems Tonga faces.

As one noble explained, there are still significant barriers, particularly nobles' tendency to focus on their lineage and estates while shoring up their own power, rather than thinking of the whole country. This has affected the Namoa; for example, they are only involved in community chapters in the villages that are associated with their family. Yet, a male member of the group in his early 20s claimed, 'Namoa has brought us nationalism', meaning that they now choose what is best for the group as a whole, not just their own family line. The TNLDF also seems to have succeeded in linking the Namoa more closely with other young people in Tonga, through the community chapters. The leader of a key youth organisation in Tonga told me that the Namoa are now more involved with the wider community—'hanging out' with other youth in their village, sitting in kava circles with commoners, attending town hall meetings, and so on. She described the relationships between nobility and commoners as 'closing up'. This has also been influenced by the community projects with which the Namoa have been involved. Some Namoa members in Kolomotu'a have joined homework sessions with other village youth that are run by teachers. Others are involved with coaching other youth with their homework. If this continues, the TNLDF is considering bringing in other extra-curricular activities such as traditional dancing, in which the Namoa could be involved with village youth.

All of this is occurring at a time when it seems that commoner youth are far less interested in Tonga's traditional leadership than previous generations. A Tongan-based journalist told me in 2013 that during her regular visits to high schools to give classes in media studies, she found that youth had little interest or knowledge of the royal or noble families and their activities. Even within those families, some young people are uncertain about the future of Tonga's hierarchical social structure. The wife of a noble expressed concern about her daughter, who lived overseas and who was 'seeing things differently' and questioning her position, despite her parents' attempts to convince her that there is a cultural expectation of her to 'look after' their people. Undoubtedly, the nobles have already lost some of their authority; as one told me: 'The days when you tell someone something to do and they do it because of who you are, those days are done'. One of the aims of the TNLDF is to encourage people to think critically about leadership, to hold leaders to account—but even the commoner board members do not envisage an end to the nobility, regarding traditional leaders as fundamental to Tongans' identity. As a leading member of the TNLDF told me: 'You can't be Tongan without nobles'.

Conclusion

Whether or not the work that the TNLDF has done with the Namoa will change Tonga's leadership or commoners' views of traditional leaders, remains to be seen. With the support of Princess Lātūfuipeka, they have attempted to use both the Namoa and the National Leadership Code to emphasise the cultural aspects of Tongan leadership as a way to restore legitimacy to traditional leadership in Tonga. The early emphasis of the TNLDF's activities with the Namoa was strongly on tradition and culture and the reaffirmation of the existing roles of the nobility, yet, over time, they focused increasingly on the implications of change and ongoing social and environmental issues. They have encouraged the Namoa members to be 'developmental leaders' and have tried to restore trust in the royalty and nobility by having the Namoa interact with people at the village level, through the community chapters, so they are regarded as having the best interests of the people as their priority. TNLDF is acting to prolong the role and authority of the traditional leaders while trying to prevent the next generation from abusing the privileges and power of their position and to make them more likely to uphold their responsibilities as leaders. This is a tricky balancing act, but the TNLDF board is convinced that this is the only way to effect real change in Tonga.

This was not what the PLP had in mind for the activities of this coalition, which caused significant tensions between them. PLP was looking for more immediate effects on the current leadership, while the TNLDF insisted on focusing on the future and pinning its hopes on long-term, gradual change. In addition, the board members argued that because so many of the Namoa members were disconnected from Tongan culture, with some not even speaking Tongan, they would be unable to meet the expectations of their roles once they reached adulthood, so they required the TNLDF's intervention through its workshops and other activities.

The Australian government closed PLP at the end of 2017, so the TNLDF lost its funding. The members of the TNLDF board all assured me that they will continue the work regardless of funding,[16] and certainly they are all passionate about nurturing a new generation of traditional leaders who, ideally, will uphold the principles of the National Leadership Code. It will be fascinating to see what happens, including with the future of the Namoa.

16 The most recent post on the TNLDF Facebook site is from July 2018, but this does not necessarily mean the coalition is inactive; the sole staff member paid through PLP funds was responsible for updating the site and lost his position when the funding ceased.

Acknowledgements

The opportunity to work for the PLP enabled me to work with all the people associated with the TNLDF and with members of the Namoa, and I'm grateful for their time and patience. Special thanks to Drew Havea, Siale 'Ilolahia and Manitasi Leger, whose dedication and unflagging enthusiasm is inspiring. Thanks also to Michael O'Keefe from La Trobe University who suggested me for this work and who co-authored some of the early reports for PLP. The work was facilitated by the Institute for Human Security and Social Change at La Trobe University.

References

Barbara, J & Haley, N 2014, *Analytical framework to engage with developmental leadership in the Pacific*, Pacific Leadership Program, Suva.

Bott, E 1981, 'Power and rank in the Kingdom of Tonga', *Journal of the Polynesian Society*, vol. 90, no. 1, pp. 7–81.

Brown Pulu, T 2011, *Shoot the messenger: The report on the Nuku'alofa development project and why the Government of Tonga dumped it*, Taimi Publishers Limited, Kingdom of Tonga.

Brown Pulu, T 2012, '"Ma'afu's word is in the hills": What is a noble's role in a democratised Tonga?', *Te Kaharoa*, vol. 5, pp. 138–208, doi.org/10.24135/tekaharoa.v5i1.78

Feinberg, R 2018, 'The future of a Polynesian chiefdom in a globalising world: Anuta, Solomon Islands', in J Connell & H Lee (eds), *Change and continuity in the Pacific: Revisiting the region*, pp. 136–150, Routledge, London, doi.org/10.4324/9781315188645-9

Fraenkel, J 2017, 'Tonga's Premature Royal Dissolution', *East Asia Forum*, viewed 11 September 2017, www.eastasiaforum.org

Hau'ofa, E 1994, 'Thy kingdom come: The democratization of aristocratic Tonga', *The Contemporary Pacific*, vol. 6, no. 2, pp. 414–428.

Hogan, T & Singh, P 2018, 'Modes of indigenous modernity: Identities, stories, pathways', *Thesis Eleven*, vol. 145, no. 1, pp. 3–9.

James, K 1992, 'Tongan rank revisited: Religious hierarchy, social stratification, and gender in the ancient Tongan polity', *Social Analysis*, no. 31, pp. 79–101.

James, K 1994, 'Tonga's pro-democracy movement', *Pacific Affairs*, vol. 67, no. 2, pp. 242–263. doi.org/10.2307/2759419

James, K 1997, 'Rank and leadership in Tonga', in G White & L Lindstrom (eds), *Chiefs today: Traditional Pacific leadership and the postcolonial state*, Stanford University Press, Stanford, pp. 49–70.

James, K 2003, 'Is there a Tongan middle class? Hierarchy and protest in contemporary Tonga', *The Contemporary Pacific*, vol. 15, no. 2, pp. 309–336, doi.org/10.1353/cp.2003.0042

Lawson, S 1994, *Tradition versus democracy in the Kingdom of Tonga*, Research School of Pacific Studies, The Australian National University, Canberra.

Lee, H 2017, 'CEDAW smokescreens: Gender politics in contemporary Tonga', *The Contemporary Pacific*, vol. 29, no. 1, pp. 66–90, doi.org/10.1353/cp.2017.0003

Lindstrom, L & White, G 1997, 'Introduction: Chiefs today', in G White & L Lindstrom (eds), *Chiefs today: Traditional Pacific leadership and the postcolonial state*, Stanford University Press, Stanford, pp. 1–18.

Marcus, G 1977, 'Succession disputes and the position of the nobility in modern Tonga', *Oceania*, vol. 47, nos 3–4, pp. 220–241, 284–299, doi.org/10.1002/j.1834-4461.1977.tb01288.x

Marcus, G 1980, 'Role distance in conversations between Tongan nobles and their "people"', *Journal of the Polynesian Society*, vol. 89, no. 4, pp. 435–453.

Moala, K 2002, *Island kingdom strikes back: The story of an independent island newspaper—Taimi O Tonga*, Pacmedia Publishers, Auckland.

Morton, H 1996, *Becoming Tongan: An ethnography of childhood*, University of Hawai'i Press, Honolulu.

Pascht, A 2014, 'Chiefs for the future? Roles of traditional titleholders in the Cook Islands', in W Rollason (ed.), *Pacific futures: Projects, politics and interests*, Berghahn, New York, pp. 152–171.

Pauwels, S (ed.) 2015, 'Chiefdoms and chieftaincies in Fiji: Yesterday and today', *Journal de la Société des Océanistes*, vol. 141, no. 2, pp. 189–198.

Petersen, G 2015, 'At the intersection of chieftainship and constitutional government: Some comparisons from Micronesia', *Journal de la Société des Océanistes*, vol. 141, no. 2, pp. 255–265, doi.org/10.4000/jso.7434

Powles, G 2013, *Political and constitutional reform opens the door: The Kingdom of Tonga's path to democracy*, 2nd edn, University of the South Pacific Press, Suva.

Powles, G 2014a, 'The Tongan monarchy and the Constitution: Political reform in a traditional context', *SSGM Discussion Paper 2014/9*, The Australian National University, Canberra.

Powles, G 2014b, *The Kingdom of Tonga's path to democracy*, USP, Suva.

The Whatitdo 2014, 'Exclusive Interview: HRH Princess Angelika Tuku'aho Highlights Young Tongan Traditional Leaders', *The Whatitdo, Inc.*, viewed 20 February 2015, www.thewhatitdo.com/2014/06/02/exclusive-interview-yttls-president-hrh-princess-angelika-mataaho-tukuaho/

Tora, I 2018, 'Tongan Parliament votes: Pohiva storms back', *Islands Business*, vol. 44, no. 1, p. 18.

6

Youth Leadership in Fiji and Solomon Islands: Creating Opportunities for Civic Engagement

Aidan Craney

Introduction

The strength of civil society across communities in Oceania varies. The hierarchical nature of 'traditional' communities can act as a limiting factor in citizens' active participation in civil society, with Oceanic societies generally prescribing the roles that each member of the community is allowed and entitled to perform. Thus, despite the long histories of group decision-making processes for most Pacific societies, it remains that power is primarily wielded by adult men (McLeod 2015; Prasad 2017, p. 331; Sahlins 1963), though senior women have greater influence in some matrilineal societies, particularly outside Melanesia (McLeod 2007, pp. 10–12, 2015).

Despite this, change has been present in recent years, resulting in an expanded and emboldened civil society sector in certain spaces. The combination of enhanced information flow through telecommunications technologies, the growing levels of educated citizens and the influences of globalisation such as through the expansion of the international development industry—including through regional multilateral bodies—has resulted in civil society groups and development organisations critically engaging with and, at times, challenging authority in the region (Brimacombe 2017; Brimacombe et al. 2018; Titifanue et al. 2017). Moving from 'sporadic' responses to immediate issues of concern, such as Fiji's 1987 military coups (Slatter 2006, p. 29), these groups, both formal and informal, are now engaging in sustained campaigns that are both sociocentric and issues based.

Notably, the increasingly politicised civil society activities of the recent past have largely been driven by, or made inclusive of, youth. This is despite the continued minimisation of the roles that they play and have the potential to play in their communities. Particularly in fields related to social justice, such as gender rights, sexuality rights and climate change, young people are at the vanguard of change and are forcing their way into the public consciousness and conversation.

This chapter discusses how a growing cohort of young people in Fiji and Solomon Islands are creating spaces for themselves to act as social justice activists and advocates for advancing youth opportunities. Through three case studies, I present examples of how these young people are resisting the structural minimisation of youth in Pacific societies to assert their rights to be full and active citizens. The chapter draws on data that were collected during fieldwork conducted in Fiji and Solomon Islands in 2015 for my doctoral thesis, in which I examined the social roles and livelihood opportunities of youth in these countries. I show how some young people in the Pacific are finding ways to proactively and pro-socially engage in critical civil society, despite the cultural expectations of their subservience.

The Structural Minimisation of Pacific Youth

The influence of hierarchy in Oceanic societies can scarcely be overstated. Social roles are generally well established and align with an individual's lineage, gender and age (Brimacombe 2017, p. 144; Cox 2017, p. 77; Jolly 1994; Morton 1996, pp. 22–24). Other factors with greater variability such as ability, sexuality, education, occupation and marital status also play a part. For youth, such hierarchy underscores the roles and influence that they can have in their communities.[1] This is commonly marked by

1 Definitions of 'youth' in the Pacific vary. The term is usually applied to people aged 15–35 who have not married, are not parents and/or have not achieved other milestones that are socially associated with adulthood, such as being employed.

an expectation of deference and a lack of deliberative participation. In the words of Tura Lewai, a civil society and gender rights activist from Fiji: 'Young people are taught to be seen but not heard'.

This marginalisation of youth voices extends to youth representatives often not being young themselves. Kaajal Kumar, a youth and civil society activist from Fiji, spoke to me of the propensity of such representatives to be disconnected from current trends and issues affecting youth, but to be holding on to the position of influence that they have obtained. She told me:

> What you see in the Pacific—you come across young people who are 30 or 40, who are in the youth movement. If you look at [name of organisation], the person holding the youth desk, how old is that person? Because it took them time to get there, they have an ideology. And the youth movement, the way it functions, is that our ideas keep changing.

Discouraging youth participation enculturates young people to occupy a subordinated position in society. In a report on increasing youth participation in the Pacific, commissioned by the World Bank, youth development advocates Shasheen Jayaweera and Kate Morioka (2008, p. 11) explain that in a Pacific context, 'Young people are expected to accept authority without question, to the extent that they are discouraged from sharing their ideas and suggestions with elders'. Despite this, examples exist of young Pacific people expressing a desire to be more actively involved in the planning and decision-making processes of their communities, countries and cultures. At the 2nd Pacific Youth Festival in 2009, over 300 young people from across the region declared: 'As young people, we are important human resources to development, and have an important role to play in building families, communities, institutions and nations; and in all sectors, both formal and informal' (SPC 2009, p. 2).[2] This sentiment is mirrored in the responses that Jayaweera and Morioka were exposed to from young Pacific people discussing their wishes to be engaged citizens. They point out that: 'Whilst some cultures actually discourage young people from expressing their views, it was the heartfelt desire of youth to become active citizens who could make a worthwhile

2 A further example of youth minimisation: though two Pacific youth festivals were organised in 2006 and 2009 to provide youth from across the region to engage in visioning and decision-making processes, a third such festival is yet to occur.

contribution to their nation' (2008, p. 10). Moreover, it is evident in the growing examples of young people inserting themselves into spaces of active civic participation, as highlighted in the case studies in this chapter.

The minimisation of youth engagement in home and village settings is replicated in the formal policies and processes of decision-making. Such minimisation even flows through to academia, with Fijian youth researcher Patrick Vakaoti writing in relation to youth civic participation in Fiji that 'literature on Fiji's political history has failed to offer any detailed analysis about young people's involvement in politics' (Vakaoti 2012, p. 8). Regionally, this minimisation is most notable in the repeated lack of mention of youth in the progress reports of the Pacific Plan (Noble et al. 2011, p. 16) and similar documents outlining the foci and ambitions of the 18 member states of the Pacific Islands Forum. It was further reinforced in April or May of 2018, when the youth-focused page on the Pacific Islands Forum Secretariat, which had remained 'under construction' (PIFS n.d.) for many years, was removed entirely from the website. Such examples act as evidence not only of the assumed lack of influence of youth within Pacific societies, but of the recurrent failures to acknowledge, understand and address their realities.

Whether by design or simply reflecting notions of tradition, the result of the youth voice being ignored amounts to a structural minimisation of the worth and potentiality of youth. To borrow a term from citizenship scholar David Owen (1996), youth are not considered to be active citizens, but instead 'apprentice-citizens' who need to be managed, rather than consulted, and taught, rather than learned from (see Bessant 2004; Harris 2006). As Jayaweera and Morioka (2008, p. 11) noted, 'Even if adults understand youth concerns, they are perceived as unlikely to prioritize them or take action to address them'.

Rationalising Power Imbalances

Several youth activists and advocates spoke to me of the frustration that they felt within Pacific youth communities regarding the lack of opportunities present for their active engagement in civil society. Primarily, their participation is considered by youth and youth advocates to be overlooked by decision-makers rather than explicitly opposed. As Patrick Mesia, a youth-focused development worker from Solomon Islands, said to me:

> Because of some of the cultural context here in Solomons, like the big man system, the elders in some places dictate what should happen sometimes for a young age group like that. They don't give them space and when they hear them raising issues, they ignore it as being from a *pikinini* [child] point of view.

This ignorance of youth engagement was discussed as being reflective of cultural practices that do not place importance on the role of youth as potential decision-makers and active citizens. In these scenarios, youth and adults alike are unlikely to consider active youth involvement in decision-making processes. Some informants, however, shared their experiences of youth populations who were resisting their minimisation rather than passively accepting it. These communities were marked by young people, who were forthright in their intention to be engaged members of their societies, meeting opposition from adult communities who were unaccustomed to assertive youth populations. Not content to be considered citizens in waiting, these young people were agitating to be viewed and included by their societies as active citizens.

Salote Kaimacuata, a child protection specialist at UNICEF Pacific and former magistrate in the Fijian judiciary who oversaw juvenile hearings, informed me that this is a problem throughout Oceania. She reflected on her experiences of working with young i-Kiribati women for UNICEF Pacific:

> I-Kiribati youth have been asking for a long time: 'Can we sit there?'; 'Can we participate?'; 'Can we input? Because our time will come sooner than we want, and we need to learn now from you and be mentored by you'.

Mamta Chand, a women's human rights activist from Fiji, described her dismay at the women's movement's rigid leadership structures and lack of acknowledgement of successes, saying:

> When we are in the intergenerational spaces, young women are told, 'You're not leaders. You're the leaders of tomorrow.' It was really frustrating. We would say, 'We are leaders of today. We are doing things. We are mobilising young women. We've mobilised young women to go and vote. We did that ourselves.' They refused to see us as leaders of now, of today. They say, 'No, when we die you become leaders.' We are leaders. We are leading. They refuse to accept that.

Usaia Moli, a youth advocate and former chair of the National Youth Council in Fiji, conveyed the same experience of engaging with the resistance of adult leaders to active youth citizenship. He said:

> No longer they can point to us and say, 'You'll be the leaders of tomorrow', because we are making changes right now. We look at every issue that comes up around the country and we have become champions on these issues in our own way. We represent the country in international meetings and presentations and everywhere we go, but yet they keep telling us, 'You are the leaders of tomorrow. Your time will come.' Our time is now. I don't have to wait a few more years.

Across the Pacific, opportunities for invited, engaged participation of youth in civil society are few. This is evident in formal spaces, such as the limited representation of youth interests in formal governance systems, including parliaments (Noble et al. 2011, p. 19). Less obvious are how social expectations are placed on youth, which limits their ability to be decisive about choices that will affect their long-term livelihoods, such as the pressures placed on children and youth to pursue education and the employment pathways that are associated with status rather than matched to their individual attributes or likely future livelihood opportunities (Nilan et al. 2006). Further, Fijian youth researcher Mereia Carling and Solomon Islands youth group leader John Firibo shared with me that when youth attempt to create space for themselves to represent their views, they are derided for disrespecting how their cultures operate and for disrespecting the wisdom of vesting authority in their elders.

Even with all these constraints to their active citizenship, growing numbers of young Pacific peoples are forging their own pathways to being active and engaged members of their societies, prosecuting the case that young people can and should be involved in decision-making processes. The following three case studies provide evidence of this. The first documents the influence that a small group of young people in Fiji were able to have on shaping public discourse ahead of the 2014 general election. The second discusses how a regional climate change–focused advocacy group is refusing to remain silent in the face of catastrophic environmental destruction. The last assembles examples of how young people in Fiji and Solomon Islands are creating spaces for the development of youth skills and voice in various contexts.

Case Study I: Be the Change

Before the Fijian general election of 2014—the country's first election since the 2006 coup d'état—Roshika Deo decided to run for parliament. With a professional background in law and international development, as well as a long history of social justice activism, Deo sought to use the campaign process to highlight the inequities that she noted in her home country, providing a voice for youth and women.

Deo built a small support team and consulted with established parties about standing for them, before choosing to run as an independent. As she explained:

> In the beginning we went to two political parties. We sat in meetings, spoke to people and we realised that they were very much conformist and there were rigid hierarchies. I realised that if I went in that party, I would only be perpetuating the same systems that are there by being part of it. I wouldn't be doing anything new. Nothing would change.

When determining to run as an independent, however, Deo decided to acknowledge the significant support network that she was building and labelled her campaign as 'Be the Change'.

Running on a social activist platform, Deo and Be the Change challenged social and political orthodoxy by not only openly discussing issues such as abortion, domestic violence and same-sex marriage, but by taking progressive positions on each of these issues, which contrasted with the conservative stances of the major parties. Her campaign shaped much of the public narrative of the election by pushing these boundaries. She told me:

> *Fiji Sun* [newspaper] was running an opinion article, so the candidates could write opinions and submit. Parties could write so I said, 'Be the Change is like a party. It's functioning like a party, so let's write.' Then I started getting other young people to write together with me. When we wrote about mental health issues, the next two or three days after we noticed that the media had started asking all the candidates about mental health. Once, when we wrote about LGBTIQ rights, on [television station] Fiji One, they asked all the candidates about same-sex marriage.

Of the campaign's influence, Deo said:

> We raised a lot of issues that no one else was talking about: things around LGBTIQ rights—no one used to talk about it, so as soon as we started talking about, the media started talking about it; violence against women—no one talked about violence against women as comprehensively as we did; also demilitarisation—people did talk about militarisation but we talked about it in terms of the impact on young people and women, moving away from generic discussions on militarisation. It was a bit more abstract, so we started contextualising it.

The campaign not only influenced media reporting and forced other candidates to discuss uncomfortable positions, it also opened Deo up to significant criticism from across the community, which regularly went beyond analysis of her political positions. She was criticised for her stance on gender, religion and culture, among other subjects (Chattier 2016; Palet 2014). She even told me:

> They had a [picture of a] full-born dead baby that they circulated all over Facebook, saying 'Roshika Deo supports abortion'. Very aggressively and loudly, I got attacked in that space.

The effect of such criticism did not silence Deo, however. She continued her campaign, narrowly falling short of being elected.[3] Her influence can be seen in her ability to attract over 1,000 votes in the general election, over 14,000 likes on the Be the Change Facebook page (Chattier 2016) and by the ability of her campaign to dictate much of the election's narrative. Demonstrating the capacity for organised youth to influence civic discourse, Roshika highlighted to me the motivation that she took from some of the more distasteful forms of criticism that she received when she realised why it was occurring, stating that 'we're challenging the status quo'.

Case Study II: 350 Pacific

350.org is a global grassroots social movement focused on combating human-induced climate change (350.org n.d.). The organisation has a diversified structure, with the main office based in New York and other

3 Due to eligibility legislation, Deo was not able to contest the 2018 election as a result of spending too great a period of time outside of the country undertaking study following the 2014 election.

satellite bodies throughout the globe, representing cities, countries and regions. Most of its members are volunteers who engage in advocacy campaigns that can be locally led or coordinated through a regional office.

350 Pacific is the arm of the organisation representing the region that incorporates Australia, Aotearoa/New Zealand and the Pacific Islands,[4] with a permanent staff member based in each of Australia, Aotearoa/New Zealand and Fiji.[5] There are active 350 Pacific groups across 15 Pacific states. Though membership across the 350 global network is not restricted by age limits, the Pacific groups almost exclusively consist of persons aged under 35. Their membership reflects their belief that, as it is young people who will mostly feel the effects of human-induced climate change, they should lead the efforts to combat it.

The Pacific-based group, who identify as the 'Pacific Climate Warriors', have not let their age negatively affect their engagement in advocacy and reform programs across the region, as well as beyond. Rather than relying on recognised government, private sector or civil society leaders to guide climate change advocacy and reform efforts, the members of 350 Pacific have insisted on having their voices be heard by domestic, regional and international leaders and change makers.

Traditional methods of advocacy that they have engaged in include direct lobbying to decision-makers and facilitating demonstrations (350 Pacific n.d.). Overcoming some of the barriers that are related to geography and timeliness, 350 Pacific has engaged in electronic campaigns to contact local representatives, as well as share images and videos of their daily climate-affected realities with the global community (Carter 2015, p. 26).

To register an effect that is both current and sustainable, 350 Pacific members have recognised that ideas of leadership that their communities held are vital to influencing change, but rather than ceding authority to those seen as leaders purely because of their age, they should instead question what leadership looks like. Fenton Lutunatabua, 350 Pacific's Fiji-based Communications Coordinator, explained to me that the organisation seeks to embed a sense of ownership and leadership in

4 350 Pacific was created by a group of volunteers whose values aligned with the global 350.org movement, which developed into a formal partnership. Its volunteers are recruited through member networks.

5 As at the time of fieldwork in 2015.

the communities that it works with, by responding 'to the needs of the community … in ways that make sense to them so they can take full ownership of and encourage leadership from the ground up'.

Beyond this, 350 Pacific actively targets young Pacific people that it considers agents of change to become members and to lead their home country initiatives. Regional representatives include members of the Pacific Youth Council, Commonwealth Youth Council and senior staff from Pacific-based development organisation offices. In regard to their worth to the movement, Lutunatabua claimed:

> These people are well connected. They're leaders in their own right. Really, they're doing the climate movement favours. Do we take claim to developing them? No. They have built their own reputations, they have networked so well, they have empowered so many people. It is us just connecting with them and trying to look at ways in which we can take their experience with the justice movements that they're in and apply that to the climate justice movement.

These youth leaders have been influential in securing positions in regional decision-making processes, such as the drafting of the current Pacific Youth Development Framework (SPC 2015).

The most disruptive 350 Pacific campaign to date occurred outside the Pacific Islands and focused on the damage being done to the planet by the region's neighbour, Australia. In 2014, 30 young Pacific people blockaded the largest coal port in the world in Newcastle on traditional canoes, with scores of non-Pacific people joining in support, stopping all 10 scheduled ships passing through (Packard 2014). The success of this action led to a 350.org repeat blockade in 2016 (Connell et al. 2016). Explaining the action, Lutunatabua stated that the purpose was:

> To send a very clear message to the fossil fuel industry saying that, as Pacific Islanders, we will do what it takes to stand up for our Pacific and show the world that, if they continue to expand the fossil fuel industry, that's literally exporting destruction to the Pacific.

The campaigns and influence of 350 Pacific illustrate how some Pacific youth are identifying gaps in how issues of social justice are being addressed by their leaders. Where such deficits exist, young people are acting decisively to fill these gaps as advocates and activists.

Case Study III: Emerging Youth Activists

Throughout Fiji and Solomon Islands—and particularly in the capitals of Suva and Honiara—a growing cohort of youth activists is creating spaces for other young people to develop personal and professional skills, as well as acting to influence policy agendas. The most obvious space in which this is occurring is the various youth councils at regional, national and subnational levels.

It is in the youth councils that young people like the Honiara Youth Council president, Harry Olikwailafa, have been able to develop their leadership skills and their exposure to decision-making processes and professional networks, to reach positions in which they can advocate for positive outcomes in youth policy planning. Harry has worked with youth councils and non-government organisations at local and regional levels to create and provide feedback on programs and policies. It was this experience that provided him skills and confidence, and that prompted him to pre-emptively create a youth policy paper to present to elected representatives following the 2014 general election during the period of government consolidation.[6] As Harry told me:

> I went to the camps at the different hotels and I sat with the elected members of parliament and presented the policy paper. I said, 'When you rub shoulders to form a government, remember young people'.

Beyond formal youth councils, young people have in recent years also begun to create their own organisations to develop youth capacity and participation. Kaajal Kumar, from Fiji, created the Aspire Network in 2012, with the mission of 'Developing Young People to Develop the Future Generation through Democratic Innovations' (Aspire Network 2012). Kaajal informed me that she wanted to create opportunities beyond youth councils, as their representative structure limits the amount of young people that they can upskill and expose to active civic engagement. To achieve such ends, the Network has engaged in activities such as hosting 50 Fijian youth at the Young Fijian Leaders Parliament Forum and Youth Parliament, which was established by the network in 2014.

6 Solomon Islands politics follows an ad hoc tradition whereby elected independent representatives are courted to create coalition governments. To try to secure numbers, aligned representatives are segregated into 'camps' at different locations to try to prevent them from being courted by opposing groups (Fraenkel 2008; Wood 2015).

A former member of the Fijian National Youth Council, Elisha Bano, takes a different approach to developing youth skills in active civic engagement. In 2014, she established ACT Fiji, standing for Advocacy through Creative Techniques. As Elisha explained to me:

> It's a youth advocacy group where we are trying to use creative mediums to advocate on social issues. There are three mediums that we are targeting: social media … theatre, and … graphic arts.

Elisha is one of a growing number of Fijians using artistic endeavours to influence civic discourse through what is referred to in Fijian critical civil society as 'artivism'.

Finally, from a more formal development perspective is the example of Sandra Bartlett. At the age of 27, Sandra was hired to manage the employment training program in Solomon Islands, Youth@Work. Unlike the examples of Harry, Kaajal and Elisha, Sandra's history as a youth advocate is purely professional. Hired based on her education and business background, Sandra utilised her age to be a mentor to the youth participants of the program, while also using her professional skills to create a positive image of youth to businesses, communities and media in Honiara. With more than 500 young people completing the training and internship program between 2009 and 2015, Sandra noted that:

> The big success, the social change success, is that we've put youth development on people's minds. In Solomons, it was always, 'youth are a problem; youth are a time bomb; it's an issue, it's an issue …', but now they see that youth are doing things.

Unlocking the Potential of Pacific Youth

Despite conceptions of 'tradition' that normalise youth minimisation, there is a small but growing recognition that providing opportunities for young people to develop their skills is required not only as a safeguard against antisocial behaviours and civil unrest, as per conventional readings of youth bulge theories (Sukarieh & Tannock 2017; Urdal 2006), but it is also required to create and sustain positive developmental futures for the great ocean states of the Pacific. This is particularly true in institutional settings that address youth development issues directly or indirectly. Many of my informants discussed this with me. Luisa Senibulu, who has run anti-corruption workshops with young people from across the region, said:

> Youth have a lot to contribute. It is often said that they are the leaders of tomorrow. They have a lot of capacity. They have a lot of knowledge that we don't really utilise.

Former chair of Fiji's National Youth Council, Usaia Moli, stated:

> If you're going to plan for the future, then it is only right that you include those that are going to be there, and that is the young people.

These sentiments were shared by Mereia Carling, who has researched youth citizenship in Fiji and who is the primary author of the current Pacific Youth Development Framework. She said:

> We are never going to solve the problems that we want to solve by ignoring what young people think and not involving them. We are creating problems when we don't involve young people.

Beyond this, some young people continue to demonstrate their willingness to be leaders of their communities. This is particularly evident in responses to issues that are observed as having social and economic consequences. On issues of climate change and civil rights, it is youth who are making themselves experts and demanding that their voices be heard. No two examples better display this than the work of 350 Pacific in relation to climate change and Roshika Deo's 'Be the Change' political campaign of 2014. These examples support political scientist Patrick Kaiku's (2017, p. 7) criticism of the application of youth bulge theories in Melanesian societies: 'Where the youth bulge discourse generally depicts young people as impulsively violent and conflict-prone, it disregards youth-led initiatives that are worth knowing and supporting'. Notably, in each of these cases, the youth that were involved created the space for their engagement in areas in which deficits existed that the traditional ideas of leadership had not filled and reinforced—social justice–led politics, climate change and youth civic engagement.

The active and open participation of a growing number of Pacific youths in civil society reflects a growing sense of both optimism for change and despair at the status quo. Though the numbers of actively and civically engaged youth remain small, their influence is growing. This shift cannot be attributed to one singular cause. Fijian academic and social commentator Jope Tarai reflects that one reason may be an increased awareness for the youth's potential to drive change, saying: 'The projected youth population in the elections is 47 per cent, so we hold the highest majority of the mandate, so to speak'.

A combination of access to information, a growing network of youth who are engaged in critical civil society, disenfranchisement at the state of politics and a renewed focus on democracy throughout the region also appear to be playing a part.

Access to information has long been recognised as important for shaping individual and collective thought patterns. From Alexis de Tocqueville's (1947) assertion in 1835 that the strength of democracy in the US was largely due to a free and informative media, through to the influence of television on the civil rights movements globally in the mid-twentieth century (Klarman 1994, p. 11; Winter & Eyal 1981), the flow of information has shaped politics and political engagement. As critical race and gender activist and author bell hooks (1990, p. 3) wrote, 'Watching television in the fifties and sixties, and listening to adult conversation, was one of the primary ways young black folks learned about race politics'. So, too, does it appear that the increasing reach of internet communications and, particularly, social media is expanding the scope of youth knowledge and engagement in civic discourse (Brimacombe et al. 2018). Sionlelei Mario is a civil society activist from Fiji who has worked on civics education programs in Fiji. She explained to me how social media is opening up channels of dialogue across the citizen spectrum of Fiji, saying:

> Social media has a lot of groups that are discussing stuff. Policy people are having discussions, youth are having discussions and then there are others who have gone past their time and they're still talking.

Facebook provides a platform that is seemingly increasing opportunities for civic discussion for Pacific peoples, old and young alike. 'Yumi Toktok Stret' is a Facebook page focused on Vanuatu civil society, with over 100,000 followers. A similar page existed in Solomon Islands between 2011 and 2018 called 'Forum Solomon Islands International' (FSII), which, at its peak, had over 23,000 followers. One of the facilitators of FSII, Benjamin Afuga, discussed with me the potential power of social media to communicate public sentiment to leaders and to agitate for social change, stating:

> We believe that people's views on Facebook can be a useful tool to bring issues across to our leaders and others who might have an answer to these things.

Disenfranchisement with the current state of politics further appears to be influencing increased youth civic engagement. Multiple interviewees spoke of the political processes that discriminate against marginalised communities and that push the concerns of youth to the side as motivating their own engagement. Jope Tarai expressed his frustration that:

> The current power structures that we have in Fiji are pro-elite, anti-youth, anti-poor. Not them personally, but the way the parliament is structured.

Such an assertion is echoed by Harry Olikwailafa, who stated:

> We have a lot of good policies but the political will behind those policies [is lacking]. Sometimes you can see the political interference at administrative level.

It is important to note that these issues are not contained to the Pacific. In a study of seven youth communities across Central, North and South America, sociologists Jessica Taft and Hava Gordon (2011, 2013) identified frustration with political systems as a driver of youth civic engagement. Taft and Gordon (2013, p. 98) even suggested that youth engagement in activist civil society demonstrates that 'these youth are deeply committed to meaningful democracy and participation'. Rather than embodying identities that are focused on individual ambition and achievement—shaped by forces of modernisation, including international development discourses of capabilities and empowerment (Cornwall & Brock 2005; Kleine 2010; Makuwira 2018)—several Pacific youth are finding ways to engage in their societies to benefit what they perceive as the common good. The case studies presented in this chapter indicate that a desire to work for 'common good' interests resonates with civically minded Pacific youth.

This commitment to democratic engagement with civil society was a recurrent theme in the interviews that I held with young civic activists. Young people engaged in critical civil society in Solomon Islands considered it their duty to promote the interests of youth and to hold the government to account for its transgressions and corruption. John Firibo, a youth group leader in Solomon Islands stated:

> In the schools, especially when it comes to history, we talk a lot about the politicians and there is a growing tension between us and the politicians. Many of us are trying to stamp out corruption in a way that they will see us, they will hear us and maybe make change.

In Fiji, this sense of frustration among youth interviewees regarding their marginalisation from civic and political practices was even more palpable due, at least partially, to the fact that 2014 had seen those aged under 30 years voting for the first time in the eight years since the beginning of military rule. The 'coup babies', as they are known (Vakaoti 2014, p. 5), appeared to revel in the opportunity to finally exercise their democratic rights and to openly discuss their concerns with friends, family and the public. Sionlelei Mario of Fiji explained this enthusiasm:

> I'm in my 20s and most of my friends are around that age group and, for most of us, it was our first time to vote. We thought we had some obligation since we were sensitised in that area of national development and youth roles [as civically engaged young people]. We needed to get involved with other young people who are just coming out of their late teens to discuss what we think your role is, what your level of interest is in the general elections and what does it mean as a young person to actually tick that box [on the ballot paper] at the end of the day.

This should not be taken as a generalisation of youth approaches to engage with governance structures. Indeed, the youth activists who I interviewed were notable precisely for the depth of critical engagement that they have with political agents and structures in comparison with their peers.

Conclusion

The case studies of Be the Change, 350 Pacific and the emerging youth activists of Fiji and Solomon Islands demonstrate not only that there are youth willing to engage in meaningful ways in the shaping of their societies, but also that they have the skills to do so. Providing opportunities for young people to be positively engaged in civil society opens the prospect for a far greater number of youth to affect the futures of their communities, countries and the Pacific region for positive developmental change. The case studies also document the ability of young people to create their own opportunities for civic engagement when none are provided.

Appropriate modes of participation are too often determined through an adult-centric lens. Parents and elders minimise youth participation daily and yet expect young people to be able to engage in systems that are designed for and by adults—and only when the adults believe that engagement is necessary or beneficial. As Vakaoti (2014, p. 24) found in a study of youth civic engagement for Fiji's Citizen's Constitutional Forum, 'Nuclear families, schools and social media were identified as popular spaces where young people could express their opinion. Adult spaces like community and church meetings were the least comfortable spaces for young people'. The specific mention of online platforms as spaces for youth civic engagement supports my own observations and data drawn from informants. Thus, it appears appropriate that when desiring youth engagement and participation, thought is put into where, when and how young people will feel most comfortable and valued to share their knowledge and opinions.

Again, it must be noted that the youth activists discussed in this chapter are not representative of the everyday civic engagement practices of all Pacific youth. For most, deference and passivity are the norm, guided by notions of 'tradition' and the social expectation that they 'be seen but not heard'. As Vakaoti (2012, p. 11) wrote, 'This is the enduring challenge for young people's participation in Fiji: how to successfully negotiate the past and the present?' Against the sociocentric backdrop of traditional communities and the increasing global influence of materialism and individualism, their challenge is to negotiate change in the roles that they play in society and in the roles that their societies play in the global environment. Chris McMurray (2006, p. 5) summarised this difficulty:

> Especially difficult for young people is that many of the values and practices of a modern society are in direct conflict with those of their traditional societies. Traditional societies tend to resist change and questioning of their identity, whereas modern society promotes freedom and democracy, new ideas, discussion and debate.

Overcoming hierarchical hindrances to youth participation requires more than soliciting information from young people regarding issues that are important to adults or organisations that they represent. For the long-term, meaningful participation of young people, youth need to be empowered to appreciate that their contributions can be valuable, and people in decision-making positions need to truly recognise their value. Ideas of who is 'expert' enough to have their opinions considered have provided insight into the power with which knowledge is observed to be held, both by governing powers (Brownhill 2009, p. 360) and from Western centres of thought, such as academia and bilateral aid agencies (Mahiri 1998). Reversing this trend is not simple. It requires the commitment of experts, policymakers and young people alike to be open to the possibilities of youth engagement leading to positive outcomes. Examples such as those from Be the Change, 350 Pacific and the growing networks of youth activists and advocates demonstrate that such outcomes are possible.

Acknowledgements

My utmost gratitude to the communities, youth activists and advocates whom I met and spoke with in Fiji and Solomon Islands. My research is simply a reflection of their knowledge and lived experiences. Thank you also to La Trobe University for the financial assistance that supported the period of fieldwork from which the data represented in this chapter were collected.

References

350 Pacific n.d., *We Don't Normally Do This Here in Kiribati …*, 350 Pacific, viewed 6 December 2016, 350pacific.org/we-dont-normally-do-this-here-in-kiribati/

350.org n.d., *Home Page*, 350.org, viewed 6 December 2016, 350.org/

Aspire Network 2012, *Aspire Network*, Facebook, viewed 17 October 2018, www.facebook.com/pg/aspirenetworkfj

Bessant, J 2004, 'Mixed messages: Youth participation and democratic practice', *Australian Journal of Political Science,* vol. 39, no. 2, pp. 387–404, doi.org/10.1080/1036114042000238573

Brimacombe, T 2017, 'Pacific policy pathways: Young women online and offline', in M Macintyre & C Spark (eds), *Transformations of gender in Melanesia*, ANU Press, Canberra, doi.org/10.1002/app5.253

Brimacombe, T, Kant, R, Finau, G, Tarai, J & Titifanue, J 2018, 'A new frontier in digital activism: An exploration of digital feminism in Fiji', *Asia and the Pacific Policy Studies*, vol. 5, pp. 508–521.

Brownhill, S 2009, 'The dynamics of participation: Modes of governance and increasing participation in planning', *Urban Policy and Research,* vol. 27, no. 4, pp. 357–375.

Carter, G 2015, 'Establishing a Pacific voice in the climate change negotiations', in G Fry & S Tarte (eds), *The New Pacific Diplomacy,* ANU Press, Canberra, doi.org/10.22459/NPD.12.2015.17

Chattier, P 2016, *Fiji's Roshika Deo—Outlier, Positive Deviant or Simply Feisty Feminist?*, Developmental Leadership Program, viewed 30 November 2016, www.dlprog.org/opinions/fiji-s-roshika-deo-outlier-positive-deviant-or-simply-feisty-feminist.php

Connell, T, Carr, M & Kirkwood, I 2016, 'Newcastle Harbour coal blockade: Live updates', *Newcastle Herald,* 8 May 2016, viewed 23 June 2017, www.theherald.com.au/story/3894106/newcastle-harbour-coal-blockade/

Cornwall, A & Brock, K 2005, 'What do buzzwords do for development policy? A critical look at "participation", "empowerment" and "poverty reduction"', *Third World Quarterly,* vol. 26, no. 7, pp. 1043–1060.

Cox, J 2017, 'Kindy and grassroots gender transformations in Solomon Islands', in M Macintyre & C Spark (eds), *Transformations of gender in Melanesia,* ANU Press, Canberra, doi.org/10.22459/TGM.02.2017.03

de Tocqueville, A 1947, *Democracy in America: A new translation by Arthur Goldhammer,* Library of America, New York.

Fraenkel, J 2008, 'The impact of RAMSI on the 2006 elections', in S Dinnen & S Firth (eds), *Politics and state building in Solomon Islands,* ANU E Press, Canberra, doi.org/10.22459/PSBS.05.2008.06

Harris, A 2006, 'Introduction: Critical perspectives on child and youth participation in Australia and New Zealand/Aotearoa', *Children, Youth and Environments,* vol. 16, no. 2, pp. 220–230.

hooks, b 1990, *Yearning: Race, gender, and cultural politics,* South End Press, Boston.

Jayaweera, S & Morioka, K 2008, *Giving South Pacific youth a voice: Youth development through participation,* International Bank for Reconstruction and Development/World Bank, Suva.

Jolly, M 1994, 'Hierarchy and encompassment: Rank, gender and place in Vanuatu and Fiji', *History and Anthropology,* vol. 7, nos 1–4, pp. 133–167, doi.org/10.1080/02757206.1994.9960843

Kaiku, P 2017, 'Re-thinking the youth bulge theory in Melanesia', *Contemporary PNG Studies: DWU Research Journal*, vol. 26, pp. 1–14.

Klarman, MJ 1994, 'Brown, racial change, and the Civil Rights Movement', *Virginia Law Review*, vol. 80, no. 1, pp. 7–150.

Kleine, D 2010, 'ICT4What?—using the choice framework to operationalise the capability approach to development', *Journal of International Development*, vol. 22, no. 5, pp. 674–692.

Mahiri, I 1998, *Comparing transect walks with experts and local people*, vol. 31, International Institute for Environment and Development, London, pp. 4–8.

Makuwira, J 2018, 'Power and development in practice: NGOs and the development agenda setting', *Development in Practice*, vol. 28, no. 3, pp. 422–431, doi.org/10.1080/09614524.2018.1433816

McLeod, A 2007, *Literature review of leadership models in the Pacific*, State, Society and Governance in Melanesia Program, The Australian National University, Canberra.

McLeod, A 2015, *Women's leadership in the Pacific*, Developmental Leadership Program, University of Birmingham, Birmingham.

McMurray, C 2006, 'Young people's participation in the Pacific—facilitating factors and lessons learned', paper presented at the Children's Rights and Culture in the Pacific Seminar, UNICEF, Suva.

Morton, H 1996, *Becoming Tongan: An ethnography of childhood*, University of Hawai'i Press, Honolulu.

Nilan, P, Cavu, P, Tagicakiverata, I & Hazelman, E 2006, 'White collar work: Career ambitions of final year school students', *International Education Journal*, vol. 7, no. 7, pp. 895–905.

Noble, C, Pereira, N & Saune, N 2011, *Urban youth in the Pacific: Increasing resilience and reducing risk for involvement in crime and violence*, United Nations Development Program Pacific Centre, Suva.

Owen, D 1996, 'Dilemmas and opportunities for the young active citizen', *Youth Studies Australia*, vol. 15, no. 1, pp. 20–23.

Packard, A 2014, *Coal Ships Stopped. The Warriors Have Risen!*, 350 Pacific, viewed 6 December 2016, world.350.org/pacificwarriors/2014/10/20/coal-ships-stopped-the-warriors-have-risen/

Palet, LS 2014, *Roshika Deo: Fiji's Feminist Voice*, OZY, viewed 30 November 2016, www.ozy.com/rising-stars/roshika-deo-fijis-feminist-voice/34034

PIFS n.d., *Youth*, Pacific Islands Forum Secretariat (page discontinued), viewed 5 February 2018, www.forumsec.org/pages.cfm/newsroom/documents-publications/youth.html

Prasad, S 2017, 'Governance paradoxes and pathways in Pacific Island countries', *Pacific Dynamics,* vol. 1, no. 2, pp. 325–339.

Sahlins, M 1963, 'Poor man, rich man, big-man, chief: Political types in Melanesia and Polynesia', *Comparative Studies in Society and History,* vol. 5, no. 3, pp. 285–303.

Slatter, C 2006, 'Treading water in rapids? Non-governmental organisations and resistance to neo-liberalism in Pacific Island states', in S Firth (ed.), *Globalisation and governance in the Pacific Islands*, ANU E Press, Canberra, doi.org/10.22459/GGPI.12.2006.02

SPC 2009, *The Suva Declaration from the 2nd Pacific youth festival: Actioning the youth agenda*, Secretariat of the Pacific Community, Suva.

SPC 2015, *The Pacific youth development framework 2014–2023*, Secretariat of the Pacific Community Suva, Fiji.

Sukarieh, M & Tannock, S 2017, 'The global securitisation of youth', *Third World Quarterly*, vol. 39, no. 5, pp. 854–870.

Taft, JK & Gordon, HR 2011, 'Rethinking youth political socialization: Teenage activists talk back', *Youth & Society,* vol. 43, no. 4, pp. 1499–1527, doi.org/10.1177/0044118X10386087

Taft, JK & Gordon, HR 2013, 'Youth activists, youth councils and constrained democracy', *Education, Citizenship and Social Literature,* vol. 8, no. 1, pp. 87–100, doi.org/10.1177/1746197913475765

Titifanue, J, Kant, R, Finau, G & Tarai, J 2017, 'Climate change advocacy in the Pacific: The role of information and communication technologies', *Pacific Journalism Review,* vol. 23, no. 1, pp. 133–149, doi.org/10.24135/pjr.v23i1.105

Urdal, H 2006, 'A clash of generations? Youth bulges and political violence', *International Studies Quarterly,* vol. 50, pp. 607–629, doi.org/10.1111/j.1468-2478.2006.00416.x

Vakaoti, P 2012, 'Mapping the landscape of young people's participation in Fiji', *SSGM Discussion Paper 6*, State, Society and Governance in Melanesia Department, The Australian National University, Canberra.

Vakaoti, P 2014, *Young people and democratic participation in Fiji*, Citizens' Constitutional Forum, Suva.

Winter, JP & Eyal, CH 1981, 'Agenda setting for the civil rights issue', *Public Opinion Quarterly*, vol. 45, pp. 376–383.

Wood, T 2015, 'The 2014 parliamentary elections in Solomon Islands', *Electoral Studies*, vol. 39, pp. 153–158, doi.org/10.1016/j.electstud.2015.03.006

7

Entrepreneurship and Social Action Among Youth in American Sāmoa

Aaron John Robarts Ferguson

Introduction

Like many high schools across the mainland US, grad-week in American Sāmoa is a lively time of celebrations for youth and their families. Days at the beach, class trips to the movie theatre and *umu* (earth oven barbeque) all serve as a lead-up to the graduation ceremony in which hundreds of families will come to honour the accomplishments of their graduating youth. But, behind these celebrations lies the fact that within a few short months, as many as half or more of those graduating youth will be leaving the islands on which they grew up. Youth leave to seek jobs to support their families, pursue education and find a new life in the Samoan diaspora, moving to destinations as varied as Hawai'i, Alaska, the Pacific Northwest (US) and California. As Samoan youth age, they are increasingly exposed to a local discourse of success and opportunity that reinforces the defined pathways that draw youth away from the islands. This discourse emphasises success as an exterior 'other' to be pursued away from the local.

Throughout the day-to-day conversations during my research in American Sāmoa, both youth and adults expressed worry about the perceived lack of opportunities. The successes and failures of youth and their effect on the *'āiga* (family) and *nu'u* (village) were frequently used as a measure of island success and prosperity for the Samoan people. Worries about youth economic opportunities would thus often segue into worries about the economic state of the island as a whole. Across ages, my contacts evoked a deep concern for the future of the islands' youth and the limits that youth must navigate in their transition to adulthood. These worries manifested when considering the status of the education system, the morality of youth and their attainment of classic Samoan ideals, such as *usitai* (discipline), and in frequent references to the 'disconnect between youth and elders'. Three pathways have emerged as the most prominent and referenced futures available for young Samoans: military careers, sports scholarships to colleges on mainland US and work at on-island tuna canneries. Recent scholarship on American Samoan youth has focused on the significance of sport in the production of youth futures (Kwauk 2014; Uperesa 2014a, 2014b). This chapter instead explores how youth entrepreneurship is an alternative for young Samoans to attain social and economic capital. Through three illustrative cases, I demonstrate how certain youth have made substantial contributions to re-signifying 'business' as a category of *fa'asāmoa* (the Samoan way) or 'Samoanness'. By representing business as a form of social action that is motivated by service to the greater community, they thereby articulate global youth culture within their local context.

This chapter is based on two and a half months of ethnographic fieldwork in American Sāmoa between May and August 2015, involving networking, semi-structured interviewing and focus groups with young people between the ages of 15 and 30, as well as with their families and community members of various ages. I begin by examining contemporary scholarship on Samoan youth specifically, followed by a discussion of relevant anthropological literature on globalisation, youth and social capital more broadly. Following that, I introduce three case studies, each of which focuses on a youth business owner whose experiences exemplify the successes and challenges that youth face related to the discourse of restricted opportunities. The first is centred on Pacific Origins, a clothing company built around the juxtaposition of global and local culture through acts of capitalistic value creation, showing how skilfully intertwining global and local influences can lead to a prosperous business and social life on-island. The next case considers Sāmoa's Finest, a *tatau* (tattoo) shop run by local Army reservist, Sonny Lavea, and highlights the topics of land ownership and military service, illuminates factors that enable success for youth business owners and reveals certain barriers that might impede business creation. Finally, the third case examines

Sāmoa Office Supply, a one-stop shop for office supplies and electronics. Run by 28-year-old Jordan Lotomau, this example details *fa'asāmoa* as materialised in the realm of business and further demonstrates how these youth have tied their entrepreneurship to social action.

I analyse each case along five interconnected conceptual categories: economic capital, social capital, technology utilisation, mediation of global and local influences, and the articulation of business as a form of social action. These were the most potent themes that emerged during my research into youth futures and, while they are not exhaustive, they allow access to a wide range of relevant factors in a concentrated manner. Hopefully, they help the understanding of some of the central questions animating this research: How do youth come to make these complex decisions about their future? What alternatives exist when youth feel unfulfilled by the conventional futures afforded to them? How do contemporary youth feel connected with *fa'asamoa*? I conclude that youth entrepreneurship in its formulation as a form of social action and as a re-envisioning of participation in local life, while restricted by certain factors, is a valuable alternative that helps Samoan youth relieve the tension between life on-island and a life in the diaspora.

Globalisation, Capital and the Anthropology of Youth in Sāmoa

The most current scholarship on Samoan youth has focused on youth involvement in sport, as observed most notably in the work of Fa'anofo Lisaclaire Uperesa and Christina Kwauk. In 'Seeking New Fields of Labor', Uperesa details how American football has become a central channel for youth future development and explores the connection between football, the history of US imperialism and how local structures of opportunity have evolved in American Sāmoa (Uperesa 2014b). At the heart of this process is the ever-present question of American Sāmoa's territoriality—specifically, the uncertainty of American Sāmoa's status throughout its history as a US territory (Droessler 2013). Regarding football as the intersection of 'local and imperial interests', Uperesa demonstrated how football has become a 'conduit' bringing Samoans through mainland educational institutions (Uperesa 2014b). This is further supplemented in 'Fabled Futures', in which she underscores the extent to which Samoan youths' navigation of the enmeshed logics of the football industry is central to the transnational movement of youth (Uperesa 2014a). For young Samoans, the often-referenced preponderance of Polynesians in the NFL, and the now multi-generational history of prominent Samoan footballers, serves as a potent force that draws young Samoans off-island. This construction of the so-called 'Polynesian pipeline' effectively legitimates football as a powerfully desirable paradigm for achieving economic prosperity for young (male) Samoans. The limitations of this 'pipeline' (for girls especially) is a reality rarely addressed in public discourse on youth futures.

'No Longer Just a Pastime' builds on this analysis of the role of sports in youth futures, instead focusing on rugby in (independent) Sāmoa (Kwauk 2014). Her exploration of sports as a path to success, a veritable ticket to 'the blessed life', particularly shows the extent to which sport has become instilled within contemporary Samoan culture as a legitimate means of 'personal and professional development' (Kwauk 2014, p. 304). Highlighting that sport itself is an alternative to traditional economic training (such as agricultural work, or professional and vocational education), Kwauk (2014, p. 304) showed how this alternative is essentialised as a form of *tautua* (service) to the *'āiga*. With sports development directly contributing to the transnational extraction of Samoan youth, life on-island is problematised when success becomes a reality that is exclusively exterior to island life. In such a climate, 'concerns about youth unemployment are thus concerns about whether and how youth can become productive contributing members of their *āiga* in an evershifting and uneven global society' (2014, p. 316). Though primarily focusing on youth sport development to reach deeper issues such as the legacy of colonialism and health development strategies, the current scholarship has accomplished much to diversify the scholarly attention on youth in Sāmoa expanding into new grounds since the work of Margaret Mead.

Indeed, the legacy of Margaret Mead's *Coming of Age in Samoa* (Mead 1973) remains pertinent and she is still a well-known name among Samoans. The book brought Mead and anthropology into focus in the US, but it became a source of controversy regarding subject representation and anthropological method (Shankman 1996). Despite the contentions that emerged since its publication, it is significant as the first anthropological contribution to the study of youth in the Samoan. While it perhaps has more to reveal about the writer and the state of anthropology at the time, it remains a useful source to reflect on certain features in the life of Samoan youth—namely, the importance of age-based respect and obeisance, the intricacy of family life and an introduction to core values of Samoan culture.

Additionally, Mead's ethnography is representative of a cross-cultural or comparative approach that dominated the anthropology of adolescence at the time, but which has transitioned to an 'anthropology of youth' (Bucholtz 2002, p. 1). This has brought forth a more encompassing approach with fewer limitations because of its lack of adult-centric, teleological perspectives of youth. Mary Bucholtz contrasts such perspectives that considered adolescence a mere stage of incompleteness on a transition to adulthood with an approach that views youth as a 'flexible and contestable social category', one in which youth is not a 'trajectory' or aim, but an identity (Bucholtz 2002, pp. 528, 532). This theoretical shift is significant because of the greater appreciation that it allows for the agency of youth in the process of their own sociocultural definition and formation as a peer group.

Globalising youth research, as Bucholtz highlighted, is an endeavour that is not so much 'cross-cultural as it is trans-cultural' (Bucholtz 2002, p. 543). Critically, this transcultural approach enables recognition of the shared experiences of youth as a social group across the Pacific, a connection that is evoked directly by the lived experiences of the youth examined in this chapter. It can be observed, for example, in their engagement with intercultural, digital diasporic spaces that proved to be essential grounds for their business development, or in their use of entrepreneurship as a tool to resolve tensions that they faced in regard to the lack of adequate employment, a reality that many youths face throughout the Pacific Island community (Secretariat of the Pacific Community 2015, p. 24). This transcultural, and even trans-oceanic, approach is also reflected in recent scholarship, including Kwauk's and Uperesa's works in the Samoan islands and Mary K Good's work on gender dynamics and experiences of marginalised youth as they interpolate influences of globalisation with notions of morality and 'modernity' (Good 2012, 2014).

There are several key features from the broader anthropology of globalisation to keep in mind precisely because of the ever-growing influence of 'the global' in the lives of Pacific youth. The first is that globalisation has 'dislodged' culture from certain locales (Inda 2006, p. 11). This dislodging encourages the conditions that allow a blending of global and local influences that youth must, in turn, interact with. The example of American football as a prism that reveals American Sāmoa's history of imprecise colonial relations with the US is one prominent example that shows this in operation, but it can be observed in the general influence of globalisation in the Samoan archipelago as a whole (Macpherson &

Macpherson 2009). In such circumstances, certain youth can capitalise on the mastery of the negotiation between those two realities, as will be demonstrated in the examples of Pacific Origins and Sāmoa's Finest. Insofar as globalisation implies a 'heightened entanglement of global and local', those in a position to 'disentangle' those realities become powerful agents in the process of defining youth identity locally (Inda 2006, p. 9).

Due to the acceleration of 'flows of capital, people, goods, images, interactions and processes', those with the means to access appropriate technology may find themselves poised to take advantage of this increased mobility of cultural flows (Inda 2006, p. 9). In this connection, the value of social media and the internet as a tool of commercial expansion places contemporary Samoan youth in a unique position to create new economic opportunities in which previous generations were more limited. It also acts as prime influence on the constitution of diasporic communities into a kind of 'digital diaspora', in which youth on the islands and those in trans-oceanic spaces knit together their ability to engage in shared experiences (such as the passing of a beloved public figure) (Burroughs & Ka'ili 2015). Youth on-island especially benefit in this regard from a higher likelihood of having regular internet access at school, as compared to many households that are still without adequate connection to the internet. The incorporation of technology has brought significant advantages in each case reviewed here. Sāmoa Office Supply sells computer and office technology and also functions as a small internet cafe. Pacific Origins and Sāmoa's Finest both interact extensively through social media with the youth of the Samoan diaspora and with other Pasifika communities. This showcases how social connections that cross 'time and space' are now 'less dependent on circumstances of co-presence' and how nodes of economic capital are increasingly inseparable from a sizeable, dispersed network that is independent of locale (Inda 2006, p. 9). Throughout these examples, the youth's ability to manage the interwoven global and local realities prove to be pivotal components of their business success.

Pacific Origins

It seems that there are more airways for the young Samoan than roadways. Arriving as I did at the beginning of summer, I was unprepared for more than half of my initial youth contacts to leave within even just a few weeks of meeting them. They followed grooves formed by the many who travelled before them, and whether in search of economic prosperity or sporting success, the paths they took were well worn. For those with the financial means, such as Tai Saifaga, these channels afford access to transnational networks and experience of life off-island. After leaving business school at the University of Hawai'i (UH) Mānoa with his degree unfinished, by age 23, he became an award-winning business owner with a shop in a prime location in a commercially developed centre of Tutu'ila. A forward-thinking young man, Tai is thrilled by opportunities to share the vision of his company and his vision for its growth. His company is an effort to create meaningful connections to the past through clothing, so that youth can 'wear [their] heritage'. By offering clothes that blend global fashion with locally designed motifs, Pacific Origins becomes an intermediary of global and local culture and a commodity is constituted through which youth acquire a certain connection to Samoan culture. This act of economic value creation is intimately tied with the accrual of social capital that is generated in part by Tai's mastery over this process of intermediation and through his role as a purveyor of desirable products. Social capital is generated from local artist patronage by sponsoring events for American Samoan youth, and it is reinforced through the use of social media. Tai is thus able to articulate his business as a form of *tautua* to his *'āiga*, his island, and his fellow youth, all in an effort, he says, to 'help inspire his generation to be leaders and connect with their heritage'.

Before opening a storefront, Pacific Origins was run out of Tai's dorm room at UH Mānoa, a compelling story that was articulated skilfully when he and I met. However, it was Tai's experience at the American Sāmoa Community College, before UH Mānoa, that inspired him to create Pacific Origins:

> From 2009 to 2011, I was in the community college, and my friends and I would practically live in the art room, but the stuff would just sit in the room; you'd have one art show a semester, but only a few would sell, if that.

Seeing a potential market for Pacific designs, Tai first began selling at UH Mānoa, but later decided to leave college and return to American Sāmoa to expand his business at home, deftly taking advantage of an already established network of business and social contacts that was cultivated through friendships, family ties and interpersonal acuity. Indeed, the speed of our mutual connection on a shared interest in youth streetwear and entrepreneurship demonstrated neatly how Tai had learned to thrive in the fabric of global youth fashion. That our rapport was built so readily on this basis emphasised our shared experience as youth despite the distance in space and time between our upbringings.

We spent much of our conversations exploring the core mission of Pacific Origins, which rose beyond just selling inspiring clothing pieces. As Tai described, it involved the creation of culturally relevant clothing that blended elements of global youth streetwear with traditional Samoan and Pacific visual motifs, which was exemplified in the motto 'wear your heritage'. Another key element was the involvement of local youth artists in the production of these wearable signifiers of cultural heritage for youth Samoans. Online, statements about the art and its relevance to youth life are paired with items to generate trans-historical and transnational semiotics: 'Wherever we travel, we carry a piece of our traditions with us. Embrace your lineage'. The storefront itself is a mix of Pacific Origins clothing and popular youth streetwear that Tai orders online or buys when travelling. Travel is promoted as a prominent element in the lives of youth, and special sales are often posted for 'flight nights'—the two days of the week that passenger flights leave the territory. Given this shared reality of travel and migration, many shirts feature designs that Tai hoped would represent Samoan culture for youth abroad. Others are more locally focused, such as one design that was dedicated to an honoured reverend who had recently passed away, or another that was designed for a local school's sports team; even so, both offer a distinct window into island life and the shared cultural experience of the many friends and family who have left the islands.

By transcending the basic demands of mere clothing, Pacific Origins purposefully crafted pieces that offer youth enfranchisement within a community of 'forward thinkers', youth-centric artists and others who cultivate a new relationship with art and heritage. Tai himself actively crafts such a persona through a fashioned presentation, a kind of informal uniform no less constitutive than the tie and button-ups adorning any local Mormons. Sleek, manicured and contemporary fashion is a badge of connection to a scene of global youth fashion, even when one is seemingly far from the production centres of what's 'in' on the street. All it takes is a keen eye to recognise it and, in Tai's case, to reformulate it within the Samoan context.

This interplay of global influence and local culture is elemental to the selection process of what clothes to print. As Tai explained, 'It's been a learning experience trying to cater to the local kids with the streetwear, but also to the off-island market with the island-wear'. The internet functions as a medium of transmission between these two domains. Social media platforms such as Instagram, Facebook and Twitter are vehicles of communication between Samoans locally and abroad. Spaces on the internet become inhabited in a distinct socio-spatial way, much like their Pacific brethren in Tonga (Burroughs & Ka'ili 2015). Frequent travels by the young afford opportunities to cultivate trend awareness and marshal that knowledge (and buying power) into local credibility and into being fashioned by such interconnection.

For a youth entrepreneur like Tai, the internet is the technological framework through which economic success is attained. Brand awareness for his business was built through an interaction with thousands of followers across different platforms and by the consistent online activity—including special sales, updates on upcoming events such as open mics (freestyle talent and art exhibitions) and hints at new apparel. It was on the internet that Tai first perceived the broader potential for Pasifika designs. 'What really inspired me honestly, was Tumblr,' Tai explained. After starting his own blog and seeing the major interest in 'Poly-designs' online, Tai recognised the potential for combining Polynesian patterns with contemporary youth streetwear. Tai observed many of his artistic friends 'drawing on whatever they could get their hands on: CD covers, lampshades, shoes'. Later in Hawai'i, he designed his first shirt by combining a trending T-shirt design with 'poly-motifs'. After becoming popular in Hawai'i, often selling out of his suitcase or dorm room, Tai decided to move home and centre the business on his home island. Embedding himself on-island proved to be a pivotal choice for his business ethos, as it firmly oriented it within a unique position that was astride the connections between local and global.

Since his move back home, community involvement has become a key part of how the business became a mode of social action rather than just a clothing company. Classic ideals of power and political involvement would have motivated young Samoans to look forward to attaining *matai* titles, becoming a church leader or obtaining government positions. In response to the limited availability of those classic routes, many of the youth may be left to contemplate other means of contributing to the betterment of the islands. Tai consciously develops his vision of social action with this in mind, which leaves him in a unique position to pursue alternative pathways.

Tai described his business model as the 'art of expressing island culture through exclusive merchandise'. Expressing business as an 'art' is a significant shift in vision from what many of my contacts described as the 'disinterested' approach that they noted as common to many Samoan businesses. The company purposefully valued youth art to support the artistic character of youth as *a social class*—this meant not just the neighbourhood youth or his network of friends, but any youth with the talent to craft stylised island designs. One way this was materialised during my visit was through offering valuable wall space (a significant sacrifice for a small fashion store) for an ongoing art show, giving youth a new space to share their artwork and further promoting a connection between enigmatic visual traditions in a culturally relevant manner. Many works of art dealt with historic themes and core elements of Samoan culture that the youth felt they needed to comment on, or that they felt disconnected from and, through this art, they tactically confronted the distance that some felt with the past. One pertinent example hanging in the shop was a painting of a *taupou,* a ceremonial role performed by the daughter of a village *matai* (chief). This otherwise classic depiction of Samoan culture was disrupted by the untraditional colours of the *taupou,* who stared forward while gleefully sticking her tongue out. This showed the kind of artistic *play* with which youth could reformulate classic motifs within contemporary constructs of space, time, culture and place. Tai placed great focus on finding ways to feature such art on shirts, giving youth the opportunity to visibly represent their interpretation of Samoan culture wherever they may be.

Alongside artist collaborations, Tai also sponsored events such as monthly open mics (by offering performance slots for any artists who signed up) that featured music, poetry, dance and visual media. Performances were captured on video and shared through social media, which offered exposure and gave Samoan youth opportunities to share their voices across online youth spaces. The events were free and open to all young people, and Tai actively sought to create an atmosphere that promoted collaboration, artistry and inclusion.

All these elements form the foundation of Tai's business ethos, through which he pursues a specific vision of *tautua* that extends beyond the family and village and outwards to youth as a social class. These service acts are constituted as a kind of heritage-based commodity that generates appeal based on notions of 'exclusivity', a feature sought by youth who desire popular fashions from abroad and who simultaneously search for meaning that is derived locally from classic Samoan visual traditions. Founded in part on the displacement that youth felt as locals with transnationally rooted desires, Pacific Origins aimed to relieve the tension between the desires for access to global culture and the constraints of evocative notions of authenticity that are rooted in being 'local'. This case thus deals directly with questions of how youth find a fulfilling future on- or off-island, how they define what 'the good life' looks like 'on the rock' and the nature of the social action that young business owners pursued. With a goal to 'educate, encourage and inspire', Pacific Origins pursued a vision of social action that intertwined capitalistic appeals with the youth's affinity for a locally meaningful, globally influenced youth culture. Such an approach towards social action allowed for a reconstitution of that social action, as more youth are brought into this social sphere of artistically minded, transnationally oriented young Samoans. Pacific Origins built an experiential product-oriented relationship to Samoan culture through the provision of heritage items, and by promoting participation in sponsored events that contributed to an enlivened youth social atmosphere. Among youth who frequently deplored that 'nothing happens here', I encountered excitement and motivation for this kind of activity in the youth community.

Overall, this case represents an iteration of *tautua* that applies less exclusively to the family; it rather encompasses the youth of the islands and those abroad instead of just those of a particular village. In this way, a kind of 'trans-family' is created from the interaction of the youth's experience with the contemporary iterations of local and historical tradition and the realities of travel and life outside the islands. Social action, as envisioned in Tai's business, involved sponsorship of artists by cultivating his function as a role model for other youth and by providing clothes that are imbued with a relationship to Samoan heritage. At other times, his social action involved supporting local causes, such as offering donations and shirt designs to local children's sports teams. As Tai expressed it, 'Small, local contributions can go a long way. Never doubt the impact you as an individual can make in the community around you'. All these channels of action form the foundation of how he considers himself contributing to the broader social good of American Sāmoa. This articulation of social action blends *tautua* (service) and *galue* (work) and is brought to fruition not through the public sector via the classic ideal of Samoan political involvement, but rather through the infusing of youthful energy and vision into the private sector.

Sāmoa's Finest

Social buzz is not the only buzz that Samoan youth are generating. The buzzing of tattoo guns can be heard often, and the practice of *tatau* is alive in the minds and hearts of youth artists. The buzzing alone is enough to make your back quiver, even though the pain that comes is welcomed with purpose because of its deeply symbolic role in Samoan culture. The tattoo needle is transformed in the capable grip of the modern-day *tufaga*, the crafter of the *tatau,* who skilfully melds ink into the blank canvas of your skin and turns your body into a lively signifier of Samoan art. Sonny Lavea was one such artist who I met, and he did not take walk-in appointments, though he loved visitors. While most *tatau* artists came to their client's homes, he was an artist with his own studio and his walls displayed this passion for art as well his own tattoos did. Appointments were easy to set up if one had the time to wait until he was available, as his time was desirable and caught between being a family man, an active Army reservist and a young businessman. Still, one could walk in at any moment to talk design, buy new shop merchandise or even meet up for his fitness group. That openness was characteristic of Sonny and his approach to running his shop, which thrived at the intersection of deft social media usage and the combination of Sonny's skilled deployment of *tatau* as evocative signifiers of Samoan visual culture with his devoted and disciplined outlook. This case examines these features of Sonny's approach, highlights the value of land access as a paradigm in business creation and economic success, explores military careers as a kind of entrepreneurial economic venture in their own right and further illustrates the role of youth in refining contemporary iterations of traditional practices.

Tattoos are often one of the first things that come to mind when people think of Samoan culture, but in American Sāmoa, there are only a few shops. With most *tatau* artists working from home, having a shop involves a greater allotment of time and the potential for a higher level of risk because of rent and maintenance costs. Risk was commonly expressed as one of the largest barriers that prevent youth from pursuing their business ideas. Sāmoa's Finest, one of the premier *tatau* shops on the island, obviates this risk by situating the shop on family land—which is a strong potential benefit for Samoan families with land and the right location. Sonny, an Army reservist in his late 20s, turned his art into a regular source of income after returning to American Sāmoa from active military duty. Much like Tai with Pacific Origins, Sonny capitalises on his talents through the provision of cultural signifiers, albeit in a more permanent medium.

His art is one of precision, of focus. His tattooing is a steady, rhythmic hum that stops and starts, more like a pulse than anything else; it came and went effortlessly and it is part of the allure of the experience, despite the inherent discomfort involved. His studio is a mere football's throw away from the open ocean, it was renovated out of a once unused portion of a family property and it is prominent and hard to miss, as it rests on the road between shopping centres in Nu'uuli and the government and fish factory centres in Pago Pago harbour. Settled in this ideal location, his shop did not need to stand out from any other building, as the only other building was his own cousin's clothing shop next door. One day, after a visit to the shop, I noticed how close it was to the trails that wound their way up the steep and thickly forested mountains that loomed over the two-lane road caught between land and sea. At the top, old navy embattlements rested, unused. They were placed to defend Tutu'ila in the Pacific War, but now they faded into the landscape almost unnoticed. To me, it felt oddly significant to find those guns watching over the narrow stretch where Sonny, upholding a history of Samoan military enrolment, found a better use for a tattoo gun.

Much like those cannons, seeing but unseen and faded into the foliage, the history of militarisation in American Sāmoa lingers, blending into the background of life on-island. Since the last century, Samoans have continually marched through the ranks of the military, perhaps like the rhythmic pulse of a drum, or a tattoo gun. It was during deployment, of all places, when Sonny honed his tattooing skill on all-too-willing fellow soldiers who must have felt cavalier in inviting an untrained Samoan to permanently mark their bodies, trusting his cultural acumen alone. It was as good a place to start as any, but it was certainly not part of the career skills advertised in recruiting centres on-island.

For Sonny, opening a shop turned a hobby into a regular income, which was supplemented by his continued military service as a reservist. With an established shop built on years of tattooing experience, Sonny benefited from a wide range of clientele, many of whom are Samoans visiting the islands for the first time, but also from visiting non-Samoans. Key to bringing in that demographic is Sonny's social media presence.

Like many of the youth in American Sāmoa, Sonny graduated from high school and entered the military. Frequently referenced as the highest per capita–contributing state/territory to the armed forces, American Sāmoa's deep history with the US military is manifested in the prominence of military careers as a core pathway for youth. American Sāmoa was considered a prized possession of great military significance for the US imperial scheme of the Pacific, which motivated US interests in the islands (Droessler 2013).

Sonny's development of his family land is an example of a unique benefit to business-minded young Samoans; those with access and a prime location can gain an advantage by avoiding prohibitively high overheads from monthly rent and decreasing potential risk. Other youth-run businesses that I encountered, such as a barbershop and a smoothie bar, similarly used this to their advantage. Tattoo work is a particularly desirable pathway, as it requires only investment in a tattoo gun and ink; it can stay a profitable part-time hobby, or it can transition to full-time or supplementary work. Sāmoa's Finest operates for many as a connection to their Samoan heritage, especially for those who live in the diaspora. Much like Pacific Origins, Sāmoa's Finest acts as an intermediary of access to cultural forms—the *tatau* itself thus becomes a form of capital, emblematic of a bridge between contemporary and traditional Samoan visual traditions. They derive their value directly from a customer's desire for visual designations of *fa'asamoa*, and getting a *tatau* done on the island is highly appealing to Samoan youth visiting for the first time and looking for 'the real deal'. For Sonny, this desirability is both a source of obtaining clientele and of derived authentic Samoanness. In this connection, he actively cultivated links to the diaspora through frequent posts on social media, spreading his art through online spaces and generating future clientele.

As with Pacific Origins, economic and social capital are intertwined through this use of social media for promotion and awareness and as a platform for showcasing *tatau* designs and connecting with customers. Photos with customers after most sessions documented new designs and were posted on the Sāmoa's Finest Instagram account, often with the customers tagged, which built a sense of camaraderie. These pictures spread widely through the use of prominent *tatau*-related hashtags that connect the business with emerging social media discourses that venerate Polynesian design. #Polyart, #Polytattoo, #tatau and other hashtags that frequently accompany *tatau*-related social media work to transform the *tatau* from a design tradition that is rooted within each specific island to a potent site used for the confluence of broader regional influences. This is even reflective of the mixed background of any potential customer who may have relatives or ancestors from different island groups, who can have their mixed heritage represented through the syncretism of multi-island art traditions. By combining inspirations from different trends in *tatau* design and by participating in the extensive social media landscape of Polynesian designs, Sonny's *tatau* work is representative of an inter-island, trans-oceanic contemporary art form. In this scheme, these interstitial connections become as much a form of capital as his skill at wielding a (tattoo) gun. Further, this arrangement reveals a particularly Samoan context of youth business creation that relies on an influx of social capital that is built on the strong connections of Samoan youth in diasporic spaces, which is then, in turn, marshalled towards economic success.

Sonny's life as a reservist is threaded through his service to his family and island and it connects him to many Samoan families, both past and present. His everyday life and relations are intertwined with his military work. His wife is also an enrolled reservist and his children may very well grow up to be the same. It is difficult to overstate how *ever-present* this militarised life is across different social circles; yet it often simultaneously plays out in the background, undiscussed. It is, however, a viable economic pathway for Samoan youth, one which many youth take to with as much vigour and spirit as they take to sports. It could even be regarded as a kind of essential entrepreneurial opportunity, as it is difficult for so many to attain an economic livelihood and generate prosperity for the *'āiga*. For Sonny, who returned to the islands after active service, it became a foundation for his business success and the start of his family life. Military service was interlaced with tattooing from the beginning.

By successfully capitalising this form of Samoan culture for Samoans both young and old, by harnessing family resources and extensive word-of-mouth and social media advertisement, Sonny acts as a kind of gateway for tattoo-seeking young Samoans wishing to adopt a supremely valuable signifier of Samoanness. Tattooing for Sonny was simultaneously an enjoyable art, a profitable livelihood and a way for him to serve others through the production of meaningful identification with traditional Samoan art. It is supplementary, and complementary, to his work as a reservist and as a fitness instructor, all of which are viewed as his contribution to his community. In terms of social action, Sonny is typically demure and does not hold any overly grand opinions of his contributions, though he clearly values the function that he has and the service that he provides as a skilled neo-traditional *tufaga*. His military service, life as an engaged community member and role as an intermediary for some of the most valuable emblems of Samoan visual tradition are all interwoven and vital to his life as a young Samoan who returned to his island from abroad, who might have just as likely been taken away either by the economic demands or by the other military postings, like so many other military-driven Samoan youth.

Sāmoa Office Supply

Jordan Lotomau is the 28-year-old business owner of Sāmoa Office Supply, a popular shop for office supplies, printing services, electronics and more. His parents bought the business when he was young, after migrating to American Sāmoa from Sāmoa. Like other Samoan children and teens, Jordan was raised working alongside his parents at their business and he took over running the store when his father passed away. This case exemplifies a common pathway to business in Sāmoa, whereby business ownership is passed through the family. Like Tai, Jordan also studied business in college off-island and this experience led him to direct his efforts towards building a future at home rather than one pursuing business in the diaspora. Sāmoa Office Supply sells new technology to local offices and families and it functions as a small internet cafe. Numerous local businesses and government offices print their business cards, flyers and other print materials in his shop. As a result, Jordan is a well-known and respected young adult businessman.

For Jordan, his business is both an end, as it is a livelihood itself, and a means to an end, as it functions as a conduit for his vision of social action. This social action is intimately tied to his ethos of business, which is founded on discipline and cooperative family involvement in the business. Jordan's business success and the cooperation of his family allows him to pursue a vision of *tautua*, primarily through his role as a coordinator of an island-wide program that focuses on creating community service groups for Samoan adolescents. Rather than regarding business and service as separate, he enacted both in his *galue* out of the principle of offering *tautua* to his family and to the Samoan people. Much like Tai, he saw all the youth of the island as a distinct social group with specific needs. He regularly facilitated gatherings of youth whom he mentored, and he encouraged their involvement in community activities, especially acts of service aimed not just towards their elders, but also towards younger youth.

The key defining feature of Jordan's approach to business is the significance of the *'āiga.* and this speaks to the centrality of family in the decision-making process for Samoan youth as they think about their future. For Jordan, involvement with the family business was encouraged early on, when his family moved to American Sāmoa in search of economic opportunities. From the beginning, his family was very supportive of what he wanted to do. As he reflected on the value of their support, he recognised how, 'in many ways, everything was placed in front of me, so I went for it'. His parents strongly emphasised the value of education and, by the time Jordan graduated from high school, they had built the economic capital to support him through college. Jordan adopted this long-term vision himself and spent eight years off-island, including five at UH Mānoa, studying business and another three years offering volunteer religious service at the Baha'i World Centre in Haifa, Israel.

This extended period off-island proved fundamental to inspiring his personal vision and encouraged him to return to focus on a life of service to his home island. The transition to college was difficult and the academic rigour was challenging in comparison to his school experience growing up. For him, as for many Samoan youth, college was an 'eye opener' because of the difference in culture and pace of life. Life off-island was appealing in many ways and he recognised that there were more opportunities for business elsewhere; however, life in American Sāmoa was 'more straightforward' and his time away increased his appreciation for life at home. This was especially cemented by doing volunteer religious service, which strengthened his faith and helped him think more deeply about what he wanted to offer to his home island. Jordan even noticed a major difference in his involvement with the business after returning. Before, he felt more like a labourer, less interested in the direction of the business. After college and life abroad, he truly felt that he had become 'business minded'. Currently, he runs the family business and coordinates much of the family's affairs.

The story of Jordan's path to business affords valuable reflections of the extent to which entrepreneurship is fostered in American Sāmoa. In certain ways, business activities in Samoan society are actively fostered from a young age. These can be as simple as accompanying parents to work at the market, selling goods on their behalf or working as shop assistants. Samoan children and youth can frequently be observed spending time at the family business and working directly at the stores. Strong oratorical traditions, the strength of family networks and the potential for utilisation of family land all potentially serve to instil entrepreneurial characteristics. Further, it is arguable that the growth of sports development has transformed youth and their families into 'sports entrepreneurs', and accessing sports opportunities often demands a level of business acumen and even family-level coordination. Yet many of my contacts observed that youth and young adults underutilise business creation as a potential pathway. In one interview with the head of the local Small Business Development Centre (an initiative offering training courses and business assistance), this perspective was reiterated in the fact that most of the initiative's consultants were middle aged, showing that perhaps youth may need more support or training to recognise what business opportunities were available. For many of the youth with whom I spoke, when asked what kind of business they would create if no barriers existed, most responded that they had never considered it an option and, therefore, it was not an imagined possibility.

When I explored this with Jordan, he emphasised the invaluable role that his family's support played in leading him to enter business. He channelled that encouragement and early-life training, as well as the economic capital that they had accrued towards further training in college. His formal education in business, combined with his parents' experience and support, proved crucial to his ability to imagine possibilities and it nurtured his capabilities. As much as he realised the value of their encouragement, he also recognised the difficulty in starting a business if you did not have a financially prosperous background. He observed that 'there is a disadvantage for youth in business creation because it is hard to get loans if you do not already have money to start up'. Even simple things such as pressure on businesses through raised licence costs and other bureaucratic hurdles can make youth feel that business creation is out of reach, not to mention the need to contribute to the welfare of their family if they were not in a position to financially consider starting a business.

As a means for achieving economic security, Sāmoa Office Supply aided Jordan in fulfilling this all-important ability to support his family financially. He held much of the responsibility for family affairs, including taking care of his younger relatives who lived with him at his household. Understandably, family forms a core benefit to the operation of a Samoan business in many ways and this can be observed in Jordan's business ethos. Family members can act as trusted employees who occupy positions at a company and who represent an invaluable resource. Offering business positions is one way of honouring connections to relatives and close family friends. Having 'loyal, honest employees' helped diminish business maintenance costs and kept money within the family—something that Jordan emphasised often. According to his younger relatives, involvement in the business aided them in their dedication to their school work and in developing the hard work and discipline needed for their future. Jordan also sought to instil a long-term vision in them and to mentor them along their path to adulthood, replicating the accompaniment that he himself received.

Besides its family-oriented nature, the business found success directly as a purveyor of technology as a commodity of exchange. Whether in its role as an internet cafe, through offering printing services for a wide range of clients or through selling affordable and up-to-date electronics, his profession cemented an important function for the community of island businesses or for the various Samoans with limited or no internet access elsewhere. However, in this case, the form of business is less important in comparison to Jordan's approach to following his entrepreneurial vision, a vision that I described as needing tender support in the scheme of livelihood opportunities that is offered to the young. Ultimately, the example of Sāmoa Office Supply offers further contextualisation of how business can operate in tandem with core concepts of Samoanness, and it is an example of a common, family-oriented pathway to business attainment for the young.

Conclusion

From the cases explored here, it is clear that there are distinct possibilities available to youth in the realm of business creation. These possibilities can reshape youth perspectives as they negotiate their futures in light of their familial ties and community needs, and they can reorient and reshape their interaction with the landscape of opportunities that is open to them overall. To support this claim, I have drawn on my research with a variety of on-island youth, paying particular attention to these three prominent examples that elucidate how Samoan youth interact with their cultural legacy and the contemporary conditions in their approach to crafting a fulfilling and promising future for themselves on-island.

From these case studies, we can see a snapshot of how contemporary youth are actively engaged in dialogue with the received categories of Samoanness, yet how they are also reflexively redefining how Samoanness is deployed in their life contexts. For Pacific Origins, this involves articulating a sense of Samoan identity and connection to the past through which youth may simultaneously connect with exclusive global youth fashion, as well as locally produced visual art. Similarly, Sāmoa's Finest offers a connection to perceived Samoan identity through the traditional category of *tatau*. In this way, Sonny operates as a point of access for young Samoans seeking to connect to the past through body modification. Yet, Sonny is not a traditional *tufaga*, but rather a master of what could be called 'Poly-style' *tatau*, a widespread art form, given prominence through social media, that incorporates traditional-style designs and integrates them within a rapidly evolving trans-island contemporary art scene. These designs have propagated alongside the Samoans who have brought them into the spaces and places of the diaspora. What differentiates Sonny from other neo-traditional *tatau* artists is the reverence for his skill and, specifically, the legitimacy granted to him as a 'local' that affords him a position as an authentic purveyor of heritage. This forms much of his appeal and attracts plenty of clients to the door, especially Samoans returning to the island or visiting for the first time.

These two cases are exceptional to some degree. Pacific Origins represents several years of work and benefit from family economic support that allowed Tai to experiment and gradually expand his business as he learned. Land as a form of capital and an already established and successful family business were essential resources that helped him invest time and money in his clothing company, something that may have been prohibitively expensive otherwise. These factors allowed him to transcend the aversion to risk that many youth felt towards following through with a business idea. Additionally, it is hardly likely that many more apparel companies could enter the market without it becoming saturated; therefore, merely replicating such an example is not an adequate solution to the limitations to youth opportunities. Sāmoa's Finest is also exceptional to a degree, as it is one of only a few tattoo shops with a dedicated building rather than being an in-home place like most other *tatau* artists. Sonny's tattoo work was also founded on his military career, and the significance of the cross-section between his army life and his life as an artist is ripe with historical and cultural significance. Sāmoa Office Supply may then serve as a connection to the more common experience of business involvement for youth, and it acts as a kind of prism through which attitudes surrounding Samoan involvement in business may be remapped as existing conditions evolve and potential for new businesses are open to youth, even as local life and accelerating global influence become more entangled.

Finally, it is also important to acknowledge and underscore the limitations of these cases overall. Specifically, besides the economic factors already mentioned in each of these cases that enabled their success, each of these cases represent male youth experiences. Despite it being challenging at times for myself, as a male researcher, to cultivate deeper research relationships with younger Samoan women, it was clear that there was not a lack of young women and girls active in the entrepreneurial space. Indeed, during my time in Tutu'ila, I encountered numerous inspiring examples of young women pursuing business, although my connections with some of them unfortunately did not coalesce into enough rapport for me to adequately portray their experiences in the scope of this work. Future research in this topic would benefit greatly from a more thorough exploration of the gendered dynamics of youth business creation. Aside from these limitations, what remains is to explore how these examples could inform strategies for re-envisioning how youth approach their futures, especially how to respond to the tensions that youth experienced regarding globally located desires and their locally rooted existence. Much could be accomplished in the context of school and family life to support and encourage youths' ideas for business and, even further, to create new opportunities for young people to contribute substantively to the public discourse regarding what opportunities are available and how to address and prepare for the challenges they'll face in the rapidly changing environment at home and abroad. Collaborations with the American Sāmoa government to foster business creation and honour the youth contributing in these spaces would continue to elevate the potentials of this mode of youth activity, and it could even provide opportunities to bridge the apparent 'gap' between the young and their elders.

This work is primarily a contribution to the scholarly attention that has been given to Samoan youth, but it seeks to broaden the conversation by exploring the socioeconomic implications of youth business endeavours and how these contribute to actualisation of youth a social body. It also serves as the basis for future contributions on youth futures, particularly in the realm of economic strategies and youth relationships with globalisation and digital diasporic spaces. Future research would benefit in this regard by exploring how youth as a social category in American Sāmoa has emerged historically over the course of the last century. Additionally, during my research, I benefited immensely from the sense of inclusion gained by being a youth, indicating that this is a rich area for student anthropologists especially. Further, youth as a research focus was particularly potent, allowing access to a wide range of topics, while simultaneously enabling specifics to be teased out of the complexities encountered in fieldwork. Given that youth as a social class intersect with many issues that are important to Samoan society, and that the stakes of the future are laid on the shoulders of youth who are regarded as the ones who will arise to adopt the legacy of past generations, it is more important than ever to rigorously consider the conditions and character of youth experience and to develop ever more effective ways of supporting young people in attaining prosperous futures.

References

Bucholtz, M 2002, 'Youth and cultural practice', *Annual Review of Anthropology*, vol. 31, no. 1, pp. 525–552, doi.org/10.1146/annurev.anthro.31.040402.085443

Burroughs, B & Ka'ili, TO 2015, 'Death of a king: Digital ritual and diaspora', *Continuum*, vol. 29, no. 6, pp. 886–897, doi.org/10.1080/10304312.2015.1073684

Droessler, H 2013, 'Whose Pacific? US security interests in American Samoa from the Age of Empire to the Pacific Pivot', *Pacific Asia Inquiry*, vol. 4, no. 1, p. 58.

Good, MK 2012, *Modern moralities, moral modernities: Ambivalence and change among youth in Tonga*, University of Arizona Press, Arizona.

Good, MK 2014, 'The Fokisi and the Fakaleitī: Provocative performances in Tonga', in N Besnier & K Alexeyeff (eds), *Gender on the edge: Transgender, gay, and other Pacific Islanders*, University of Hawai'i Press, Honolulu, pp. 213–240.

Inda, JX 2006, *The anthropology of globalization: A reader*, John Wiley and Sons, Chichester, UK.

Kwauk, CT 2014, '"No longer just a pastime": Sport for development in times of change', *The Contemporary Pacific*, vol. 26, no. 2, pp. 303–323.

Macpherson, C & Macpherson, L 2009, *The warm winds of change: Globalisation in contemporary Sāmoa,* Auckland University Press, Auckland.

Mead, M 1973, *Coming of age in Samoa*, Dell Publishing, New York.

Secretariat of the Pacific Community 2015, *The Pacific youth development framework 2014–2023*, Pacific Community, Suva.

Shankman, P 1996, 'The history if Samoan sexual conduct and tie Mead-Freeman controversy', *American Anthropologist*, vol. 98, no. 3, pp. 555–567, doi.org/10.1525/aa.1996.98.3.02a00090

Uperesa, FL 2014a, 'Fabled futures: Migration and mobility for Samoans in American football', *The Contemporary Pacific: A Journal of Island Affairs*, vol. 26, no. 2, pp. 281–301.

Uperesa, FL 2014b, 'Seeking new fields of labor: Football and colonial political economies in American Samoa', in A Goldstein (ed.), *Formations of United States colonialism*, Duke University Press, Durham and London, pp. 207–232.

8

Youth's Displaced Aggression in Rural Papua New Guinea

Imelda Ambelye

Introduction

Papua New Guinea (PNG) has significant land resources and close to 80 per cent of all land in the country is customary owned, either by individuals or by some form of clan ownership; it is thus governed by traditional land tenure systems. Most people meet their basic needs through subsistence agriculture and a large part of the rural population and, to a lesser extent, the urban population relies on forest products, fishing, hunting and subsistence agriculture for their livelihoods (UNESCO 2007a). About 87 per cent of the population in PNG lives in rural areas, most of which are not accessible by road. The country is culturally and ethnically highly diverse, as well as deeply politically fragmented. Dealing with this fragmentation within the postcolonial nation state entails numerous economic and social challenges.

PNG's extractive industry is booming and attracting economic benefits in the form of revenue for the government, royalties for landowners and jobs for many communities and villages living around the mining, gas and oil sites. The extractive industries in PNG are a major economic driver, creating jobs, revenue and opportunities for growth and development. Theoretically, material resources are thus available to provide an enabling environment for women and youths to identify their own goals and to reconstruct their reality (Kabeer 1999). Logically, it should follow that men, women and young people in the villages who are affected by the extractive industries would be more empowered and thus better able to participate and contribute to community development, but this often does not happen (Cornwall 2016; Sholkamy 2010). Most women and youths in the villages and communities of PNG are not empowered, including those affected by the resources boom.

This chapter shows the problems and challenges that youths face in the rural villages of PNG. Youths here are those aged between 15 and 33 years. Most of these youths have been educated to secondary and post-secondary education and return to the villages because they cannot continue to live elsewhere due to limited opportunities and resources. The antisocial behaviour demonstrated by some reflects their frustration and displaced aggression. This chapter begins by examining youth in two villages and their livelihoods. Then, a case study is presented to use the theme that emerges for discussion. The main theme on antisocial behaviour and its implications is followed by a discussion of how such behaviour is a reflection of the broader social, economic and political climate of PNG.

Background and Setting

In this section, I will outline the general socioeconomic and infrastructural setting in the two villages of Lealea and Kugmumb. These two villages are where I lived and conducted my doctoral fieldwork for six months in 2015 and a month in 2017, focusing on youths, especially educated young women and empowerment. Lealea is a coastal village in the Central Province and Kugmumb is a village in the Western Highlands.

Lealea

The village of Lealea (Rearea) is a coastal village with a population of about 2,936 people (NSO 2011). It is in the Central Province of PNG, in the Kairuku-Hiri district and in the Hiri Rural Local Level Government. Kairuku-Hiri district surrounds Port Moresby and stretches from the Gulf Province to Gaire Village, southeast of Port Moresby (NRI 2010). Hiri covers four coastal villages in Hiri West, and Kairuku-Hiri District in Central Province in PNG covers approximately 30 km west of Port Moresby. Three villages (Lealea, Boera and Porebada) are Motuan and one (Papa) is Koita (the Koita are referred to as Koitabu by the Motuan people). The Motu are an essentially maritime people; villagers engage in fishing, hunting and gardening activities to sustain their daily livelihoods. Other income includes small-scale commerce (e.g. trade stores and street markets) and working for the PNG Liquefied Natural Gas (LNG) project. All villages lie within a 5 km radius of the PNG LNG facility and are classified as resource development impact areas or as communities.

Kugmumb

With a population of 702, Kugmumb is located in the Mt Hagen Rural Local Level Government, Hagen District, Western Highlands Province. It is less than 15 km from Mt Hagen (NRI 2010) and is in a province that does not have any extractive industry. Subsistence agriculture and cash cropping are common. Coffee plantations have created higher incomes for people in the Wahgi, Kuna and Komun Valleys. The land is fertile and it produces good food yields for subsistence livelihoods. Within this region, agricultural potential is relatively high, as are incomes, and access to services is reasonably good, with the exception of the steep slopes of the Hagen and Kubor Ranges (Bourke & Harwood 2009).

Kugmumb is located close to Mount Hagen, the capital of the Western Highlands. The general infrastructure in Kugmumb includes a road that links it to the capital city, which makes it easy for the town bus to drive to the village. Electricity, television reception and water supply are connected to some but not all households and mobile phones can be seen everywhere. There are primary, secondary and tertiary institutions within walking distance. The river Kum that runs through the village is used as a dam to supply the residents and surrounding villages. The water supply for the city of Mt Hagen is derived from Kugmumb and, for the city residents, it is the only source of water, apart from rainwater for some houses that have tanks.

Both Lealea and Kugmumb have access to nearby urban centres. Kugmumb is located about 8 km from Mt Hagen city and Lealea about 30 km out of Port Moresby. Generally, both villages have good transportation and road systems that link them to the main cities, schools and health centres (NRI 2010), as well as to markets, shops, electricity and water sanitation. These are general infrastructures that are usually missing in the more remote villages of PNG. Houses in Kugmumb are a mix of huts and modern houses, but those in Lealea are almost all modern, semi-permanent and built on stilts. However, inequality is evident and most households do not have electricity or proper sanitation. These are available only to those who can afford them.

General Livelihoods

People in the villages of Kugmumb and Lealea have diverse livelihoods and income strategies that are changing and becoming more complex. Agriculture and natural resources–based activities have been common and important to their livelihoods. However, households in these villages today have diversified into other activities; these strategies for this diversifying include subsistence production and production for sale at markets, as well as participation in the labour market. Jobs vary from office administration, construction and building to teaching, medical professions and others. However, youths in the villages are mostly unemployed.

In Lealea, many gardens have been neglected because of the effect of the LNG plant, which is situated on the Lealea people's customary land. However, the initial pulse of wage–labour income that originally accompanied the construction of the LNG plant has ended and people are now readjusting to gardening. A growing number of women sell both garden produce (particularly betel nut) and store goods at the markets. Youths who were casually employed during the construction phase of the LNG plant are struggling to find other means of getting employed for wage labour. The promises and dream of having more money and wealth from the LNG project has not been realised, which has been frustrating for the villagers—and especially for the youths.

Livelihoods in the villages near towns and urban centres are quite different from those further away and are changing rapidly. Robert Chambers and Gordon Conway (1992) said that a livelihood comprises the capabilities, assets (including both material and social resources) and activities that are required for a means of living. A livelihood is sustainable when it can cope with and recover from stresses and shocks, and when it can maintain or enhance its capabilities and assets while not undermining the natural resource base. Sustainable livelihood frameworks (DFID 2000; Ellis 2000) aim to conceptualise how people function within a vulnerability context that can be caused by different factors—shifting seasonal constraints (and opportunities), economic shocks and longer-term trends and how they draw on different types of livelihood assets or capitals in different combinations. The different assets include those of a financial, natural, physical, human and social kind. These are influenced by the vulnerability context, a range of institutions and processes and how they use their asset base to develop a range of livelihood strategies for achieving their desired livelihood outcomes (Scoones 1996).

Youths in both villages have faced shocks that have left them vulnerable. These shocks vary, as they were experienced by different members in the villages. For youths, shock includes becoming unemployed, discontinuation in the educational system and returning to the village, where no formal systems are in place to support reintegration. Hence, more problems arise, as the youths who miss out on employment and tertiary education demonstrate antisocial behaviour. The following case study illustrates some of the complex social effects of frustrated development aspirations in rural PNG.

Death and Violence: A Case Study

Dinga[1] died after a long illness. He had completed Year 10 at a local high school, but never continued to further his education because he did not pass the national exams. Frustrated that he was considered a failure in the village, he went to live with relatives in town and there he met his wife. They had a son when they both came back to live in the village.

Dinga was 28 years old and had been sick for months. He had been going in and out of the hospital, but he could never recover. The family reported that the doctors could not diagnose what was wrong with him. He would thus spend days in the house and village, and Christian groups would pray for him. These groups were from different denominations and would take turns praying for Dinga. He was part of the music ministry in the local Pentecostal church and played bass guitar in the music team at the church. In the weeks leading up to Dinga's death, his mother, wife and son, together with other believers, spent days and nights praying in the church, hoping for a miracle that unfortunately never came.

1 Names used in this chapter are pseudonyms.

Figure 1. Funeral service of late Dinga.
Source. Author.

The funeral was arranged. Normally, funerals in the village are week-long, official and communal activities that not only allow the family to grieve, but the community and tribe as a whole as well. The whole community gathered officially at the *ples singsing*, a common big and open space in the middle of the village. Men, women and the young are all expected to sit in the open sun and take part in the official traditional *hauskrai* (mourning as a community). Neighbouring tribes and extended relations also come to pay respect and to help, which strengthens communal ties. During this time, it is expected that no one does gardening, bush clearing, house building or any big manual jobs. Entertainment of any sort or expressions of happiness are generally frowned upon. If one is seen ignoring the mourning, it is believed that they had a part in the death, that they are pleased by the death or that they have no feelings of empathy and sympathy.

On the second day after Dinga's death, the village was deep in mourning. At about 6.00 am, the unusual quiet was interrupted only by the slow sobs of the mother, aunty, wife and some of the women in their houses. Later, around 8.30 am, they all moved to the *ples singsing* to congregate and have the *hauskrai*. Suddenly, a commotion erupted with screams and wailing, as angry men rushed to bash a woman that they believed had used sorcery to cause Dinga's death.

Everyone ran to the scene to find out what was wrong, including the people I was staying with. From far through the coffee trees, I could see enraged young men in their late teens and early 20s surround a poor woman, throwing punches at her. I struggled to identify the woman and realised that it was the wife of the late Dinga's father's cousin. She is regarded as a real family member. As I got closer, I could hear them screaming as they raged and punched her in anger.

The poor woman was helplessly fighting back to free herself, but she was overpowered by men on top of and around her who threw punches and kicks. I noticed that one was wearing large boots and kicking so hard that I thought she might be killed, but after 30–45 minutes of constant physical abuse, they finally let her go; however, it did not end there.

The men demanded that she explain why she went to the garden so early to plant peanuts and corn. Culturally, the norm is that once somebody dies, relatives are not supposed to do any gardening or other physical work. Having been caught planting, prior rumours that she had performed sorcery were now quickly 'confirmed'.

She was very bruised and traumatised. While this was going on, her husband and her 23-year-old son, about the same age as her attackers, looked on. They could not do anything, or they would too be bashed, tortured or worse. I was shocked, as I had never witnessed something like this before. Among the onlookers were university graduates, but surprisingly no one called the police; the idea was so remote, and everyone seemed to think that the police and local court system had no part to play in this. Most of the young men who bashed the poor woman were known to drink homemade 'jungle juice' (alcohol) and to take drugs, and all had dropped out of the formal education system at about the age of 16–18 years.

Two of them needed money so badly that they had to steal goods from other villagers and sell them. On one occasion, they decided to steal a huge pig from their own aunt who fed them, so that they could obtain money for their needs. They planned it for the middle of the night when everyone in the village was still asleep but, when they walked into the marketplace, they were discovered and the theft was reported to the owner. When they were caught, the police were called and the young men were quickly arrested. However, the violence related to the sorcery incident was never reported to the police because such issues are resolved at the village level with customary laws. It showed how easily vulnerable women are abused.

Antisocial Behaviour and Its Implications in Villages

The behaviour described above reveals the intense frustration felt by youth. Many young men and women hang around in the villages doing nothing after dropping out of the education system. They discover that what they have learned is of little practical use and they look for ways to vent their frustrations. Typically, they make and drink home brew and cause antisocial behaviour. When they are drunk, males sometimes steal food items from gardens, as well as break into houses for food and other items for sale (UNICEF 2005).

Lulu is a mother in her 50s. She works hard to look after children who are not her biological children. The following is the disappointment that Lulu expressed at falling victim to such behaviour:

> The other day, somebody went in and chopped the strong banana [*kenenga*] from the garden. I went to harvest it to sell the next day, but it was gone in the night. Later, I realised it was stolen by some of the young men. They are so lazy and stupid. Why can't they work?

Bopi is a man who is also in his 50s. He said that he too fell victim:

> Two weeks ago, I am building a house. I had all my building materials outside in the shed. One day I was to put the windows to my house, but I realised some were missing. I quickly investigated that some young men have taken them and sold them.

When young men see other members of the family with jobs, money and a 'better' material life than them, they take out their frustration and resentment on innocent people. In former times, stealing from family members was never an option but, because of their desperation to have money, these young men turn to antisocial behaviour such as stealing pigs to sell. Economic inequality thus contributes to the increase in violence and other forms of antisocial behaviour (Wilkinson & Pickett 2009).

The rising cost of living in PNG creates an ever-widening inequality between those who have cash incomes and those who do not (Martin 2007). This often leads to jealousy within communities between the economically advantaged and disadvantaged groups. As a result, when sorcery issues arise, people release their frustrations. The intense discontent created by economic imbalances in society is often triggered by the widespread belief in sorcery, which typically results in violent and antisocial behaviour.

The young men's violence and stealing also show that the social structures and institutions, which hold societies together, are becoming weak and are gradually crumbling. Today, a new social group is emerging in the communities. They are known as 'drug bodies', which are groups made up of young people who have no perspective in life and who have no hope for the future (UNICEF 2005). They become a danger to communities because of their association with drugs and violence. In times of social crisis such as sickness and death, sorcery accusations and retribution are often led by young drug takers.

Village elders and traditional leaders speak out and do their part, but they are no longer being respected by young people who seek identity and acknowledgement in society. Social unity within families and clan communities drops, as sorcery-related violence causes social fragmentation. Traditional values of communal life and social systems are increasingly being tested as materialism and individualism rise. This also results in the culture of greed and corruption, while the social and economic life of sharing, caring and helping is gradually losing its value. The collapse of traditional social systems promotes the culture of sorcery accusations and other violent behaviours (Forsyth 2016). The breakdown in social order and generational conflict between the old and young also leads to the increase in antisocial behaviour.

This is what a community leader from Lealea village said regarding young people's antisocial behaviour:

> Young people, especially males, would turn to drugs and brewing homemade jungle juice commonly known as 'steam'. These containers [see Figure 2] have been confiscated last month because they use these containers to brew their steam. When they are drunk and controlled by drugs, they make noise, seek attention, destroy things, act violently and fight.

Figure 2. Brewing containers confiscated in Lealea village.
Source. Author.

Another aspect of social change is that unrealised expectations of a better life lead to innocent people falling victim to violence and antisocial behaviour. Minimal support and opportunities for improved livelihoods causes social stress among people and contributes to an increase in these behaviours. Lack of economic and infrastructural development in rural areas, failure in school, failure in business and failure to find employment result in more stress. Rapid changes brought about by modernisation have changed people's perception of life and create confusion, disorientation and social tension. Promises of development and improved livelihoods do not transpire. When these expectations are not met, people resort to sorcery, drugs and violence as a means of seeking answers and making their deep concerns known.

This is what a woman aged 27 years old from Lealea had to say:

> Before the Liquefied Natural Gas was going to be extracted here, we were told that our village would have very good modern permanent houses with water running inside. We would have so much money too because we are landowners. That was all a lie, because look at us now. We are still poor and have not improved. Things are not as expected. People, especially young people, are

> turning to drugs and steam. They are lazy and do nothing. People imagine and dream of a good life. A good life is living in modern, permanent housing with electricity and proper sanitation. There would be enough money to use and save for school fees and other needs and, at the same time, they want sealed roads connecting them to cities and towns with good transportation.

The wishes of people are stronger and larger than the reality. The reality is that these wishes take time to be realised and they do not come easily; it takes hard work and effort. The resources and systems of governance, management and delivery that are in place do not work effectively; while some are aware of corruption in the system, they either accept it or do not know how to address it. Finally, people have deep belief systems that explain deaths and dilemmas for them better than what many outsiders would regard as facts. People are so deeply rooted in their belief systems that they are not able to accept alternative world views. Disease and illness have medical explanations, but these are overlooked and, instead, causality is explained through supernatural belief systems. Many people also lack knowledge about health, hygiene and healthy lifestyles. When people die from accidents or lifestyle diseases such as diabetes, innocent people are blamed. People die young due to risky behaviour and unhealthy lifestyles, yet relatives often attribute the deaths to sorcery (Urame 2015).

To make matters worse, many people in positions of authority and responsibility, such as medical workers, police, church pastors and educated elites, continue to believe in the power of sorcery and witchcraft. This implies that in PNG, the level of education, social standing, profession and leadership of many people does not play a significant role in influencing people's belief systems. For example, a young woman who recently graduated from the formal education system said:

> I completed my schooling as a Grade 12, but I never got to university because people are jealous so they used sorcery to stop me from continuing.

Implications: PNG's Social, Economic and Political Environment

Weak Political Governance and Corruption Contributes to Youth's Displaced Aggression

PNG is one of the 'weak states in a region characterised by corruption, an absence of "good governance" and "civil society" and increasingly subject to violence' (Patterson & Macintyre 2011, p. 9). The violence and antisocial behaviour are displaced aggression. Youths that are pushed out of the education system are marginalised in many ways because there is no good structural and formal leadership for them to have a voice and make decisions. Leadership is needed to have formal programs and institutions that specifically target such youths to help and integrate them into society. Unfortunately, this is absent. Leaders are caught between two worlds of traditional modern leadership that are influenced by capitalism and individualism, which has been challenging and problematic (McLachlan 2018).

PNG has kept a good record as a democratic government, but the vision of pre-independence leaders has not translated into a sense of national identity and purpose. This is because politics at the local and electoral levels are narrow and, at the national level, politics is manipulated by individuals who serve personal interests in the short time that they are in power (Kama 2017b). Such attitudes and behaviours have caused problems in the lives of common citizens like the youths. Political leaders are driven by personal and individualistic interests, not by the interests of youth.

Political parties have not developed to play the expected role of selecting candidates, articulating issues and keeping MPs accountable; there has been little development of a civil society, and the quality of governance has been poor (Kama 2017a). For example, during elections, Bitu, a man in Kugmumb, said:

> People, especially men, are cunning at elections. They go to candidates' campaign places, get money promising to cast their votes but, when at polling, they vote for their relative or someone whom they will benefit from in terms of employment or material goods. They really don't care about the policies and parties. In fact, most do not understand.

At the national level, this is what a minister said when asked why the O'Neill government could not be replaced easily:

> The reason is because DSIP (District Services Improvement Programme) is there, that's why we will be in the government and support the O'Neill-Dion government. It's not about your number of qualifications you have to lead the government; so long as you have the money, you will master the numbers (Kama 2017a).

PNG has a political system that is unstable and corrupt. A local retired public servant said this:

> Today, we have a bunch of men who have so much money that, with it, they can do anything to get into power and control—get the sweet little sixteen who just finished high school, bribe the policeman and go free if they have done wrong. Members of the tribe look up to him as a god because they represent the tribesmen. They will help more in terms of communal activities whenever such activities come up once in a while. Other than that, the rest of the time and most of his money and resources belong to themselves and their family. Even though individuals complain that such men are greedy and do not share, that does not matter. It is the name of the tribe he promotes which is their pride.

Corruption has had detrimental effects on the nation of PNG. Corruption has undermined sustainable economic development, ethical values and justice; it has destabilised the society and compromised the rule of law. It has weakened the institutions and values of our democracy. Acts of corruption at varying levels have deprived citizens of their constitutional and human rights (Kama 2017a). Frustrated citizens like youths are deprived of their rights and opportunities so they turn to violence and antisocial behaviour.

PNG has allowed corruption to grow systematically for the last 42 years. This has resulted in ordinary youths' and citizens' lives being made more difficult and in their opportunities being limited. Inefficiencies and dysfunction in the public service have impeded progress. Loopholes have been created in legal and administrative systems that allow manipulation and distortion of democratic values, which deprive citizens of their basic human rights and trap millions in poverty.

Corruption has been accepted as a norm. People regard it is as part of the way of life. This is because of PNG's so-called 'big men', who take whatever they want and do whatever they want. They have become a law unto themselves, powerful and untouchable. All citizens have become their victims. This big man culture is practised alongside democracy and modern politics causes many problems (Gewertz & Errington 2004; Wyeth 2017). Different systems of government—traditional forms and the modern introduced version—cause confusion and compound the problems.

Controlled and Mismanaged Economy Contributes to Youth's Displaced Aggression

The dual economy of PNG has a small (in terms of the number of employees) formal sector, focused mainly on the export of natural resources, and an informal sector that employs most of the population. Agriculture provides a subsistence livelihood for 85 per cent of the people (NRI 2010). There is a youth bulge.

> Youth unemployment is high in PNG, with young people in urban areas living day-to-day, often causing opportunistic crime to survive and leading lives without direction. And though the informal sector is burgeoning, life for these young people is tenuous and uncertain (McLachlan 2018).

The formal sector consists mainly of workers who are engaged in mineral production, forestry and fisheries, a relatively small manufacturing sector, public sector employees and service industries, including finance, construction, transportation and utilities. Most of the population is engaged in the informal sector. Youths' migration into major city centres in the past decade has contributed to urban unemployment and social problems.

Mineral deposits, including copper, gold and oil, account for nearly two-thirds of export earnings. The government faces the challenge of ensuring transparency and accountability for revenues flowing from this and other large LNG projects. The government still faces numerous challenges, including providing physical security for foreign investors, regaining investor confidence, restoring integrity to state institutions, promoting economic efficiency by privatising declining state institutions and maintaining good relations with Australia, its former colonial ruler. Other sociocultural challenges could collapse the economy, including chronic law and order and land tenure issues. All these factors mean that the kind of future and environment for youths is not promising. There is vulnerability and their livelihoods are not sustainable.

PNG is dependent on foreign aid because a large part of the economy and technology is foreign and controlled by transnational corporations with entities in donor countries. Most of the wealth created by these foreigners inevitably leaves the country (Mousseau & Lau 2015), with just enough that is distributed locally to keep the system operating. The foreign-owned part of economy has not stimulated local economic development nearly as much as the transnational companies have promised. PNG's economy brings wealth for elites and impoverishment for most of the population, including youths. The problem has worsened, as the government continues to borrow. The growth of national debt has emerged as a key weakness of many third-world countries (Rapley 2002). For instance, PNG's total public debt is expected to increase by more than PGK4 billion from the projected 2017 budget estimate of PGK22 billion, according to the PNG Treasury Department (Patjole 2017).

Sociocultural Challenges Contribute to Youths' Displaced Aggression

PNG faces challenges with human rights, especially in relation to women and children. A UNICEF study of orphans and vulnerable children showed that 68 per cent of women have experienced violence in the home—though this is as high as 90 per cent in some communities in the highlands provinces (UNICEF 2005). Many girls in PNG are at risk of commercial sexual exploitation, and one-third of all sex workers are under the age of 20. This is because of the pressure to meet basic needs in a struggling socioeconomic environment. Expectations from family and relatives are there too. They turn to commercial sex and other risky behaviours to survive.

For example, one young woman aged 20 said:

> I live in a settlement area; my parents do not have a job now. I did not continue to college because my parents could not afford school fees. Living in such [a] harsh environment forced me to look for money to survive. Since there is no job for people like me, I saw that the easiest way was to get money from men who had money, so I went out with them.

UNICEF reports that 80 per cent of the population is yet to have their births registered and that 22 per cent of children reside away from their biological parents. Girls and young women are the most abused and vulnerable. Some 75 per cent of children who come into conflict with the law experience police abuse (UNESCO 2007a). These figures show that youths are neglected and are the most victimised structurally.

Community obligations push against the individualism that is demanded by global market logics. These factors have an effect on communities, families and children. Marriage breakups or change of partners by one or both parents are not uncommon, putting children in the middle of new relationships. Stepfathers or non-biological members of new families can expose the child to sexual abuse, violence or neglect.

Generally, issues are complex and stem from poverty, unequal power structures and gender roles, subordinate status of women in society, women's economic dependence on men, lack of land rights and their overall lack of power in the decision-making process (Dyer 2016; Sepoe 2002). Other compounding factors are ethnic diversity and language, urban migration, abuse of alcohol and illicit drugs, polygamy and changing traditional customs. In PNG, women and young girls are a particularly vulnerable group (ILO 2011). They are vulnerable to violence and harassment of all forms.

Further, weak infrastructure, weak service delivery mechanisms, marketing difficulties and low government and civil society capacity reduce the possibilities of alternative livelihoods. With about 87 per cent of the population living in rural areas, this is a major concern (UNESCO 2007b).

Conclusion

The antisocial behaviour and other problems that youths face are a result of many factors. Displaced aggression is the result of youths looking for opportunities to release their frustrations as victims of structural deprivation. Livelihoods for some communities that are near towns or cities and those communities affected by extractive industries are becoming unsustainable. Youths and the young adults are the ones that need urgent attention. High population growth and the low median age means that the country is facing huge youth challenges, especially with the high potential for the population to grow further (NSO 2011) This puts pressure on the country to invest a large proportion of its resources in social services such as health and education, as well as in employment creation.

It is increasingly evident that the fruits of globalisation benefit mainly the elite and that, in many countries, the poor become more marginalised and more impoverished (Jason 2017). This trajectory will see more conflict and more suffering (Saskia 2014). All governments, including PNG, go to UN meetings and vote that the poor and marginalised like the youths must be given priority and that there must be more progress. The systematic reduction of poverty is the point of the development relationship. This message is repeated at the World Bank, in UN agencies, in the Asian Development Bank, the African Development Bank, the European Union and the International Monetary Fund. But, will the rural poor and this growing, deprived population of youths really feel the benefit? Development in PNG is not focused on people as the centre. People, and especially youth, are affected detrimentally because of the complex issues discussed in this chapter.

References

Bourke, M & Harwood T (eds) 2009, *Food and agriculture in Papua New Guinea*, ANU E Press, Canberra, doi.org/10.22459/FAPNG.08.2009

Chambers, R & Conway, G 1992, *Sustainable rural livelihoods: Practical concepts for the 21st century*, Institute of Development Studies, Brighton, England.

Cornwall, A 2016, 'Women's empowerment: What works?', *Journal of International Development*, vol. 28, no. 3, pp. 342–359, doi.org/10.1002/jid.3210

DFID 2000, *Sustainable livelihoods: Current thinking and practice*, DFID, London.

Dyer, M 2016, 'Eating money: Narratives of equality on customary land in the context of natural resource extraction contests in the Solomon Islands', *The Australian Journal of Anthropology*, vol. 28, no. 1, pp. 88–103, doi.org/10.1111/taja.12213

Ellis, F 2000, *Rural livelihoods and diversity in developing countries*, Oxford University Press, Oxford.

Forsyth, M 2016, 'The regulation of witchcraft and sorcery practices and beliefs', *Annual Review of Law and Social Science*, vol. 12, pp. 331–351, doi.org/10.1146/annurev-lawsocsci-110615-084600

Gewertz, D & Errington, F 2004, *Emerging class in Papua New Guinea*, Cambridge University Press, Cambridge.

ILO 2011, *Child labour in Papua New Guinea: Report on the rapid assessment in Port Moresby on commercial sexual exploitation of children and children working on the streets 2011*, IPEC, Geneva.

Jason, H 2017, 'Is global inequality getting better or worse? A critique of the World Bank's convergence narrative', *Third World Quarterly*, vol. 1, p. 15, doi.org/10.1080/01436597.2017.1333414

Kabeer, N 1999, 'Resources, agency, achievements: Reflections on the measurement of women's empowerment', *Development and Change*, vol. 30, no. 3, pp. 435–464, doi.org/10.1111/1467-7660.00125

Kama, B 2017a, *An analysis of Papua New Guinea's Political Condition and Trends through to 2025*, Lowy Institute, viewed 18 February 2018, interactives.lowyinstitute.org/archive/png-in-2017/png-in-2017-png-political-condition-to-2025.html

Kama, B 2017b, *PNG in 2017: A year of redefining deomcracy?*, Devpolicy Blog, 27 January, viewed 18 February 2018, www.devpolicy.org/png-2017-year-redefining-democracy-20170127/

Martin, K 2007, 'Your own Buai you must buy; the ideology of possessive individualism in Papua New Guinea', *The Anthropological Forum*, vol. 17, no. 3, pp. 285–298, doi.org/10.1080/00664670701637743

McLachlan, S 2018, 'Youths in PNG: Challenges to building a positive future', Devpolicy Blog, 27 January, viewed 18 February 2018, www.devpolicy.org/youth-png-challenges-building-positive-future-20180117/

Mousseau, F & Lau, P 2015, *The great timber heist: The logging industry in Papua New Guinea*, Oakland Institute, Oakland, CA.

NRI 2010, *Papua New Guinea district and provincial profiles*, National Research Institute, Port Moresby.

NSO 2011, *Papua New Guinea national population and housing census 2011*, NSO, Port Moresby.

Patjole, C 2017, *Mid-year economic and fiscal outlook report*, Loop PNG.

Patterson, M & Macintyre, M 2011, *Capitalism, cosmology and globalisation in the Pacific*, University of Queensland Press, Brisbane.

Rapley, J (ed.) 2002, *Understanding development: Theory and practice in the third world*, Lynne Rienner, London.

Saskia, S 2014, *Expulsions: Brutality and complexity in the global economy*, The Belknap Press of Harvard University Press, Cambridge, MA.

Scoones, I 1996, *Hazards and opportunities. Farming livelihoods in dryland Africa: Lessons from Zimbabwe*, Zed books, London.

Sepoe, O 2002, 'To make a difference: Realities of women's participation in Papua New Guinea politics', *Development Bulletin*, no. 59, pp. 39–42.

Sholkamy, H 2010, 'Power, politics and development in the Arab context: Or how can rearing chicks change patriarchy?', *Development*, vol. 53, no. 2, pp. 254–258, doi.org/10.1057/dev.2010.26

UNDP 2015, *Human development report: Work for human development*, UNDP, viewed 4 March 2018, hdr.undp.org/sites/default/files/2015_human_development_report.pdf

UNESCO 2007a, *Country programming document—Papua New Guinea; 2008–2013 (vol. 6)*, UNESCO, Apia.

UNESCO 2007b, *Country programming document 2008–2013*, UNESCO Cluster Office for the Pacific States, Apia.

UNICEF 2005, *The state of Pacific youth 2005,* Secretariat of the Pacific Community, Noumea.

Urame, J 2015, 'The spread of sorcery killing and its social implications', in M Forsyth & R Eves (eds), *Talking it through: Responses to sorcery and witchcraft beliefs and practices in Melenesia*, ANU Press, Canberra, doi.org/10.22459/TIT.05.2015.01

Wilkinson, R & Pickett, K 2009, *The spirit level: Why equality is better for everyone*, Penguin, London.

Wyeth, G 2017, 'Big men, no women: Politics in Papua New Guinea', *The Diplomat,* 11 August, viewed 18 February 2018, www.thediplomat.com/2017/08/big-men-no-women-politics-in-papua-new-guinea/

9

From Drunken Demeanour to Doping: Shifting Parameters of Maturation among Marshall Islanders

Laurence Marshall Carucci

Introduction

In this chapter, I explore the way in which Marshallese youth, encountering the effects of globalisation, have come to include the use of hard drugs (predominantly 'Ice' [crystal methamphetamine] and its less-purified form, meth) as strategies to adapt to the vagaries of a relatively new phase in their lives—adolescence. As others have argued, adolescence itself is a Euro-American invention that carves out a life cycle space between childhood and adulthood that found no place in gathering and fishing (or hunting) societies in which life cycle rites moved youth rapidly from childhood into adulthood.[1] Marshall Islanders certainly

1 An entire debate exists around the universality of adolescence, but the terms of the debate are largely facile. For example, Chen and Farruggia (2002) stated that 'most researchers … believe that industrialization in the late 19th century brought about the emergence of adolescence as a distinct period of the life-span' yet go on to note that 'after studying ethnographic data from more than 170 pre-industrial societies'; however, Schlegel and Barry (1991) concluded that 'almost all societies have the notion of adolescence'. Like the Human Relations Area Files' cross-cultural survey, the latter view begins with sets of functions and features. Therefore, rather than asking whether a society has a linguistic category similar to 'adolescence', Schlegell and Barry presumed that any society with initiation, then marriage, also have 'adolescence' even though many such societies initiate children into manhood or womanhood, not adolescence. Based on the Schlegel and Barry survey, Ember et al.

seem to follow this same pattern—though, at the same time, colonial/globalising encounters are hardly new. In the Marshall Islands, they have been ongoing and actively increasing for more than 150 years.[2] Linguistic change, however, lags. Therefore, local categories for children (*ajiri*) and mature adults (*rutto*) are locally derived, while no comparable collective category exists for adolescence. From the mission encounter, the category 'youth' (*iuut*) has been appropriated and deployed to discuss this group.[3] However, the entire extension of the period between childhood and adulthood is of recent derivation having been developed as an indigenous mimetic product (Carucci 2017) of the colonial/globalising era. The new life cycle category is but one element involved in the transformation of a subsistence workforce into a capitalist one, freeing up and/or incarcerating a subset of the population in a prolonged 'unemployed' status. Along with this shift, a marked subset of lifestyle activities have been created to engage the newly constructed category of social persona: 'youth'. In this chapter, I explore some of the changes that engage Marshall Islands' *iuut* as they transition from childhood to adulthood, particularly the activities of Enewetak/Ujelang *iuut* with whom I am most familiar. While many of these changes appear to engender new opportunities for youth, they also involve vastly increased levels of uncertainty and anxiety. My primary focus here is on the shifting parameters and practices within drinking circles that have occurred as the community has moved from being a highly cohesive group living on Ujelang, the most isolated atoll in the Marshall Islands, to a transnational community with residents now spread across half of the globe, from Taiwan to North Carolina, with primary residence sites on Enewetak and Majuro in the Marshall Islands as well as on the Big Island (Hawai'i).

(2017) answer their own rhetorical question, 'Is adolescence a human universal?' with 'The short answer is "yes"', even though the article began with the contention that 'almost all societies recognize adolescence'. Even in that statement, 'almost all' seems highly dubious since it lacks grounding in indigenous cosmologies. I adopt the lexical/semantic view: lacking a cultural category for adolescence provides strong evidence that, for the speakers of that language, a distinct phase of life analogous to 'adolescence' does not exist. Given that perspective, the notion that adolescence is produced as complex societies become industrialised, is most likely accurate.

2 Much earlier colonial encounters began with Saveedra in 1529, with Spain then claiming eastern sections of what came to be known as 'Micronesia' until German administration of the Marshall Islands began in 1885. Spanish colonisation had little effect on the area, however, with major Euro-American influences coming only with the whaling era and the introduction of Christianity in the mid-nineteenth century (Hezel 2000).

3 There are indigenous terms for pubescent, yet unmarried, females and males—*jiron* and *lekau*—but not a collective, gender undifferentiated term.

From Drinking Circles to Drugs

Drinking circles became an integral part of the movement between youth and adulthood in early colonial times as coconut toddy (*jekero*) and its fermented cousin (*jekmai*) were incorporated into Marshallese life, coming to these atolls from Kiribati, directly to the south. It is unclear why the making of toddy did not occur at an earlier date, but nineteenth-century folklorists date the incorporation of coconut toddy to the mid-nineteenth century, perhaps during the whaling era or the missionisation and copra eras that followed. As discussed elsewhere (Carucci 1987a), as drinking circles became indigenised within the Marshall Islands, and certainly on Ujelang and Enewetak Atolls, northwest outliers of the Marshalls where I first worked with them in the 1970s and 1980s, they were a core representational element of young men's transition to adulthood (compare with Oliver 1989). As liminal performative arenas (Turner 1969), drinking circles were most frequently organised in the sleeping houses of young unmarried men, or they were convened in hidden locales in the bush (representationally, the male sphere in opposition to the village space). While almost exclusively male, in the 1970s on Ujelang, a few women classified as 'exchangers' (*kokañ*: those who exchanged sexual favours for cigarettes, foods and other desirable items) were occasionally incorporated into these drinking circles. Two mature women without husbands and a couple of young, unmarried women were members of the *kokañ* contingent. Nevertheless, in conceptual contour, the drinking circles remained young men's affairs. Their liminal character was marked by all sorts of contra-normative evidences of their unacceptability and structurally antithetical character, as judged by mature community members. The core features of drinking circles that challenged the norms included a trifecta of missionary tabus: sex (outside of marriage), smoking and drinking. Following missionisation in 1926, each of these tabus became markers of what it meant to be a *Kūrijen* 'Christian' and young Ujelang men relished breaking those tabus. Such contrarian activities were truly the core marker of being a *lekau*—an unwed, maturing, young male—and, with one sole exception (a young Christian convert), all young men proclaimed their membership among the *lekau* through shared drinking, smoking (Carucci 1987b) and setting up trysts with women[4] (see Marshall 1978, for a comparison of drinking performances in Chuuk).

What, then, has changed since the 1970s and what has remained the same? The most marked continuity is the way in which today's young men engage in contra-normative rites of passage to mark their transition from youth to adulthood. As in the past, these performances raise the ire of mature men and women who spend a substantial amount of time chastising young men's coming-of-age activities. With some irony, mature men today, as in the past (including church members), simultaneously castigate young men for their carousing, yet, in the shadows (though often not entirely hidden from the young men or the women) they regale audiences with humorous anecdotes of their own youthful exploits of drinking, smoking and seeking out women. Despite the tabu and a host of rhetorical admonitions, a site is thus maintained that re-legitimises the liminal space for contrarian coming-of-age performances.

The changes are more notable, with each creating certain contradictions that must be confronted within the various residential locales where Enewetak/Ujelang people now reside. As noted elsewhere (Carucci 2006, 2007), the repatriation of the exiled community from Ujelang to Enewetak in 1980, following a modest but incomplete clean-up of nuclear wastes from Enewetak Atoll, involved radical shifts in everyday life. Having stripped the main islets of all vegetation and topsoil and having repatriated the community without adequate access to fuel (on which they had become dependent for fishing), few of the subsistence activities that had occupied people's time on Ujelang could be pursued. Consequently, many residents replaced gathering and fishing with bingo and cards. Lacking the options available to their carousing cousins, church members increased their focus on food exchanges, mission trips and events that more generously supported their ministers. The expansion of bingo and cards led to, or coincided with, more drinking and smoking.

4 Many such trysts were not culturally tabu, in that shared sex among cross-cousins (potential spouses) was largely acceptable. Nevertheless, by strict church doctrine, such permitted pairings were still negatively sanctioned inasmuch as only pairs that were wed within the church should engage in sex. Such was the mission-introduced rule, even though the indigenised realisation in practice could never fully inculcate the ideal. Rather, anything other than parallel cousin (sibling) relationships received little comment and no negative sanction. Not infrequently, however, drunken young men were also accused of breaking the cross-cousin proscription, of having sex with siblings or of attempting to 'damage marriages' by having sex with married women. These acts directly conflicted with higher order cultural tabus.

Many more women on the 'New Enewetak' played bingo and/or cards than had been the case in Ujelang, which also meant that they became increasingly available to participate in drinking and smoking circles. Thus, while drinking circles and smoking continued primarily to be discussed as occupations of young, unmarried men who defined themselves as non-Christian through those actions, many young women became involved in these activities as well.

When I asked Litenka, a young female participant, about this change in 2002, she said:

> Well, there is no importance to this [change]. Life on this atoll has changed forever, so you cannot go and collect pandanus fronds and make mats or make handicraft or those sorts of things, as on Ujelang. There is not a single pandanus on Enewetak … or, at least, one with fronds suitable for weaving, so we play bingo. And then some of the young men said we should come and combine with them and play cards. So, now there are many young women who play cards. Well, some of those belonging to the church are mad, but there is no reason for this thing (their being upset), because there is nothing at all on Enewetak now. What else could you do? Just remain stationary for a while or drift off aimlessly into the open ocean from the reef.

Disillusionment with life on the New Enewetak became apparent within a few months of people's return to the atoll. Since it was impossible to live *moud in Majel* (a Marshallese life) on the atoll, migration rapidly increased. This included substantial expansions in the number of Enewetak/Ujelang people residing in the government centre, Majuro and, beginning in 1991, the founding of an expatriate Enewetak/Ujelang community on the Big Island of Hawai'i (see Carucci 2012). After several years, drug use within these new communities began to include substances other than alcohol and tobacco. With the exception of marijuana and betel, this exploration of new recreational drugs did not affect young people on Enewetak, since open supply lines did not exist. Indeed, contact between Majuro and Enewetak has been reduced from what were monthly (at times, even weekly) airlines flights, to four planned supply ship trips per year since the beginning of the twenty-first century.

On the Big Island and on Majuro, the situation has been rather different. In a blind attempt to exploit every commercial opportunity, outside immigrants, many from Taiwan, received a government welcome to Majuro. The new immigrants brought superior entrepreneurial skills, resulting in the monopolisation of all sorts of trade and marketing opportunities on the atoll. Consequently, one of the largest complaints by Marshallese living in Majuro relates to their dependence on businesses that are owned and operated by Taiwanese people. Rapid in-migration also brought gang activity to Majuro and, along with those gangs, access to illegal drugs.[5]

As with many other activities on the Big Island, the presence of drugs long preceded the migration of Marshall Islanders. Nevertheless, between 1991 and 2010, young Marshallese men did not become involved in the local drug trade (other than some experimentation with marijuana, which was relatively easy to obtain). However, beginning with the second generation of Enewetak/Ujelang residents on the Big Island, that has changed. This new phase does not represent a gradual move towards a greater assimilation of Marshall Islanders into Big Island life, since significant effort is still dedicated towards community cohesion-building (separation-maintaining) Marshallese activities, such as distinct Marshallese churches and church activities, *keemem* (first birthday parties), celebrations of death and other group events. However, the involvement with hard drugs does reflect larger alterations in the continuity of transmitted identities between older and younger males and females. As is true in many societies, this disjunction affects men more than women. That is, the everyday activities of young men are hardly recognisable when compared to their adult male elders. The life course options available to them are entirely different than the normal maturation opportunities pursued by their fathers and grandfathers. As boys and maturing young men, members of older generations learned to fish, make canoes, climb coconut trees, gather other subsistence foods and build houses. Even though the rites of passage into adulthood inverted acceptable everyday practices for male elders, as remains true for today's youth, boys and young men on the Big Island now learn only a little about the subsistence pursuits that would occupy their time as adults—though, they would learn far more about house building than canoe construction. In brief, today's Big Island Marshallese youth will rarely mature to replicate and advance

5 Alcohol was also illegal on Ujelang, though that hardly prevented young men from imbibing. Imported alcoholic beverages, primarily cheap whisky and vodka, were only available during and immediately following the visit of the field trip ships that brought all sorts of other desirable commodities as well, but *jemani* and *iiej* (a fermented yeast concoction) supplemented bottled alcohol once a field trip ship had departed.

the activities of their male elders. While the same is true of young women living on the Big Island or on the mainland in the US, several domestic activities do provide a minimal sense of identity continuity through time.

The lack of a practice-grounded, shared, cross-generational identity has served to increase the rift between Big Island Marshallese elders and the community's youth. Elders now frequently complain that they are powerless to alter the actions of young men and women, even close family members. This is quite unlike the situation on Ujelang in the 1970s. Certainly, even in that era, elders complained about the contrarian activities of youth, but extended family members did not hesitate to verbally sanction what they saw as antisocial engagements of young people, be they members of their own household or more distant relatives. At the collective level, the Ujelang Council (comprised of all adult household heads) frequently assigned the youth community service work—such as cleaning the main path or repairing the wharf—if young men or, occasionally, young women did not adhere to their pronouncements regarding morally acceptable activities. In diasporic communities, including Majuro, no such organised disciplinary authority exists.[6] Drug use among youth has increased this sense of anomie for the youth themselves and for the adult members of the community.

As with other sources of alienation, the anomie derives from a lack of shared experience. While elder men tell stories of their drunken exploits as youth, none have any experience with drugs. Be it Ice, meth or some other legally restricted substance, the elders thereby discuss the drug effects on the youth as out of control: crazy (*bwebwe*), like a wild person (*einwot auwie*), lacking consciousness (*jaji lokjen*) and unfettered by custom (*ejaji manit*). While they attempt to control the actions of youth under the influence of drugs with the standard array of communal strategies that their elders applied during their drinking years, they are frequently disappointed that these constraints are not effective.

6 Within churches, some disciplining force remains inasmuch as disobedient youth, those who fail to abide by the required moral proscriptions, will lose membership in that church. However, at the community level, no analogous group membership ban can operate because it stands in direct opposition to the immigrant community's rigorous attempts to maintain a sense of group solidarity in the face of their own foreign identity (Carucci 2012).

Dealing with Drug-Affected Youth

The details of one encounter may help clarify the uncertainties that members of the Big Island Marshallese community faced, once young men and women began experimenting with hard drugs.

One Sunday in June 2017, a young man, Letōōbta (a pseudonym) came into the Ocean View church just as the morning service was under way. He was an Enewetak/Ujelang community member and, while the men were unsettled when he entered—fearing that he might disrupt the service since they had heard he was under the influence of drugs—they seated him near the front between a couple of men who were Letōōbta's relatives. While the young man was unsettled for the first short segment of the service, he then became more animated, drawing increasing attention to himself and away from the minister, elders and 'deaconesses' who were leading the service. These men and women were also close relatives of the young man. He stripped off his shirt, saying he was very hot, and stood up, pacing between the front row of seats and the ambo, the pulpit and altar. The service could not continue, so two elders, including the elder who owns the land on which the church was constructed, seized the young man under his armpits and attempted to escort him from the scene. This only enraged Letōōbta and he dug in his heels to resist the men who tried to remove him from the church. At this, other Enewetak/Ujelang relatives along with additional church members intervened, telling the elders to allow the young man to remain. They led him back to a seat next to the church president—that is, the first aisle seat in the first row (the highest-ranked chair on the male side). Letōōbta agreed to sit in that location, but he would not put his shirt back on.

The service reconvened but, a few minutes later, Letōōbta again stood up and began pacing, mumbling, gurgling and shivering, even as he reiterated that it was very hot. His hot flashes were understood by some church members as 'an attempt to throw off the evil things that had "boarded themselves upon"' Letōōbta when he took the drugs. As the youth performance group came forward and began to line up to perform some songs that they would sing at the upcoming youth conference, Letōōbta moved his chair in front of the performers, seating himself, shirtless, as though he were a special representative of the group. Some of the elders, including a highly ranked elder who owned the land, again came forward to remove him, since Letōōbta seating himself as a leader or chief of the group was too representationally discordant. The youth, at least in their purest form, are called *naan aorek* (the critical word), since in their (sexual) purity, they represent the closest thing to God. The songs that the youth planned to perform had to convey a sense of purity. Then, perhaps, that purity could be manipulated with sexually suggestive parts of their dance to generate humour among members of the audience. This complex play of innocent and then not-so-innocent simply could not be aligned with Letōōbta's restricted performative range, as he lacked both innocence and the ability to play. Defaming the church performance, his actions required a response from the elders.

As he did previously, Letōōbta resisted their efforts to remove him with great strength and determination. Finally, when the elders placed him back in his seat, one of Letōōbta's youngest classificatory mothers came and sat at his feet, stroking his legs and feet and pleading with him to not create further damage. This type of intervention by highly valorised female relatives of the young man was the same strategy that had been used on Ujelang several years prior, when Harry, an elder in the Ocean View church, had violently confronted the mayor, his mother's brother, when inebriated. As with Letōōbta, nearly the entire community became involved in calming and containing the young man. When Letōōbta's disruptive actions had continued for about 20 minutes, the minister (at the recommendation of some elders) finally suggested that everyone move out of the church for an interlude. A food exchange to celebrate an adult's birthday, which was planned for the time between the morning and evening services, was moved into the originally planned church hour and Letōōbta was escorted out and, treated as a honoured first guest, was provided with food and drink before being encouraged to leave the church grounds. Following the birthday celebration, church members and guests reconvened to finish the early Sunday service.

Letōōbta's actions instigated a lengthy series of storytelling performances and critiques of the event. Immediately after the church service, the men began talking about Letōōbta and the day's service. Clearly, they were upset at the 'damage' (*joraan*) that he had created, but they were also worried that several of Letōōbta's age mates were equally 'very damaged by drugs'. The drugs were said to be quite evil—*lukuun nana* or *nana wot im nana* (even worse than bad)—but damage to the social order was just as worrisome as the personal harm that the drugs created. After much talk, I asked how the drugs differed from the alcohol that Tobin and Joniten used to consume on Ujelang (jokingly selecting two of the many church elders present who, in their youth, had been dedicated drinkers). Most of the men posited that 'much more damage resulted from the drugs. With alcohol, a person would be drunk but', they said, 'the following day, all the drunkenness would be gone. Maybe your head would hurt, but there would be no further damage'. Of course, their theory was not entirely true, as one story that Joniten frequently told involving a drinking episode that he and Lamentijen had engaged in while living in Ujelang Town (Majuro) ended in alcohol poisoning and Lamentijen's death. Nevertheless, it was true that the young men usually recovered and that the drinking episodes were now more manageable by the community.

The men also noted that, unlike drugs, alcohol was usually consumed in drinking circles in which each participant sequentially drank equivalent amounts from a common cup, kava style, before passing the cup to the next consumer. In contrast, the older men contended that their 'sons/grandsons did not know the method of mixing drugs'. They indicated that 'a person really had to know what they were doing because, if you mixed them improperly, I am sorry, you might collapse and die. You would never die', they said, 'from making yeast or *jemani*. You might be a little sick or throw up, but die? Never'. With the drugs today, 'they (the youth) never really know. They come from other people, from the American guy in the white pickup or from others, and they (the youth) do not know the content'.

Shifting Parameters in Disciplining Youth

The communal component of drinking has also been disrupted on the disciplinary end, reflecting the changed circumstances of the community. While Ujelang people in the 1970s certainly did not believe that the Earth ended when one crossed the outer reef, they essentially believed that as soon as the field trip ship departed, the meaningful outer margin of the active community was marked by the reef's edge. Adult council members were responsible for all disciplining of inebriated youth. In sharp contrast, in Majuro and on the Big Island, policemen are not elected by the local council; they are representatives of a larger community. In these locales, not only has the Enewetak/Ujelang community come to admit that they are powerless to control the actions of their youthful members, but in the worst circumstances, they turn to the police to discipline the youth on their behalf. In both locales, community members complain when the police do not follow through in a way that they deem to be appropriate. People sometimes feel that the police are too rigorous in their enforcement attempts, but they more often feel that the police are too lax. After Letōōbta's disruption of the church service, the men complained that, recently, when they had called the Big Island police, officers had come and picked up a group of young Marshallese men who were using drugs, handcuffed them and forced them into the back of two police cars. However, instead of taking the youth to the police station and booking them, the young men were then driven down to the Ocean View Shopping Center and were released. 'For what reason were they arrested? Just to go on and toss them aside? There is no value to a policeman of this sort.' One group of elders speculated that the police were themselves involved with the drug trade and that was the reason why they did not follow through.

Perceptively, community elders in Majuro and on the Big Island recognise that the involvement of outside people and foreign substances—from the source of the drugs to their mode of manufacture, from those who sell drugs to the young men to disciplinary personnel who are now expected to control them—has substantially changed the power relations that once surrounded the contrarian activities of the youth. When people say *ejjelok ad maron ilo raan ke in* (today, we have no ability/power) in relation to the performances of youth, it is the altered social conditions encountered by Ujelang/Enewetak residents in Majuro and Ocean View (Big Island) that create those feelings of distance, of being out of control.

Often, elders primarily observe difference between today's young people and their own contrarian coming-of-age routines of 30 or 40 years ago. Fundamentally, however, the more that things change, the more they have remained the same. The liminality and inversion involved in Marshallese youth coming of age is of long standing. While we do not have any in-depth descriptions of pre–Christian era coming-of-age ceremonies, elders in the 1970s indicated that such celebrations did exist for both males and females and that they were, indeed, liminal performances. Such ceremonies were disbanded by the church, if only to re-emerge on the margins. Drinking circles were one such primary form, both a re-instantiation of liminality and resistance to the Christian attempt to tabu what was in missionary eyes tabu. Therefore, Letōōbta's disruption of a Sunday service returned the church's meta-tabu to its source, bringing the prohibited within the now sanctified space of a Sunday service. His activities were hardly new, however, since today's youth rely no less on drugs and sex to mark the passage into adulthood than did their elders. As much as the church has become a central part of Marshallese life, the American Board of Commissioners for Foreign Missions (ABCFM) proscriptions have never settled smoothly into Marshallese cultural designs.[7] Certainly, the welcoming of young women into drinking and smoking circles has been an innovation—yet, young women remain peripheral to many of the most egregious of young people's attempts to invert the cultural norms. The expansion of the array of prohibited drugs to include Ice, meth and an over-dependence on other opioid substances has certainly altered the landscape of exchange and social control in ways that are frightening and new in the eyes of community elders.

However, youth regard this differently. For them, their elders' drinking, smoking and exchanging of sexual favours are the equivalent of their own activities. Tikal, a young man who claimed to have used various experimental drugs, observed:

> Well, the elders, they say that we will really be damaged by drugs. But they do not see that at the time they were young men and women (*lekau im lijiron*), well, they were drinking and smoking and screwing. (laughs). They were damaging all of the rules of the church, just like today, but now that they are church people, deacons and elders, now they are upset with us and say the wrongdoings have just arisen in these times. They are our *bwod* 'mistakes' or 'unacceptable actions'.

In certain respects, Tikal is correct. Many of the routines that accompany the transition to adulthood have been smoothly transmitted from old to young. Not only are church prohibitions inverted, but certain favoured locales—a Marshallese youth hangout near the corner of Coral and Lotus Blossom streets in Ocean View—become the routine sites where such coming-of-age fetes occur and, in most upsetting circumstances, the reveries of the youth's identity-transforming performances slip towards a more radical attention-getting cultural activity: youth suicide (Rubinstein 1983). Such suicides are strategies deployed when young community members feel abused by their close relatives or by the Marshall Islands community at large. These youth-focused disaffections are most frequently discussed among age mates in drinking circles or, presently, in the locales where drugs are shared. In 2017, building on an established Ujelang/Enewetak history of suicide, an elaborate group

7 The ABCFM, which first brought biblical teaching to Hawai'i in 1819, became the Hawaiian Mission Society before coming to the Marshall Islands in the 1850s (and to Enewetak in 1926); but the markers of heathen debauchery that they introduced have remained as church-grounded ideals until the current day.

suicide pact was planned by young men sharing drugs on the Big Island to draw attention to their sense of disempowerment. In planning a group event, the young men hoped to transform two recent sequential suicides within the community into an age-graded social movement.

The potency of suicide lies in its ability to rapidly transform the power of those who take their own lives. As living persons and as young men moving from still-maturing youth to non-corporeal ancestors, the rank of the suicide 'victims' increases immeasurably. Such non-corporeal 'spirit' beings, what David Graeber and Marshall Sahlins (2017) term 'meta-humans', have far greater power than living humans. That power is manifest in their ability to move freely between the worlds of the living and the dead, to influence human affairs and to instigate shifts in the balance of exchange relationships between living and non-corporeal beings. The choice of method for those contemplating suicide, hanging or *lukwoj buru-* is particularly salient in terms of Marshallese communicative intent as well. The throat (*buru-*) is the seat of emotions for Marshall Islanders and youthful disaffection involving highly emotion-laden feelings/thoughts are displayed iconically for the entire community when young people hang themselves. The Big Island suicide pact involved seven or eight young men who felt that their collective suicide, following on the heels of their age mates' suicides, would communicate to community elders their collective sense of disenfranchisement. The young men specifically modelled their suicide plan from the suicide of Preteley on Ujelang in 1977. Preteley had hoped that his suicide would send a message of indignation to various elders who he believed had not treated him with the respect due to him being an offspring of the chiefly family. Big Island young men viewed their proposed actions in an analogous fashion. They hoped that their strategy would communicate their sense of disempowerment to the elders. If all the young men committed suicide at the same time, they believed that the collective action would be even more transformative. Rather than just 'one additional suicide', the community would be stricken with the loss of the death of an entire set of young men. Ultimately, one of the community elders heard about the pact and, admonishing some of the young men, their group suicide was never accomplished. Consequently, neither the disaffections of the young men, the adults' critiques of young people's drug use, nor the agreed-upon idea that the young men's current style of life was largely 'useless', changed in the least.

While Tikal and other youth regarded their shared drug use as a continuation of the practices of earlier generations, some of their analogies are problematic. Indeed, Tikal spoke of the cohesion-building components to sharing hard drugs, much as an earlier generation had observed the sharing of alcohol as creating similar bonds. What is overlooked in the suggested equivalence among today's drug choices and those in the past is the matter of internal versus external power and disciplinary control. Particularly on the Big Island, the use of Schedule 1 drugs places youth at risk of serious criminal charges. With Compact of Free Association residents under increased scrutiny under the Trump presidency, such charges may be cause for deportation (Froelich 2017). Drug charges, especially criminal charges, also follow youth for their entire life. Even though Marshallese youth claim that they share drugs much like the longstanding outer-island practice of sharing alcohol or tobacco, US law does not align with this view of sharing. Even though drug sharing undoubtedly serves as a method of creating equivalence among co-participants—as was the practice in drinking circles[8]—sharing Schedule 1 drugs risks elevating legal charges from 'possession' to 'distribution', which is a substantial leap in punishment and levels of disciplinary control.

Conclusion

As with all social and cultural practices, change equates with hybrid formulations that both perpetuate core features of the past and inscribe newly formulated innovations, often using mimetic practices in formulating new components. This has certainly been true of the Enewetak/Ujelang Marshallese, the most isolated of outlier groups in the Republic of the Marshall Islands. As the entire life stage that Europeans and Americans term 'adolescence' or 'youth' has been indigenised, it has moved from a rapid rite of transition from childhood to adulthood to a more elongated and elaborated phase of Marshallese life. The mimetic term adopted to describe this stage is *iuut* (youth). If female rites of

8 Themes of sharing are stressed not only by Marshall Islands' youth; they surface in the works of Philippe Bourgois (2009) and of Angela Garcia (2010), whose respective research among San Francisco dopefiends, and marginalised residents of the Espanola Valley (New Mexico), point to the way in which sharing and otherness are linked, helping form bonds of solidarity and inclusion among those engaging in contra-normative performances in many distinct social settings. Rocky Sexton (2010), analysing meth users' poetry, also finds solidarity themes, noting that 'in many instances, those who produce the drug will share it with friends, family, and acquaintances within local social networks, often within group use settings'.

passage in the Marshalls were once quite private and secluded affairs, male rites during the colonial era came to incorporate the ingestion of drugs, primarily alcohol and tobacco. In recent years, however, not only have women been included in drinking and smoking circles, but the use of hard drugs has begun to supplement alcohol and tobacco, particularly among young men. Such hard drugs are mainly restricted to Majuro, the Big Island and other Marshallese communities on the US mainland. They are rarely available on outer islands like Enewetak. While these hard drugs have not radically altered the routines of sharing among age mates, the power dynamics that have shifted among diasporic Marshall Islands communities more generally—with Enewetak/Ujelang people now forming part of larger Marshallese communities, and those communities being embedded as emergent minority groups in larger sodalities—have also been inscribed in rites of passage into adulthood. With lines of power that exceed the bounds of the emergent Marshallese communities themselves, the effects on youthful practices along the path that leads from childhood to adulthood have been significantly re-contoured in ways that are partially predictable. However, with both supply and sanction extending beyond local control, the entailed outcomes of such youthful practices are also quite unsettling.

References

Bourgois, P 2009, *Righteous dopefiend*, University of California Press, Berkeley.

Carucci, LM 1987a, 'Jekero: Symbolizing the transition to manhood in the Marshall Islands', *Micronesica*, no. 20, pp. 1–17.

Carucci, LM 1987b, 'Kijen Emaan ilo Baat: Smoking circles in Marshallese society', in L Lindstrom (ed.), *Drugs in Western Pacific societies,* University Press of America, Washington, DC, pp. 51–74.

Carucci, LM 2006, 'Mōņnjaar eo: The church as an embodiment and expression of community on Wōjlan and Āne-wetak, Marshall Islands', *Pacific Studies*, vol. 26, nos 3–4, pp. 55–78.

Carucci, LM 2007, 'Life in dis-place: Re-searching processes of imagining with Enewetak-Ujelang people', *Pacific Studies*, vol. 27, nos 3–4, pp. 107–133.

Carucci, LM 2012, 'You'll always be family: Formulating Marshallese identities in Kona, Hawai'i', *Pacific Studies*, vol. 5, nos 1–2, pp. 203–231.

Carucci, LM 2017, 'Mimesis and reimagining identity among Marshall Islanders', in J Mageo & E Hermann (eds), *Mimesis and Pacific transcultural encounters: In time, in trade, and in ritual reconfigurations,* Berghahn Books, New York, pp. 209–229.

Chen, CS & Farruggia, S 2002, 'Culture and adolescent development', *Online Readings in Psychology and Culture*, vol. 6, no. 1, doi.org/10.9707/2307-0919.1113

Ember C, Pitek E & Ringen, EJ 2017, *Adolescence*, HRAF, viewed 5 June 2018, hraf.yale.edu/ehc/summaries/adolescence

Froelich, J 2017, 'Trump Immigration Enforcement Puts COFA Migrants At-Risk for Deportation', *KUAF (National Public Radio) report*, 18 April 2017, viewed 12 August 2018, www.kuaf.com/term/immigration?page=2#stream/0

Garcia, A 2010, *The pastoral clinic: Addiction and dispossession along the Rio Grande*, University of California Press, Berkeley.

Graeber, D & Sahlins, M 2017, *On Kings*, Hau Press, distributed by University of Chicago Press, Chicago, viewed 5 June 2018, haubooks.org/wp-content/uploads/2018/01/On-Kings.pdf

Hezel, FX 2000, *The first taint of civilization*, University of Hawai'i Press, Honolulu.

Marshall, M 1978, *Weekend warriors*, McGraw Hill, New York.

Oliver, D 1989, *Oceania: The native cultures of Australia and the Pacific Islands*, vol. 1, University of Hawai'i Press, Honolulu.

Rubinstein, D 1983, 'Epidemic suicide among Micronesian adolescents', *Social Science and Medicine*, vol. 17, no. 10, pp. 657–665.

Schlegel, A & Barry, H III 1991, *Adolescence: An anthropological inquiry*, Free Press, New York.

Sexton, RL 2010, '"Tweaking and geeking, just having some fun": An analysis of methamphetamine poems', *The Journal of Psychoactive Drugs*, vol. 42, no. 3, pp. 377–383.

Turner, V 1969, *The ritual process*, Routledge and Kegan Paul, London.

10

Understanding Childhood in the Micronesian Diaspora by Linking Home Island Lives to Post-Migration Experiences

Mary L Spencer

Introduction

The contemporary migration of children and families from the new nations of the Republic of the Marshall Islands (RMI), the Federated States of Micronesia (FSM) and the Republic of Palau (RP) to the United States (US) Territory of Guam, the US Commonwealth of the Northern Mariana Islands (CNMI), Hawai'i and the continental US has brought serious challenges in both the origin islands and the receiving locations. Effects on these children have rarely been systematically studied. The lack of a firm description and understanding of Micronesian children's development in their home cultures and contexts further hampers both the sending and receiving communities, as they grapple with questions regarding the children's needs and appropriate ways to support them.

One purpose of this paper is to establish what is known about Micronesian childhoods in both home island and migration contexts. It pursues this objective by highlighting that knowing the contours of life in each major sub-context (i.e. home, neighbourhood, school, church and community) is important to understanding the everyday lives of Micronesian children that circulate within and around their home islands and their migration locations. This more thorough understanding is foundational for the practical support of child development, as well as for appropriate social policy. The second purpose is to project new directions for research of Micronesian children whose childhoods have been subjected to major episodes of residential movement. The emerging post-migration research with children worldwide, with those from Micronesia and particularly that conducted by indigenous Micronesian scholars holds promise for a greater understanding and policy guidance. In this chapter, childhood will be operationally defined as birth through to the late teens, unless otherwise explained.[1]

How the Flood of Contemporary Migration Is Shaping the Research Paradigm

Geographic movement is an age-old phenomenon for Pacific Islanders. The history of Micronesian migration around, away and back and forth is a fascinating one (Hess et al. 2001; Hezel 2013; Perez 2004; Spencer 2012). Many important cultural qualities of the different Micronesian groups are intricately tied to geographic movement: navigation, canoe building, arts used in trade such as weaving, and genealogy practices. Nevertheless, with the exception of the forced relocations of Marshall Islanders by the US for atomic bombing purposes, Micronesian movement was more limited during the years following the Second World War, in which the United Nations Trust Territory of the Pacific Islands (TTPI) arrangement was in place. US security practices severely limited access into the region as well as inter-entity and extra-Micronesia movements in general.[2] Many took for granted that most Micronesians would spend their lives in their heritage islands or perhaps in regional administrative locations. Some would leave on US I-20 student visas for higher education and some would leave for medical care, especially Marshallese who had been victimised by the atomic testing. However, it was widely assumed that most would return to

1 The operational definition of *child* or *children* in this chapter is flexible, but it is generally framed by the first two decades of life. A review of anthropological research in multiple Micronesian island groups reveals culturally textured developmental scenarios across the age range, differentiated by puberty events, gender roles, birth order expectations, societal status and privilege traditions (Barnett 1960; Carucci 1985).

2 Because Guam was home to a strategic military base, a Navy security clearance was needed to enter; President Kennedy's appointed governor, William Daniel, was instrumental in having Kennedy lift the requirement in 1962 (Sanchez 1987).

assume leadership positions at home. Neither the scale of movement nor the nature of globalisation that this new phase of the postcolonial period would bring to the Marshall Islands, Kosrae, Pohnpei, Chuuk, Yap and Palau had been widely foreseen.[3]

It was not until several years after the 1986 RMI and FSM Compacts of Free Association with the US were finalised that Guam, CNMI, Hawai'i and several US mainland states began to realise the heights to which the population influx from these new countries would rise. Palau's 1994 Compact with the US heightened this realisation. When the predominantly adult-male composition of migrants to Guam and Hawai'i shifted to include women, children and elders, the residents, educators, health providers and social workers in the receiving areas realised how little they knew about their new neighbours and how much more understanding was needed. Similarly, it would not be enough for the Freely Associated Micronesians to understand local child development that is preparatory for a lifetime spent on the home island. It became necessary for them to also understand what children who leave will experience in new settings and how they can be prepared for this before they depart. Stakeholders and individuals in the migration settings, especially those who play major roles in children's lives, needed information on Micronesian children's family, community, culture and past experiences to nurture them in positive ways. There was a lack of information and strategies that could facilitate the process of working through differences quickly. This led to frictions in places where high rates of post–Compact Micronesian migration occurred. In reaction, US federally funded 'Compact Impact' projects were established in the early 1990s (Smith et al. 1997).

On Guam, there were needs-assessment surveys performed for each major Micronesian culture/language group that identified the problems and critical needs of the families. The projects were primarily conducted by leaders and members of these same groups and guided by the university social science faculty. Resulting lists of prioritised problems, needs and recommendations proved to have long-term usefulness to multiple agencies on Guam. The projects also developed an indigenous leadership pool and provided them with employment experience in their new home. Evolved remnants of these 'Compact Impact' projects continue,

3 The Northern Mariana Islands, the other post-war entity of the TTPI, opted to join the American family by becoming a US Commonwealth. By order of President Jimmy Carter, the CNMI constitution went into effect in 1978 (Farrell 1991).

even now, in Guam, CNMI and Hawai'i. Even so, a conversation today with professional human service personnel in any of these places would readily reveal questions and stories that speak of much misunderstanding. These voids of understanding and lack of appreciation for the rich *funds of knowledge* that Micronesian migrant children and families bring with them appear to be commonplace in the post-migration contexts.[4]

Practical imperatives in the educational, health, social services and economic domains of the Micronesian migration sites are shaping the childhood research paradigm for Micronesian migrant children. Cross-context investigations that include the heritage island location prior to migration as well as the migration destination are now needed. What do the children and their families bring with them? What demands and experiences do they face once they arrive? How do the post-migration experiences in different locations compare, especially when children experience multiple stepping-stone relocations? What is the fit between the heritage resources and the demands of the new context? What are the consequences of the gaps and misalignments for the children? What adjustments are made and to what end? What experiential factors in the new location protect them and hold a promise for enhancing their development? Is there a feedback loop between the migration experience and the heritage island location throughout the history of the migration cycle? That is, what collective learning about migration success factors gradually accumulates over a period of years and decades of the migration process? These are just some of the broadest questions that arise and that could be addressed by a cross-context research design that is focused on the circulation of Micronesian children.

Cross-Context Research Literature on Micronesian Childhoods

A review of the literature was conducted to bring to the forefront the lessons learned on Micronesian child development in both the broad migration contexts—home island and migration destination. For increased explanatory power, the research was further organised by sub-context—

4 See Gonzalez et al. (2005) for a full discussion of the 'funds of knowledge' concept relative to children and families who have migrated to the US.

family home, school, church, neighbourhood or community. Also noted was the type of research design. The findings were first summarised for the home island and then for the migration context.[5]

Home Island

Family Home

The only direct observations used to document and describe the family homes of Micronesian children in their islands of origin have been ethnographies or short-term case studies. Ethnographies were conducted by Thomas Gladwin and Seymour Sarason (1953) and Fischer (1950, 1956) on Romonum Island, Chuuk Lagoon; by Mary Thomas (1978) and Juliana Flinn (1982, 1992a, 1992b) on the Western Chuuk islands of Nomonuito and Pulap, respectively; and by Donald Rubinstein (1979) on Fais Island and Anne Douglass (1999) on Woleai, both sites in Yap State, FSM.

More recently, I conducted 12 observational case studies with children of Romonum Island, Chuuk FSM (Spencer 2015). All were enrolled in school (young were aged 6–8 years; middle were aged 9–10 years; and old were aged 11–14 years). I found considerable concordance of results across this study and the earlier ethnographic studies in Romonum and four other locations in Micronesia regarding the nature of children's play and work activities, and in their interactions with significant adults.[6] The play activities of the children (e.g. young children digging holes, making little boats, drawing in the sand, playing tag, middle and older children running races or participating in organised games) were similar across the studies. However, many of the traditional activities that were documented for children of Fais, Nomonuito and Woleai are now unknown to Romonum children—although some of these were observed there in the late 1940s (e.g. canoe building).

5 Contact the author for an annotated listing of references for each setting within home or migration context.

6 See Spencer (2015, pp. 161–165) for a summary comparison across these researchers.

Figure 1. A young Romonum girl tends to a cooking fire in the family compound.

Source: Author.

Figure 2. An eighth-grade Romonum boy returns from a fishing trip with neighbours.

Source: Author.

The human environment in all sample homes in my study was multigenerational, with an extended family composition and a wide age range in which multiple simultaneous activities were underway. Developmental trends were uncovered in the frequencies of child engagement over a range of activities that were documented for the sample of children. These differed from those documented for the same children at school. The differences revealed that gender and age contrast and relate to the nature of adult and child interactions and roles in the home. The work engagement for children of all ages was large. Younger girls engaged in work more often than younger boys. Middle and older-aged boys performed more work than the same-aged girls. Older boys had virtually no play activity and no hanging out/spacing out time at home—their time was dominated by work.[7] Only younger children had the freedom to be purposeless and idle. Young and middle boys played or hung out until work commitments were imposed by the family.

Direct home instruction was not prominent on Romonum; rather, the children's teaching and learning at home more often consisted of a child learning through a gradual, observational and experiential process with an adult or older child, and through repetitive practice (i.e. the 'intent community participation tradition' or the 'guided repetition tradition' as described by Rogoff et al. [2007]). Sibling care of younger children was pronounced (Spencer 2015).

In all the observational studies of children that were cited, researchers engaged with theoretical questions relating to the mechanisms of child development. The relative resilience of these theoretical considerations mirrors the historical changes in professional acceptance of specific theoretical tenets and empirical methods of research. My study demonstrated how contemporary digital photography and recording can be conducted at modest cost and combined with more traditional observation and interview methods to effectively document child and family life in remote Micronesian settings.

School

Considerable resources have been applied to school studies in Micronesia. FSM, RMI and RP have all had student achievement testing programs for many years. Typically, these programs produce annual academic achievement reports for English-language reading and mathematics. For some Micronesian entities, results in other subjects such as home-language literacy and science are also reported. Testing programs are relatively new and are not yet organised for longitudinal research. Improvements in sampling, quality of test instruments and reliability and validity characteristics may make longitudinal or predictive results possible in the future. Several large multi-year US federal contracts for educational support services (e.g. Pacific Resources for Education and

7 Tudge's (2008) system for coding child observations was applied to the video records of Romonum children's activity samples. At times, sample children would sit or stand in sustained quiet and inactive mode, sometimes by themselves and sometimes with other children. We coded those instances as 'hanging out/spacing out'.

Learning; the McREL Regional Education Laboratory for the Pacific) have trained education specialists and addressed a US federal research and development agenda.

In my Romonum Island case study and research in the school setting, school and FSM census data revealed that only 56–74 per cent of the children in Grades 1 to 8 attend school. For the 1–12 grade range, only 44 per cent of school-aged Romonum children are attending school. The 2010 census statistics for the entire Chuuk Lagoon area, of which Romonum is one island, indicate that 66 per cent of the school-aged population are enrolled in high school, with 56 per cent males and 71 per cent females. This percentage would be much lower for Romonum and the many similar lagoon islands where there are no junior or senior high schools. For those who do not attend school, one might conclude that their lives appear much as the observation findings for home settings. However, further observations of children who do not go to school are warranted. In the observations of school children, 80 per cent of the time of the three age groups combined was spent on lessons. Only 2–18 per cent of their time was spent hanging out/spacing out, with variations depending on age and gender. For older students, comprised of a small group remaining after years of attrition by age mates, very little time was spent in off-task, unproductive ways.

Indigenous priorities, viewpoints, traditions, content, teaching methods and administrative directives were apparent throughout the overall school experience. Although US textbooks and teacher support materials were prominent, Chuukese oral language was ubiquitous in teacher–student communication in the earlier grades, with teachers gradually using some English instructional content in Grades 5–8. A local culture curriculum was taught several times a week by a male and female culture teacher, and it was somewhat integrated into the other subjects. The greatest emphasis in the formal instruction was on the symbolic knowledge of literacy and numeracy—all with US textbooks and Chuukese teacher narratives. The three learning traditions described by Barbara Rogoff et al. (2007) were all documented to varying degrees, but the assembly line learning tradition was dominant—that is, in the typical school experience, a single teaching expert would conduct a lesson to a group of students in an authoritative style. Lessons requiring rote memory activities were common. When used, the intended community participation teaching–learning method was most likely to be found in the culture lessons. At times, a mix of teaching approaches was apparent. There were no science materials, but several teachers taught science content based on their own traditional knowledge or they taught by an individual teacher sharing content that he or she had independently found in a science book.

Church

No studies directly focusing on children were found for the church sub-context on the home island. Flinn's (2010) book relates to some degree to the role of the churches in child development on Pulap Atoll, Chuuk and FSM. I have previously mentioned the perceived importance of the role of churches throughout Micronesia to children's development and practice of literacy and linguistic skills (Spencer 1992). Studies that better document the lives of Micronesian children as they engage with churches would fill a gap in the evidence that is available on the lives of children in various Micronesian cultures.

Figure 3. Groups of children take turns reciting memorised bible verses to a large child and parent audience during Children's Sunday School at the Lelu Church in Kosrae, FSM. Just one prominent example of the role the church plays in literacy development and the role that rote memorisation plays in learning activities.

Source: Author.

Neighbourhood and Community

Ethnographic and case studies conducted on home islands typically incorporate some aspects of children's compounds, neighbourhoods and communities. The social arrangements and physical attributes of these contexts in close relationship to child development have received little direct study. The best research resources for glimpsing these arrangements are the studies on Romonum by Gladwin and Sarason (1953), Fischer

(1950, 1956) and Spencer (2015); by Thomas (1978) and Flinn (1982, 1992a, 1992b) on the Western Chuuk islands of Nomonuito and Pulap, respectively; and by Rubinstein (1979), Douglass (1999) and Spencer (2018) in Yap, on the island of Fais, Woleai Atoll and Ulithi Atoll, respectively.

In the summer of 1985, I conducted observations of children on the Falalop Island of Ulithi Atoll over six weeks, during which I also taught University of Guam courses at the Outer Island High School to teachers from a wide range of the Yap outer islands. I documented young children often playing in groups and engaging in peer teaching (Spencer 2018). For example, children aged approximately 5–10 years old were observed playing music with homemade instruments and singing together, walking paths in small mixed-age and gender groups, peer teaching dance and games, detailed teaching of the seated stick dance to a dance partner, tree climbing, playing in sand piles, ocean swimming, drawing, kung fu acrobatics, and quiet sitting and hanging out. Culturally based and contextually defined rules of silence appeared to direct the children's behaviour when in the company of adults. Even during their free summer days, families and neighbours stimulated literacy development via books to read and opportunities to draw and write. The children had many opportunities to shadow and assist family adults; for example, as they conducted daily work such as collecting flowers and making leis, contributing to the food preparation process, or assisting men bringing in canoes full of freshly caught fish.

One aspect of my courses in Ulithi was the study of the role of culture in child cognitive development. In one assignment, teachers read and discussed Susan Philips's (1972) study of the teaching–learning methods that she documented with Warm Springs Indians in Oregon. Afterward, teachers from Lamotrek, Woleai, Farraulap and Ulithi provided individual written descriptions of how children's lives and learning in their own cultures might compare with Philips's findings. Student comments included the view that within their families, there is a private proprietary nature to knowledge. The owner of knowledge carefully selects who will receive his or her knowledge, based on the respect and care that this person has given to the knowledge owner's family member; on their demonstrated care for the good of the community; on their ability to respect the knowledge; and on their need to be secretive about it themselves. The sole female Ulithian teacher said, 'The most important aspects from my culture, about the person who wants to learn, come from listening to and observing their parents, family members, and people within their community'. She also noted that customs, stories and legends were important in this process. She further explained that the composition of groupings in her culture were important to learning: 'There is always the division of men and women in almost anything: learning skills, working, playing, etcetera'.

Some obvious variables related to child development in the communities of Micronesia, which are of interest for future research, included a) high versus low island geography and island size, because of the resource differences and relative remoteness that these physical features endow on the inhabiting families; b) the degree of technological access; c) the modernity of communication and travel facilities; d) the access to health, education and commercial resources; e) the continuity of cultural control of the home island; and f) the nature and extent of the home island's immigration and emigration activity. These variables all have the power to shape children's lives on the home island and to maintain influence on children who circulate to other places.

Post-Migration

Family Home

Documentation of the lives of Micronesian children in their family homes in post-migration contexts is rare. Of the two relevant studies to date on children's post-migration home lives, the interview study by Katherine Ratliffe (2010) focuses on the implications of Micronesian migrant family obligations for education. She conducted interviews with 26 adults from the FSM, RMI and Palau, mostly in Hawai'i. Many of the informants were educators. Others had worked in entry-level jobs as janitors, fast food workers and drivers, or they were homemakers. Seven were recent migrants or had children in US schools. They explained that their traditional cultural responsibilities to their immediate and extended families—in both Hawai'i and their home islands—continued to play major roles in the lives of both children and adults. These obligations included maintaining connections with their distant families, keeping them informed about their lives, asking permission for many things or even returning home when needed. Obligations often revolved around life transition events such as births, graduations, home building, illnesses, marriages and deaths. Based on her interviews and review of the literature regarding other migrants, Ratliffe (2010, p. 680) concluded that 'the actions that a person takes to fulfill traditional and other obligations to family members are part of the maintenance and development of both personal and ethnic identities both in Micronesia and after emigration'. Children will be fully engaged in these obligations and will likely be absent from school when their participation is needed by the family.

In their 2012 study on Oahu, Hawai'i, Kaneshiro and Black selected four 13- and 14-year-old Marshallese and Chuukese migrant children who had been found eligible for special education services. With the support of interpreters, the children were individually interviewed about pictures that they themselves had taken in their homes with disposable cameras provided by the researchers. Afterward, they and their families reviewed the written summaries for accuracy. Researchers concluded that a common strength among the children's home experiences was family cooperation; for example, the child performed housekeeping, cooking and childcare responsibilities that benefited the whole family. Grandparents sometimes provided temporary housing, as well as advice and supplementary funds.

School

Post-migration outcome data for Micronesian children in educational settings should be robust due to the intensive academic testing required by US federal and state education policy. My examination of Guam Department of Education databases in 2012 revealed that Micronesian migrant data were identifiable and systematically collected (Grandjean & Spencer 2013). Hawai'i State Department of Education academic databases also contain regularly collected achievement data; however, Hawai'i has resisted coding Micronesian students' ethnicity identifiers in a manner that would permit analysis (Ault 2013, pp. 3–5). In both locations, technical issues of missing data may pertain due to such factors as exclusion from testing of students with limited English proficiency. Documentation of the extent to which Micronesian migrant children are thriving academically in US schools is legally required by Title VI of the *Civil Rights Act 1964* (US Department of Education 2018). The absence of this information and the lack of action to acquire it may eventually require US federal regulatory intervention. The potential for positive change stemming from such intervention is substantial. When students identified as English-language learners (ELLs) are discovered, whose ability to participate in or benefit from US public school instruction on the basis of language or minority race or ancestry, Title VI requires that the school district takes 'affirmative steps to ensure that the English learner students can participate meaningfully and equally in educational programs and service'. This includes providing 'an educationally sound language assistance program' with 'qualified staff and sufficient resources to instruct ELL students', 'monitoring the progress of ELL students in learning English and doing grade-level classwork, remedying any academic deficits' and 'evaluating the effectiveness of *their* ELL programs'.

Paul (2003) was an early observer of the post-migration school lives of Micronesian children in Honolulu. She was a woman who had married into Pohnpeian culture and worked as a volunteer teacher's assistant in elementary classrooms, and reported teachers describing the Micronesian children as 'bad' and 'lazy'. She was surprised at the teachers' public criticism of the students in ways that humiliated them and brought them to tears. Steven Talmy (2006, 2009) published detailed observational studies of Micronesian students in Honolulu high school classes, most of whom had to relocate to Honolulu from the Marshall Islands and Chuuk. Academic English as a Second Language (ESL) print literacy was a significant problem for all, regardless of their island origin. Talmy also detailed a social environment that was presented to these students by teachers and classmates in which intimidation and degradation were thoroughly engrained.

In Walter et al.'s (2011) survey study of Chuukese migrants to Guam, education ranked only second to jobs as what they liked best about Guam. Becoming a teacher was the highest-ranked dream job. However, racism and discrimination ranked as what they liked the least about Guam. Relationships between the Micronesian community on Guam and the Guam Department of Education (GDOE) have not always been smooth. However, collective action of the Micronesian migrant community has tended to motivate GDOE improvement efforts. A major crisis occurred when, in the 2010–11 school year, a series of schoolyard events at a middle school became the subject of a contentious televised oversight hearing of the Guam Legislature on the subject of bullying (Spencer 2012). A small group of Micronesian migrant students who had been expelled continued to come to school on the school bus. Once at school, they retreated into a jungle area through holes torn in the school's back fence. From this sanctuary, they and other students yelled insults and threw rocks at students and school personnel in the schoolyard. Shortly afterward, the GDOE Superintendent organised a public meeting with the Chuukese community in which mutual concerns and recommendations were shared. This positive event forged inter-group connections and the

GDOE promised to hire a number of bilingual school aides who could assist newly migrated Micronesian students. It was mutually acknowledged that Chuukese students had also been victims of bullying.

Maria Pong, a Micronesian migrant parent living in a northern Guam neighbourhood, demonstrated how true Walter et al.'s (2011) finding is regarding the importance of Guam's educational opportunities to parents like her. School bus service was often lacking in her neighbourhood due to unpaved roads that became impassable after hard rains. One day, she learned of an urgent plea to parents from the school to be sure that their children came to school the next day for the annual testing activities. When the school bus failed to pick up the waiting children, Maria walked all 47 of them to the school several miles away. Guam DOE thanked her at an appreciation ceremony (Ngirairikl 2011a).

In an observation study of several Chuukese children in K–5 elementary classrooms on Guam, I reported that a nurturing and caring instruction of Micronesian students was observed in numerous contexts (Spencer 2012). However, the lack of best practices and resources needed for them was also sometimes apparent. There were no instructional aides or teachers who could communicate with the young students in their home languages. ESL materials were scarce and many training needs were evident—for example, how to use GDOE curriculum standards and performance indicators, effective bi-literacy strategies for ESL and regular classrooms, strategies for infusing higher order thinking skills and how to plan and carry through a course of study for students who lack prior or adequate schooling when they arrive. Most troubling was the reaction of one teacher to children who, as an appropriate sign of respect in Chuukese culture, did not make direct eye contact with the teacher. Repeatedly, the teacher spotlighted these children before the entire class, scolding them for not looking directly at her. Multiple times, she cupped her hand around the child's jaw and rather roughly pulled the student's face upward. In a more recent study, a group of teachers at a school with many Micronesian migrant students conducted systematic observations of a sample of these students. They used an observation instrument, the Sheltered Instruction Observation Protocol (Echevarria et al. 2013), which is designed to document the extent to which eight categories of best instructional practices for ELLs occur. The engagement of these educators and their principal in this action research project demonstrates their intentions of learning and applying effective instructional methods for the Micronesian migrant students in their care.

Based on her adult interview study regarding the implications of Micronesian family obligations for education in Hawai'i, and informed by her review of the literature (e.g. Heine 2002), Ratliffe (2010) provided six suggestions on how educators can support Micronesian families so that they can successfully navigate US school systems: a) ask them about their home islands; b) ask them who the decision-makers are in the family; c) give alternative options for gender-sensitive educational practices; d) become familiar with laws and practices regarding guardianship and provide relevant paperwork and instructions for completing it;[8] e) identify members of the different Micronesian communities who can bridge communication between families and schools; and f) build on the cultural importance of personal relationships by creating opportunities for relationships to develop.[9]

Church

Few studies of Micronesian migrant children relative to direct post-migration church experiences have been identified. Kaneshiro and Black's (2012) study in Hawai'i with four Marshallese and Chuukese pre-adolescent children demonstrates the potential for such inquiry. They documented that family participation in church activities, and the cultural association of these particular churches, were regular and formative experiences. Church members also assisted these students and their families by making a variety of financial opportunities available, such as providing activities in which the children could earn money or obtain domestic goods.

During Kupferman's (2009) interviews with Kosraean mothers living in Honolulu, a local Kosraean church was identified as a main feature in the lives of the mothers and children. They credited it as being an important source of personal support and of Kosraean language and culture exposure for their children. Allen (1997) conducted a study of Marshallese migrants in Enid, Oklahoma, and found two very different Marshall Island communities, one composed of chiefly families and the other composed

8 The presence of migrant Micronesian children on Guam who have travelled without their parents or who live with adults other than their parents continues to confuse and worry many educators, health providers, public safety, airport or other governmental personnel. This concern is usually due to lack of information about the cultural traditions of the children's heritage islands. In some locations in Micronesia as many as 90 per cent of children experience adoption. Adoptive parents are usually aunts and uncles, or grandparents, and the secrecy so often present in US adoptions usually does not apply (see Rauchholz 2008, 2012).

9 For example, at Upi Elementary School on Guam, the principal invited Micronesian parents and community members into the school for literacy instruction on evenings and weekends.

of Kili Atoll recipients of US nuclear compensation and relocation funds. To unite themselves and create shared traditions, they organised a new church that became central to their lives in Enid. Although children's experiences with the church and its effects on their lives have never been reported, Allen documented its centrality to community life. Its activities affect not only the lives of Enid Marshallese children, but they extend to the home islands because of its vigorous work to provide educational scholarships and arrange for student home stays in Oklahoma.

Neighbourhood and Community

The meagre body of post-migration research sometimes addresses Micronesian children's neighbourhoods and communities, usually through needs-assessment surveys of adults that include reflections on resource access issues, challenges, adjustments, schooling and attitudes relevant to families and children (e.g. Walter et al. 2011). A direct and systematic research focus on children in the neighbourhood or community context is missing.

Journalistic sources have provided some of the most insightful views of post-migration, neighbourhood/community experiences of Micronesian migrants. In Honolulu, Kandell and Foley (2012) related the story in words and photos of young Micronesian men representing multiple cultures and a newly discovered cross-cultural unity, creating a basketball 'league of their own'. Twenty teams, playing more than 90 games a year in gyms all over Honolulu, culminated their 2012 season with the All-Mike Basketball tournament. A Marshallese community leader, Dr Wilfred Alik, was quoted as saying, 'The fact that we were there changed a lot of people's thinking. It's often a struggle just to gain access to public courts. Many were downright scared, but sitting in the Blaisdell Arena, the feeling—that sense of empowerment—was palpable'. The teams include teenagers. The tournament is a pride-inspiring experience for children and spectators of all ages who come from Micronesian migrant communities throughout Oahu.

A situation involving sex trafficking of minors has been the most serious community problem on Guam involving Micronesian youth. Referred to as the Blue House case, it was closely reported by journalists of the *Guam Pacific Daily News* and prosecuted by both local and federal law enforcement (e.g. Aguon 2011; Matthews 2011; Thompson 2011). A Guam bar owner recruited minor girls and young women from their home islands in Chuuk. Their testimony revealed that they were held hostage, called degrading names and forced to perform sex acts to work off their debts to the bar owner. At least one girl was beaten and forced to have an abortion when she became pregnant. Another is raising her child from one of these customer unions. The girls flew to Guam on the promise of working at a restaurant. The bar owner was convicted on all counts and sentenced to life in prison.

Other journalists followed community activities and debates that focus on the effects and terms of the Compact of Free Association on Guam (e.g. Ngirairikl 2011b, 2011c). Journalistic attention has been given to the Guam Contactor Association's Trades Academy and the Center for Micronesian Empowerment, who created a model for employment training and life skills (e.g. Pacific Daily News 2011).

The University of Guam faculty in the Women and Gender Studies Program, funded by a grant from the American Association of University Women and the Island Girl Power organisation, provided a summer program for Micronesian teens (Thompson 2009; Thurber 2009). The girls met at the university, were mentored and encouraged to attend college and were given computer journal writing projects. They converted these journals into dramatic monologues and performed them for an audience. Some of the mentoring relationships continued for several years after the summer program.

For Guam's *Pacific Daily News,* journalist Ngirairikl (2011d) reported a project that the Guam Humanities Council conducted with teenage Micronesian migrants: *The Micronesian Question—Issues of Migration, Identity and Belonging on Guam.* The 57 participating Micronesian teens carried out a youth-centred photography and creative writing project using community conversations and civic reflections. After learning photographic techniques, they created large storyboards that they displayed and explained in settings such as high schools and shopping centres. Project Director Monaeka Flores described the major themes of their productions as reflections on their education, culture and identity, faith and community. One participant, Richy Santipas, was quoted as saying that the activity allowed him to find his voice: 'I'm not scared anymore to stand up and tell people they're wrong when they talk about stereotypes like it's the truth'. When someone in his class said that it was a Chuukese tradition for men to drink alcohol, get drunk and fight, Richy told them it was ridiculous and untrue.

Personal and Interpersonal Development

The pre-migration personal and interpersonal development of Micronesian migrant children influences the meaning, trajectory and effect of their experiences in all the settings of their everyday post-migration lives. A research thread has emerged that illuminates the importance of indigenous and migrant children's protective factors and risk management. The personal and interpersonal wellbeing of adolescent Micronesian children, regardless of home location, must be taken as a bright-line priority due to the exceedingly high suicide rates among this demographic category (Rubinstein 1992; Twaddle et al. 2011).

Noting the high rates of problematic social and behavioural outcomes for the youth of many Pacific Island societies, Okamoto et al. (2008) examined the risk and protective factors that Micronesian migrant adolescents in Honolulu experienced. On the basis of interviews with nine different focus groups consisting of 41 Chuukese, Pohnpeian and Marshallese middle and high school students, Okamoto et al. reported that the youths had experienced stress that was associated with their migration to Hawai'i. This included poor housing conditions; racism, especially in school; dirty neighbourhoods; interethnic gang fighting in school and the community; and pervasive substance abuse in their communities. On the reverse side of this deficit portrait, the students described traditional cultural practices (e.g. celebrating Micronesian holidays and election results from the home island; preparing for and attending traditional funerals; attending church and singing religious songs) and culturally specific prevention programs (e.g. drug and violence prevention involving mentoring and networking in the context of familiar language and customs) that they believed buffered the adverse effects. Ratliffe (2010) concluded that when Micronesian migrant children perform traditional obligations, they are developing and maintaining their Micronesian ethnic identities.

These results are interesting when compared to the findings of a recent, rigorous three-year longitudinal study of the effectiveness of certain *protective factors* with indigenous Māori adolescents in New Zealand (Stuart & Jose 2014). Stuart and Jose's study may have heuristic value for future research with Micronesian migrant children because of the mutual Pacific Island origins of the Māori and Micronesians. The three-year longitudinal study with Māori youth (aged 9–15 years old) found that culturally specific protective factors were associated with the levels of adjustment that are typical for the adolescent years. Further, the degree of both family connectedness and ethnic identity predicted initial levels of positive wellbeing. The state of wellbeing over time was significantly predicted by family connectedness, and it was marginally predicted by ethnic identity. Stuart and Jose concluded that while normative developmental processes tend to result in decreases in adjustment with their Māori sample during middle adolescence, appropriate supports can significantly buffer these reductions in wellbeing. They reported that the results are similar to studies showing a normative decline in the wellbeing of children of other ethnic/racial origins in middle adolescence, and that the results of the study are consistent with the health and wellbeing framework postulated by practitioners working with the Māori population (Durie 1997). Important to this framework is the quality of *whānau* (extended family) relationships that are the foundation for healthy intergenerational cultural transmission. The finding that ethnic identity positively predicted wellbeing for Māori youth was congruent with international research (e.g. higher self-esteem, fewer behavioural problems and higher academic achievement: Umana-Taylor et al. 2002) and with research focused on marginalised groups (e.g. Phinney 1990). Stuart and Jose noted that ethnic engagement by itself was not enough. Development of healthy adjustment also required that the feelings that an individual held toward his or her ethnic group needed to be positive and potent—that is, engagement coupled with pride and identification with the ethnic group. For Micronesian migrant adolescents, we might hypothesise that engaging in traditional cultural practices (e.g. cultural dance and forms of work), family obligations (e.g. preparing for and participating in funerals) and exciting and fulfilling community activities (e.g. community sports) constitute protective factors.

Summary and Conclusions

The research reviewed in this chapter sheds light on the contours of Micronesian children's lives in their family homes, neighbourhoods, schools, churches and communities—on the home islands, as well as post-migration. Empirical research is meagre in both contexts. There are few studies directly documenting the post-migration lives of Micronesian children in their family homes. However, research in these and other settings is increasing in frequency, depth, breadth and quality. There are some disturbing outcomes regarding the treatment of Micronesian migrant children, particularly in public schools and community experiences.

There are also a growing number of reports of promising practices and opportunities for Micronesian migrant children and instances of positive diaspora community organisation and socioeconomic progress. Research on risk management and protective factors suggests that cultural dimensions that are shared by multiple Pacific Island populations may provide protection against post-migration difficulties if applied in the new environment.

Children occupy multiple contexts within their home islands and each context may have different and important developmental consequences that transfer with the children to their respective migration sites. Direct observations were reported on the lives of a sample of children in their family homes and school on their home island in Chuuk State—a district that contributes the highest level of migration from Micronesia to the US. The industry and labour contributions of the children, beginning early and increasing with age, were remarkable. The role of play and cultural expectations regarding children's exhibition of speech were reported. Outer island Yap teachers outlined key dimensions of family teaching–learning practices. Features of home island lives in all of these locations will matter later in post-migration contexts, as children strive to adapt to the expectations and routines of the people and institutions there.

Contrasts were found between the home island–learning patterns of children in homes when compared to schools. Home island schools structured instruction much like US post-migration schools. However, large numbers of Micronesian migrant children have never attended school or have only attended intermittently before moving to US destinations. The school attendance profiles of individual children will probably not be known to receiving educators. Second, most Micronesian migrant children will not be proficient in English when they arrive. Judging from earlier research, US schools may not always provide effective ESL or bilingual instruction for them. The home learning patterns documented for Romonum children could be interpreted as flexibility across contexts featuring didactic instruction, teaching and learning that is grounded in repetition and recitation, as well as collaborative apprentice-like development. Such flexibility could be important to success in school and other settings following relocation—but only if those in the receiving locations provide linguistic access and take responsibility to learn how the funds of knowledge that the children have brought with them can be applied.

New Directions

In reviewing the emerging research and journalistic reporting on phenomena surrounding the migration of Micronesian children to US destinations, it has been encouraging to see the expanding voices of indigenous researchers and authors.[10] Their involvement in research with Micronesian children and communities holds promise for increasing depth, relevance and validity of results. In a 2014 interview with Palauan researcher David Rehuher, co-author of the Okamoto et al. (2008) article on family obligations of Micronesian migrant children in Honolulu, he discussed practical research implementation problems that arise when indigenous researchers are absent from the enterprise. For example, tasks such as preparing and sending letters, or making personal approaches to families to secure informed consent for the participation of minor children in research require indigenous language and culture support. Also, unrealistic expectations may arise in assuming that indigenous culture or language associates can communicate with Micronesian migrants from multiple different Micronesian cultures besides their own. The multiplicity of mutually non-intelligible Micronesian languages and variant cultures is often not fully understood by the non-indigenous research community. These factors threaten the quality of data collection and interpretation if inappropriate language–culture matches are made between data collectors and research participants. If requests for participation, or instructions for providing informed consent, are not made in the families' respective indigenous languages—or if follow-up communication in their indigenous languages is not available—the sample will likely be skewed and minimised. In such cases, the study may become unfeasible.

Rehuher, who works with suicide prevention programs across the University of Hawai'i campuses, shared compelling advice from Micronesian migrant family members as they cooperated with research discussions. They urged him not to focus solely on the problems of their migration. Their message, in effect, was that they know about the bad things, but what can they do to make things good? Their advice reminds researchers of the classic dangers of leaning too heavily on the *deficit* model

10 Works of the following ethnic Micronesian scholars were consulted for this paper: RP: C Filibert, O Ngiraireki, DR Ongalibany; FSM–Chuuk: M Cholymay, N Cholymay, J Peter, A Walter; RMI: H Heine; FSM–National government employees from the Department of Education and the Division of Statistics, Department of Economic Affairs; Guam-Chamorro: M Aguon, M Castro, M Flores, F Cruz Grandjean, CG Meno, EJG Perez, M Perez, MC Salas, PC Sanchez.

of designing research in ways that only document the problematic and the anomalous (e.g. Valencia 1997). Besides the stigmatising effects when that approach is over-used, it leads to the under-identification and under-study of the whole range of positive social and behavioural possibilities. Indigenous researchers, because of their cultural and linguistic capital, may be in the position to perceive options for *promising, positive* or *best practice* research models. For example, Chuukese researcher Novia Cholymay was part of a research team that interviewed Chuukese students and parents in Honolulu and reported their recommendations for *building bridges, not barriers* by inviting Chuukese family involvement in Hawai'i schools (Iding et al. 2007). In another example, Micronesian migrant adolescents in the Guam Humanities Council project authored their own stories and created photo-documentation of their migration experiences. Incorporating their oral traditions, they presented these personal histories in multiple public forums on Guam (Ngirairikl 2011d).

One clear conclusion that emerges from my close-up examinations of Chuukese children's home and school lives on their home island (Spencer 2015) is that the activities and patterns of learning in the two contexts were in contrast. Had only one of these settings been observed, one would greatly misjudge the diversity of experience that the children actually enjoy. The paucity of empirical documentation of the home lives of Micronesian children leads to an underestimation of the richness and the extent of experience, depth of skill building and the resulting intellectual capital that Micronesian children bring to both their home island and their post-migration contexts. Classroom observations such as those reported in Hawai'i by Paul (2003) and Talmy (2006, 2009), or on Guam by Spencer (2012), caution that many educators in the migration destination schools lack knowledge of the richness of the Micronesian migrant learners' backgrounds. Enriching the appreciation of receiving adults and institutions for the cultural funds of knowledge that migrating Micronesian families bring with them could represent a new and positive research and application direction.

References

Aguon, M 2011, 'Several witnesses presented at Cha trial', *KUAM News*, 10 February, viewed 11 February 2011, www.kuam.com/story/14003118/2011/02/10/prosecution-presents-several-witnesses-at-cha-trial?clienttype-printable

Allen, LA 1997, 'Enid "Atoll": A Marshallese migrant community in the midwestern United States', PhD thesis, University of Iowa, Iowa.

Ault, P 2013, 'Distribution and academic achievement of students from the Freely Associated States (FAS) to Hawai'i', paper presented at the Fish out of water: The educational experiences of migrant students from Micronesia in Guam and Hawai'i symposium, American Educational Research Association, McRel Pacific Center for Changing the Odds, San Francisco, 27 April – 1 May.

Barnett, HG 1960, *Being a Palauan*, Holt, Rinehart & Winston, New York.

Carucci, LM 1985, 'Conceptions of maturing and dying in the "middle of heaven"', in DA Counts & D Lanham (eds), *Aging and its transformations: Moving toward death in Pacific societies*, University Press of America, Maryland, pp. 107–129, 275–313.

Douglass, A 1999, 'Childrearing and adoption on Woleai Atoll: Attachment and young children's responses to separation', PhD thesis, Harvard University, Massachusetts.

Durie, M 1997, 'Whānau, whānaungatanga, and healthy Māori development', in P Te Whaiti, P McCarthy & A Durie (eds), *Mai I Rangiatea: Māori wellbeing and development*, Auckland University Press, Auckland, pp. 16–19.

Echevarria, J, Vogt, ME & Short, DJ 2013, *Making content comprehensible for English learners: The Sheltered Instruction Observation Protocol (SIOP) model*, 4th edn, Pearson Education Inc., New Jersey, pp. 288–293.

Farrell, DA 1991, *History of the Northern Mariana Islands*, Public School System, Commonwealth of the Northern Mariana Islands, Saipan, CNMI.

Fischer, A 1950, *The role of the Trukese mother and its effect on child training: A report to the Pacific Science Board of the National Research Council on research done under the program entitled scientific investigation of Micronesia, Contract N7–onr–291, Task Order IV*, The Office of Naval Research & The National Academy of Sciences, Washington, DC.

Fischer, A 1956, 'The role of the Trukese mother and its effect on child training', PhD thesis, Radcliff College, Massachusetts.

Flinn, JB 1982, 'Migration and inter-island ties: A case study of Pulap, Caroline Islands', PhD thesis, Stanford University, Stanford.

Flinn, JB 1992a, *Diplomas and thatch houses: Asserting tradition in a changing Micronesia*, University of Michigan Press, Ann Arbor, doi.org/10.3998/mpub.12389

Flinn, JB 1992b, 'Transmitting traditional values in new schools: Elementary education of Pulap atoll', in S Falgout & P Levin (eds), 'Theme issue, transforming knowledge: Western schooling in the Pacific', *Anthropology & Education Quarterly*, vol. 23, no. 1, pp. 44–58.

Flinn, JB 2010, *Mary, the devil, and taro,* University of Hawai'i Press, Honolulu, doi.org/10.21313/hawaii/9780824833749.001.0001

Gladwin, T & Sarason, SB 1953, *Truk: Man in paradise. Viking fund publications in anthropology, no. 20,* Wenner-Gren Foundation for Anthropological Research, Inc., New York.

Gonzalez, NE, Moll, LC & Amanti, C 2005, *Funds of knowledge: Theorizing practices in households and classrooms,* Lawrence Erlbaum Associates Inc., Mahwah.

Grandjean, FC & Spencer, M 2013, 'Academic characteristics of Guam's Micronesian migrant learners: An information platform leading to successful solutions', paper presented at the Fish out of water: The educational experiences of migrant students from Micronesia in Guam and Hawai'i symposium, American Educational Research Association, McRel Pacific Center for Changing the Odds, San Francisco, 27 April – 1 May.

Heine, H 2002, *Culturally responsive schools for Micronesian immigrant students,* Pacific Resources for Education and Learning, Honolulu.

Hess, J, Nero, KL & Burton, ML 2001, 'Creating options: Forming a Marshallese community in Orange County, California', *The Contemporary Pacific,* vol. 13, no. 1, pp. 89–121.

Hezel, FX 2013, 'Micronesians on the move: Eastward and upward bound', in RC Kiste & GA Finin (eds), *Pacific Island Policy,* vol. 9, East-West Center, Honolulu.

Iding, M, Cholymay, N & Kaneshiro, S 2007, 'Building bridges, not barriers: Inviting Chuukese family involvement in Hawai'i schools', *Journal of Pacific Rim Psychology,* vol. 1, pp. 10–13, doi.org/10.1375/prp.1.1.10

Kandell, A & Foley, R 2012, 'A league of their own: What do you do when you're trying to fit in in a new country? Play ball', *Hana Hou! The Magazine of Hawaiian Airlines,* vol. 15, no. 5, pp. 111–115.

Kaneshiro, SM & Black, RS 2012, 'Strengths and resources of Micronesian students in a Hawai'i middle school', *Pacific Educational Research Journal,* vol. 14, no. 1, pp. 43–66.

Kupferman, DW 2009, '*Lutlut* in a strange land: Kosraean immigrant perceptions of schooling in Hawai'i', *Micronesian Educator*, vol. 13, pp. 19–34.

Matthews, L 2011, 'Violence alleged in trafficking case trial', *Pacific Daily News,* 12 February 2011, p. 5, viewed 12 February 2011 (story removed), www.guampdn.com/article/20110212/NEWS01/102120311/Violence-alleged-in-trafficking-case-trial

Ngirairikl, O 2011a, 'Mother who walked kids to school honored', *Pacific Daily News*, 25 May 2011.

Ngirairikl, O 2011b, 'FAS migrants focus of Calvo, Mori meeting', *Pacific Daily News,* 1 February 2011.

Ngirairikl, O 2011c, 'Feds to study compact-impact aid', *Pacific Daily News,* 8 February 2011.

Ngirairikl, O 2011d, 'Youth exhibit aims to educate', *Pacific Daily News,* vol. 5, no. 22, 1 June 2011.

Okamoto, S, Mayeda, D, Ushiroda, M, Rehuher, D, Lauilefue, T & Ongalibang, O 2008, 'Risk and protective factors of Micronesian youth in Hawai'i: An exploratory study', *Journal of Sociology & Social Welfare*, vol. 35, no. 2, pp. 127–147.

Pacific Daily News, 2011, 'GCA Trades Academy', 17 February, p. 3.

Paul, KA 2003, 'Is there a problem here? The history of Micronesian immigration and its affect on the experience of Micronesian children in Hawai'i's schools', Master's thesis, University of Hawai'i, Honolulu.

Perez, M 2004, 'Insiders without, outsiders within: Chamorro ambiguity and diasporic identities on the US mainland', in LHN Chiang, J Lidstone & RA Stephenson (eds), *The challenges of globalization: Cultures in transition in the Pacific-Asia region,* University Press of America, Maryland, pp. 47–72.

Philips, SU, 1972, 'Participant structure and communicative competence: Warm Springs children in community and classroom', in CB Cazden, VP John & D Hymes (eds), *Functions of language in the classroom,* Teachers College Press, New York, pp. 370–394.

Phinney, J 1990, 'Ethnic identity in adolescents and adults: Review of research', *Psychological Bulletin*, vol. 108, pp. 499–514, doi.org/10.1037/0033-2909.108.3.499

Ratliffe, KT 2010, 'Family obligations in Micronesian cultures: Implications for educators', *International Journal of Qualitative Studies in Education*, vol. 23, no. 6, pp. 671–690, doi.org/10.1080/09518390903468339

Rauchholz, M 2008, 'Demythologizing adoption: From the practice to the effects of adoption in Chuuk, Micronesia', *Pacific Studies,* vol. 31, nos 3–4, pp. 156–181.

Rauchholz, M 2012, 'Discourses on Chuukese customary adoption, migration, and the laws of state(s)', *Pacific Studies,* vol. 35, no. 112, pp. 119–143.

Rogoff, B, Moore, L, Najafi, B, Dexter, A, Correa-Chávez, M & Solis, J 2007, 'Children's development of cultural repertoires through participation in everyday routines and practices', in JE Grusec & PD Hastings (eds), *Handbook of socialization, theory, and research*, Guilford Press, New York, pp. 490–515.

Rubinstein, D 1979, 'An ethnography of Micronesian childhood: Contexts of socialization of Fais Island', PhD thesis, Stanford University, Stanford.

Rubinstein, DH 1992, 'Suicidal behaviour in Micronesia', in KL Peng & WS Tseng (eds), *Suicidal behaviour in the Asia-Pacific region* Keng Ridge, Singapore University Press, Singapore, pp. 199–230.

Sanchez, PC 1987, *Guahan, Guam: The history of our island*, Sanchez Publishing House, Hagatña.

Smith, KD, Smith, ST, Aguilar, V, Coulter, PM, Woo, G & Spencer, M 1997, 'Contemporary Micronesian communities on Guam: Acculturation, conflict and economic prospects', in K Sudo & S Yoshida (eds), *Contemporary migration in Oceania: Diaspora and network,* The Japan Center for Area Studies, National Museum of Ethnology, Osaka, pp. 45–64.

Spencer, ML 1992, 'Literacy in Micronesia', *ISLA Journal of Micronesian Studies*, vol. 1, no. 2, pp. 289–328 (page discontinued), www.uog.edu/dynamicdata/CLASSIslaJournalMicroStudies.aspx?siteid=4&p=44

Spencer, ML 2012, 'Paths of Central Caroline Island children during migration and times of rapid change', *Pacific Asia Inquiry: Multidisciplinary Perspectives*, vol. 3, pp. 7–29.

Spencer, ML 2015, *Children of Chuuk Lagoon: A 21st century analysis of life and learning on Romonum Island,* Micronesian Area Research Center, Mangilao.

Spencer, ML 2018, 'Glimpses of Ulithian and other Yap Outer Island learning traditions for children', in RA Stephenson & ML Spencer (eds), *Ulithi Atoll, Micronesia: Recalling the past, reaffirming the future,* University of Guam Press, Mangilao, Guam, pp. 184–214.

Stuart, J & Jose, PE 2014, 'The protective influence of family connectedness, ethnic identity, and ethnic engagement for New Zealand Māori adolescents', *Developmental Psychology*, vol. 50, no. 6, pp. 1817–1826.

Talmy, S 2006, 'The other other: Micronesians in a Hawai'i high school', in CC Park, R Endo & AL Goodwin (eds), *Asian and Pacific American education: Learning, socialization, and identity*, Information Age Publishing, Greenwich, pp. 19–49.

Talmy, S 2009, 'A very important lesson: Respect and the socialization of order(s) in high school ESL', *Linguistics and Education*, vol. 20, pp. 235–253.

Thomas, MD 1978, 'Transmitting culture to children on Namonuito Atoll, Caroline Islands', PhD thesis, University of Hawai'i, Hawai'i.

Thompson, E 2011, 'Cha wants new trial or appeal, Trap says', *Guam Pacific Daily News*, 21 February 2011, pp. 1, 4, viewed 21 February 2011 (story removed), www.guampdn.com/article/2011022/NEWS01/102210303/Cha-wants-new-trial-or-appeal-Trappsays

Thompson, H 2009, 'Voicing our pathways to education', *AAUW Final Grant Report*, American Association of University Women, Guam Branch, Mangilao.

Thurber, D 2009, 'Noh way: A modern interpretation of an ancient form', Master's thesis, College of Liberal Arts & Social Sciences, University of Guam, Mangilao.

Tudge, J 2008, *The everyday lives of young children*, Cambridge University Press, New York, doi.org/10.1017/CBO9780511499890

Twaddle, IKB, Spencer, ML, Perez, EJG, Meno, CG & Castro, M Jr 2011, 'Building capacity for suicide prevention in Guam: Culturally responsive practices for Pacific Islanders and Asian Americans', *Pacific-Asia Inquiry, Multidisciplinary Perspectives*, vol. 2, pp. 121–134.

Umana-Taylor, AJ, Diversi, M & Fine, MA 2002, 'Ethnic identity and self-esteem among Latino adolescents: Making distinctions among the Latino populations', *Journal of Adolescent Research*, vol. 17, pp. 303–327, doi.org/10.1177/0743558402173005

US Department of Education 2018, *Race and national origin discrimination: Overview of the law*, US Department of Education, viewed 20 November 2018, www2.ed.gov/policy/rights/guid/ocr/raceoverview.html

Valencia, RR (ed.) 1997, *The evolution of deficit thinking: Educational thought and practice*, Falmer Press, Washington, DC.

Walter, A, Salas, MC & Li, N 2011, 'Survival in a new home: Chuukese migration to Guam—toward educational and organizational change', *Micronesian Educator*, vol. 15, pp. 17–30.

11

Young Pacific Male Athletes' Experiences of Mental Wellbeing in Elite Rugby Union and Rugby League

Caleb Marsters and Jemaima Tiatia-Seath

Introduction

Young Pacific athletes in New Zealand and Australia have been increasingly linked to depression, suicide and other such adverse events, as demonstrated in Australasian media, social networking sites and recent academic studies (Horton 2014; Lakisa et al. 2014; Napier 2015; Panapa & Phillips 2014; Rodriguez & McDonald 2013; Tiatia-Seath 2015). While these events and the prominence of Pacific athletes in elite rugby union and rugby league suggest that mental health support should be a priority for this group, gaps remain in the literature relating to the mental wellbeing of young Pacific male athletes, particularly in New Zealand.

Pacific peoples constitute 7.4 per cent of New Zealand's population (Statistics New Zealand 2013), yet Pacific males account for just under 50 per cent of all provincial rugby union players in New Zealand (Field 2013) and 42 per cent of all rugby league players in the National Rugby League (NRL), an elite professional rugby league competition based in Australia and New Zealand (National Rugby League 2016). These percentages are greater in areas with higher Pacific population density, such as Auckland, where Pacific peoples constitute 14 per cent of the population but comprise 55 per cent of club rugby players and 67 per cent of the New Zealand Warriors, an Auckland-based professional rugby league team in the NRL (Craig 2018). These figures are expected to rise, as a large proportion of junior representative rugby union and rugby league players have Pacific heritage (Craig 2018; Field 2013).

While this success is an achievement to be cherished and celebrated, there are many transitions and challenges that are associated with participating in elite youth sports and in finding a career in professional sports. Young Pacific athletes are often living away from home for the first time, learning how to deal with freedom and independence, forming new social and professional relationships and are making financial decisions and contractual commitments alongside their familial obligations and on-field pressures to train and perform well (Lakisa et al. 2014; Marsters 2017; Panapa & Phillips 2014; Zakus & Horton 2009). These factors can influence the mental health of some young athletes.

Several studies identified that elite athletes may be at an increased risk of experiencing certain mental disorders, such as depression (Doherty et al. 2016; Hughes & Leavey 2012), anxiety, distress and substance abuse (Gouttebarge et al. 2015a, 2015b; Roberts et al. 2016). Other studies, however, have found that the prevalence of mental illness among elite athletes is comparable to the general population (Gulliver et al. 2015; Markser 2011; Rice et al. 2016; Schaal et al. 2011). Nevertheless, the true rate of mental illness among elite athletes remains unclear, given the paucity of quality research investigating the mental health status of elite athletes.

Setting the Scene

What Is Mental Wellbeing?

The World Health Organization (2014) defined mental wellbeing as a state in which an individual can realise their own potential, engage in positive relationships, be resilient in the light of typical life stresses, earn a living and contribute to their community. It is important to note that mental wellbeing is distinct from positive affect, which can come and go, as wellbeing is a stable state of wellness, satisfaction and contentment (Galderisi et al. 2015). Mental wellbeing is often referred to as the foundation of health, but it can also be a goal in itself, with the restoration of mental health a key aspect of mental wellbeing (Keyes 2013).

Pacific Peoples in New Zealand

'Pacific peoples' is an umbrella term used to group different ethnic affiliations and peoples that identify as belonging to one or more of the Pacific subregions of Polynesia, Melanesia or Micronesia (Dunsford et al. 2011). In New Zealand, Pacific peoples account for 7.4 per cent of the total population and are expected to comprise 10 per cent of New Zealand's total population by 2026 (Statistics New Zealand 2013). Over half of Pacific peoples, 54.9 per cent, are younger than 25 years old and are mostly New Zealand–born (62.3 per cent), and they are increasingly diverse—with a large number of Pacific young people identifying with multiple ethnic groups (Craig et al. 2008; Statistics New Zealand 2013). People with mixed Pacific and non-Pacific heritage do come under the Pacific peoples umbrella (Tukuitonga 2013). While Pacific peoples are commonly regarded as a homogenous group that is based on its members' similarities, shared experiences, cultural attributes and belief systems, each Pacific ethnic group has their own separate and unique cultural identities, languages, customs, social structures, belief systems, ideologies, histories and worldviews (Finau & Tukuitonga 2000; Ministry of Health 2008). In this discussion, 'Pacific peoples' refers to people who self-identify as belonging to one or more of the seven largest Pacific population groups in New Zealand: Cook Islands, Fiji, Niue, Samoa, Tokelau, Tonga and Tuvalu (Tukuitonga 2013).

Pacific Male Athletes' Participation in Elite Rugby Union and Rugby League

Pacific athletes remain central to the cultural and economic growth of both professional rugby codes in New Zealand and Australia, and increasingly in Europe (Zakus & Horton 2009). Pacific athletes have become key 'commodities' in the global rugby union and rugby league labour markets, and the number of Pacific males playing professionally is expected to increase exponentially worldwide (Zakus & Horton 2009). The NRL illustrates the growing prominence of Pacific athletes in professional rugby league. In 1996, Pacific athletes comprised only 12 per cent of the NRL's playing rosters, but Pacific athletes today comprise 42 per cent of the players in the NRL and over 50 per cent of players in the NRL's under-20 league—a gross over-representation compared to the relatively small Pacific populations in New Zealand and Australia

(Field 2013; Ng Shiu & Vagana 2016; Panapa & Phillips 2014). Similar trends are prevalent in rugby union (Besnier 2014; Grainger 2008; Zakus & Horton 2009).

Pacific athletes have become well known for their natural athletic ability, unwavering determination and robust physical traits, which contributes to why Pacific males are highly sought after in both codes of elite rugby—an argument that warrants justified critique, as it fuels the racist stereotype that Pacific athletes are 'all brawn and no brain' (Besnier 2014; Chen 2014; Grainger 2008). The growing visibility of Pacific rugby players in both codes has made a career in professional rugby an attractive prospect for young Pacific males, both financially and as a means to validate their 'masculinity' and attain treasured social and cultural capital for both individual and family alike (Besnier 2014; Horton 2014).

Rugby is deeply entrenched in most Pacific communities, which furthers the tendency for young Pacific males to pursue a career in professional sports (Crocombe 1976; Horton 2014). However, for every Pacific athlete that enjoys a long and prosperous career in professional rugby, there are scores of young Pacific males who do not make it professionally and who, in some instances, experience significant challenges when transitioning away from sports (Besnier 2014; Schofield 2015). Many stressors remain for athletes who can secure professional playing contracts, on top of the fact that a career in both codes of professional rugby is often short, averaging three to four years per player (Price 2007). Alongside greatly publicised expectations and familial responsibilities, this uncertain and high-pressure environment can hamper the mental wellbeing of some athletes (Horton 2014; Teaiwa 2016).

Pacific Mental Wellbeing in New Zealand

Pacific Perceptions of Mental Wellbeing

Pacific perceptions of mental health, both traditional and contemporary, differ to those found in mainstream literature. Without making any conclusive generalisations, Western views of mental health are often based on clinical and biomedical paradigms and tend to take an individualised stance (Alefaio 2009; Bush et al. 2009; Pulotu-Endemann et al. 2004; Tiatia 2012; Tukuitonga 2013). Fuimaono Pulotu-Endemann et al. (2004) argued that this is the case because Western perceptions of mental health tend to be derived from clinical perspectives that must be objective in their explanations of mental health so that medical diagnoses can be standardised. In most instances, this undermines the subjective nature of mental wellbeing (Pulotu-Endemann et al. 2004). In contrast, Pacific perceptions of mental health are more holistic and are based on collectivism, in which the family forms the foundation for individual and community wellbeing (Pulotu-Endemann et al. 2004).

As most Pacific peoples hold fast to collectivism, it is important to acknowledge the effect of the 'relational self' on Pacific perceptions of mental health (Alefaio 2009; Samu & Suaalii-Sauni 2009; Tamasese et al. 2005). Bush et al. (2009, p. 142) provided an apt description of the concept of the relational self:

> It is a total being comprising spiritual, physical and mental elements which cannot be separated. It derives its sense of wholeness, sacredness and uniqueness, from its place of belonging in family and village, genealogy, language, land environment and culture.

Pacific perceptions of mental wellbeing can be organised into three categories: traditional perceptions, contemporary perceptions and a blend of both (Vaka 2014). Each perspective provides insight into the way that mental health is understood by Pacific peoples and their differing worldviews that are prevalent in Pacific communities (Mila-Schaaf & Hudson 2009). Factors related to cultural efficacy, religious centrality, mixed ethnicities and Pacific connectedness can lead to differing worldviews, which contributes to this wide spectrum of views of mental wellbeing (Le Va & Te Pou O Te Whakaaro Nui 2009). While most young Pacific peoples in New Zealand may lean towards contemporary perceptions of mental wellbeing, the holistic and collectivist concept of wellbeing remains for Pacific youth (Bathgate & Pulotu-Endemann 1997; Puna 2013; Puna & Tiatia-Seath 2017).

The Mental Wellbeing of Young Pacific Male Athletes in New Zealand

There is currently a paucity of literature that examines the mental wellbeing of young Pacific male athletes in New Zealand, despite a growing evidence base on the mental wellbeing of Pacific peoples in New Zealand and on Pacific participation in the New Zealand rugby union (Grainger 2008; Schaaf 2006; Te'evale 2001). There is, however, an emergent field of research that explores the lived experiences of Pacific male rugby league players in Australia (Horton 2014; Lakisa et al. 2014; Panapa & Phillips 2014; Rodriguez & McDonald 2013). While this research provides invaluable insight into the lived experiences of Pacific athletes, there remains a gap in the literature that focuses specifically on the mental wellbeing of young Pacific male athletes. Due to the limitations in the literature regarding this group of athletes, relevant evidence from non–athlete specific Pacific research is used to discuss the mental health context that is related to this group.

Without generalising, the young Pacific male athlete population fall into multiple demographic groups that experience unique disparities in mental health outcomes: Pacific males, Pacific youth and Pacific male youth. Each of these demographic groups experiences higher rates of mental illness and are less likely to access mental health services or to engage in help-seeking behaviours when compared with other New Zealanders (Foliaki et al. 2006; Gulliver et al. 2012; Kessler et al. 2007; Rickwood et al. 2007; Teevale et al. 2016; Vaswani 2011). For example, the onset for more than half of all diagnosed mental illnesses in New Zealand occurs at 18 years or younger, 16–34-year-olds experience the highest rates of mental illness in comparison to other age groups and Pacific males experience the highest rates of admission to acute mental health services in New Zealand—these are all demographics that young Pacific male rugby players fall into (Gulliver et al. 2012; Kessler et al. 2007; Ministry of Health 2008; Oakley Browne et al. 2006; Rickwood et al. 2007).

Pacific youth also face increased challenges to achieving and maintaining mental wellbeing, often exhibiting substantial resilience in the face of adversity (Fa'alili-Fidow et al. 2016; Siataga 2011; Suaalii-Sauni et al. 2009). These disparities are concerning, as 50 per cent of the Pacific population are under the age of 22 and the Pacific youth population in New Zealand is expected to grow exponentially over the next 10 years (Statistics New Zealand 2015). These statistics may or may not be similar for young Pacific male athletes, but they do provide insight into the mental health experiences of young Pacific males in New Zealand.

Suicide and Young Pacific Male Athletes

Although uncommon, suicide is a concern for young Pacific males in New Zealand. Young New Zealanders aged 15–24 years old experienced the highest rates of suicide among OECD countries in 2016, and the attempted suicide rates were three times higher for Pacific youth in comparison to non-Pacific and non-Maori youth in New Zealand (Teevale et al. 2016; Tiatia-Seath et al. 2017). The recent suicide deaths of several young Pacific rugby union and rugby league players in New Zealand, Australia and Europe suggest that these trends may be similar among this group of athletes (Cadzow 2013; Horton 2014; Schofield 2016; Tiatia-Seath 2015).

Summary

In summary, this evidence provides a strong rationale for this research and emphasises the need for further exploration into the mental health of young Pacific male athletes in New Zealand. Reflecting on these concerns, this chapter aims to address two key components of mental health for young Pacific male athletes that seem to have been overlooked in the current literature: how young Pacific male athletes define mental health and what shapes young Pacific male athletes' perceptions of mental health. We will also discuss the implications for researchers, mental health professionals and professionals working with young Pacific male athletes in high-performance environments.

Methodology

This chapter is derived from a Master's of Public Health, which investigated young Pacific male elite athletes' perceptions and experiences of positive mental wellbeing. A qualitative methodology was utilised to explore young Pacific male athletes' perceptions and experiences of positive mental wellbeing at the elite level (Hammersley 2013; Smith 2015).

Researcher's Positionality

The lead researcher (Marsters) brought to this research an 'insider–outsider' perspective (Dwyer & Buckle 2009). He is an insider because he is a young Pacific male undertaking research in his Pacific community, and an 'outsider' because he has never played sports at the elite level. This means that although he may be from the culture under investigation, he did not have complete knowledge of the subcultures and intersectional identities that exist (Asselin 2003; Dwyer & Buckle 2009; Puna & Tiatia-Seath 2017). To address the lead researcher's 'outsider' status, his supervisor, who had previously played both codes of rugby at the elite level, supported the integrity of the research. An advisory group consisting of former Pacific elite athletes, current coaches, managers, psychologists and academics with understandings of the professional sports environment and Pacific cultures were also reference points throughout the research. Their knowledge and understanding increased the feeling of confidence in the credibility and rigour of the methodology that was used in this research.

Development of the Semi-Structured Interview Guide

The interview guide consisted of 11 question zones. The question zones comprised semi-structured, open-ended questions that captured participants' perceptions and experiences of mental wellbeing. The use of a semi-structured interview guide ensured consistency between interviews, without negating the autonomy of participants to openly express their personal thoughts and experiences. Adopting this approach allowed for the collection of rich and in-depth data on participants' views and experiences of mental wellbeing in the context of their own lived experiences. The interview schedule was developed in consultation with experts in the field of Pacific athlete wellbeing and Pacific youth mental wellbeing and from a review of national and international literature.

Recruitment

Purposeful sampling was used during the recruitment stage. Purposeful sampling is often employed in qualitative research to ensure that the recruitment of information-rich participants is relevant to the phenomena of interest (Liamputtong & Ezzy 2005; Palinkas et al. 2015). The inclusion criteria for participation was self-identified Pacific heritage, aged 16–24 years, living in Auckland and engaged in an elite rugby league or rugby union program.

To recruit participants, an advertisement was disseminated among the researcher's personal and professional sporting networks to advertise, promote and recruit potential participants. Personal networks included connections via Facebook. The advertisement was also emailed out to elite rugby union and rugby league organisations that had large numbers of young Pacific athletes. These organisations showed interest in the study and shared the advertisement on their websites, among their networks and via social networking sites such as Facebook. This approach was very effective, as there were many 'shares', which broadened the advertisement's reach among the target population.

Although this approach was effective, purposive snowball sampling was also used to speed up the recruitment process. It was employed by asking recruited participants to share the research advertisement with other Pacific athletes who met the recruitment inclusion criteria. Typically, participants shared the advertisement with their teammates. Purposeful snowball sampling helped the researcher to build trust and rapport with potential participants. For example, potential participants were more likely to respond to the advertisement if they knew someone who had already participated in the interview process. This approach aligns closely with the Health Research Council of New Zealand's (2014) Pacific Health Research Guidelines, which emphasise the importance of establishing trust and positive relationships when undertaking research with Pacific communities.

A 'participant information sheet' outlining the details of the study was sent electronically to those who responded to the study advertisement. Participation was voluntary and each participant was given the opportunity to ask questions before arranging a convenient time and location for the face-to-face interview. At the face-to-face interviews, the study details were clarified again before the interview was commenced.

Participants

Twenty young Pacific males participated in this study. The average age of the participants was 19.5 years. The ethnic make-up of participants included those who identified as Tongan (n = 9), Samoan (n = 6), Samoan/European (n = 1), Samoan/Niuean (n = 1), Cook Islands Māori (n = 2) and Fijian (n = 1). Regarding the sports played, seven participants played rugby league and 13 played rugby union. Four participants were not contracted to any sports club, three were on age-group development contracts, seven were on semi-professional contracts and six were on full, professional contracts. The youngest participant was aged 16 and the oldest was aged 24. A summary of participant demographic information is provided in Table 1.

Table 1. Demographic summary of participants

	Age	Ethnicity	Area of residence	Code	Contract
1	22	Tongan	Central Auckland	Union	None
2	22	Samoan	South Auckland	League	Semi-professional
3	18	Samoan	South Auckland	Union	Semi-professional
4	19	Tongan	Central Auckland	Union	Professional
5	19	Tongan	Central Auckland	Union	Professional
6	23	Tongan	West Auckland	League	None
7	23	Fijian	West Auckland	League	None
8	19	Samoan/ NZ European	West Auckland	Union	Professional
9	19	Tongan	Central Auckland	Union	Professional
10	16	Cook Islands	South Auckland	Union	None
11	21	Samoan/Niuean	Central Auckland	League	Professional
12	16	Tongan	South Auckland	League	Development
13	17	Samoan	East Auckland	Union	Development
14	18	Tongan	South Auckland	Union	Development
15	19	Samoan	West Auckland	Union	Semi-professional
16	18	Samoan	West Auckland	Union	Semi-professional
17	19	Tongan	South Auckland	Union	Professional
18	19	Tongan	South Auckland	Union	Semi-professional
19	24	Samoan	West Auckland	League	Semi-professional
20	19	Cook Islands	South Auckland	League	Semi-professional

Data Collection and Analysis

The one-on-one, face-to-face interviews were conducted in July 2016. Participants selected the time and location for their interview. Locations included local rugby clubrooms, local fast-food establishments, libraries and participants' homes. Interviews lasted between 45 and 90 minutes and were audio recorded, with the participant's permission. All interviews were conducted in English. Interviews were reflective of the Pacific research methodological approach known as *talanoa*, which provides a safe and culturally appropriate environment for Pacific research participants by using Pacific traditions and protocols during interviews (Vaioleti 2006).

A grounded theory approach was used to analyse the data collected from interviews. Grounded theory is an inductive method involving the use of constant comparative analysis to analyse data (Glaser 2017; Glaser & Strauss 1967). Constant comparative analysis utilises three stages of analysis to create emergent categories and to develop theoretical models to explain the data collected and phenomena studied (Corbin & Strauss 1990). A key function of constant comparative analysis is that data analysis and data collection occur simultaneously, which allows for the two processes to influence one another so that the researcher can focus on, and gain a deeper understanding of, the developing concepts (Glaser & Strauss 1967). Data analysis was repeated until saturation was reached and no new concepts emerged from the data. This allowed for strong theoretical understandings of the phenomenon to emerge (Corbin & Strauss 1990). All interviews were transcribed verbatim by the researcher.

Findings and Discussion

This study entered relatively new ground, with a focus on what mental wellbeing means for young, elite, Pacific male athletes. Participants regarded mental wellbeing holistically, emphasising the importance of family, friends, spirituality, sports and a healthy lifestyle balance. Athletic performance played a central role in participants' definitions of positive mental wellbeing. Last, participants considered personal development, both in and away from sports, important when defining mental wellbeing. Narratives that relate to holistic wellbeing and the balancing of the relational self are presented as findings under five key themes: family support, reciprocating family support, the need for a 'well-balanced' life, athletic performance and personal development.

Family Support

All participants described the love, support and reassurance of family as essential elements when defining mental wellbeing. Participants agreed that having a positive relationship with family was central to living a positive life and to overcoming any challenges along the way. It was acknowledged that family support helped athletes remain grounded, focused and motivated to self-improve. Participants deemed such attributes essential to achieving and maintaining success at the elite level. The following quotes highlight the importance of family support for young Pacific male athletes:

> I feel on top of the world aye, but sometimes I get a bit too overboard. So, I remember how I came from humble beginnings. It's not the amount of stuff I have, but the love I get from family and others that makes me feel complete. It helps me keep a positive attitude and remain humble. It's helped me grow. Everyone supporting you makes you feel good; it makes you hungry for more and makes you want to challenge your weaknesses and improve yourself. (P15)

> The biggest one for me is family support. Getting that external appreciation from your family, that positive vibe coming from them, a reassuring vibe. It just gives you that happiness inside. (P2)

Consistent with the Pacific mental health literature, a loving and supportive family was the central element of mental wellbeing for this group. This finding illustrates the relational nature of mental wellbeing for these athletes. Additionally, family support intensified athletes' determination to succeed and helped participants remain humble—which were traits that participants perceived as beneficial to supporting mental wellbeing at the elite level. Several other studies have also found family to be a powerful motivator for Pacific rugby union and rugby league players (Horton 2014; Lakisa et al. 2014; Panapa & Phillips 2014; Schaaf 2006). In the context of mental wellbeing, this may prompt young Pacific male rugby union and rugby league players to place additional pressure on themselves to succeed professionally, which may in turn increase their risk of high anxiety levels (Rice et al. 2016). Not wanting to 'let the family down', for example, may heighten the fear of failure, which would naturally hinder mental wellbeing during stressful or challenging times, which is a well-known phenomenon in the current scholarship relating to Pacific athletes (Horton 2012, 2014; Lakisa et al. 2014; Panapa & Phillips 2014; Rodriguez & McDonald 2013). It would be beneficial to investigate the effect of this phenomenon on mental wellbeing in future research.

Reciprocating Family Support

Participants noted the importance of reciprocating family support when defining mental wellbeing. Making their families proud and helping their families financially were the two common forms of reciprocity described, as expressed by the following:

> It's just being able to provide [financially] for family, and just keeping the family happy. Making them proud. (P4)

> I would probably say being able to help, to help family and others. But only when you're at the top of your game, because it's hard to help someone when you're struggling yourself. (P3)

Another central aspect of positive mental wellbeing for these athletes was being able to reciprocate family support, generally by making their families proud and by providing financial stability. This profound desire to reciprocate familial support is prevalent in most studies involving Pacific athletes (Horton 2014; Lakisa et al. 2014; Panapa & Phillips 2014; Rodriguez & McDonald 2013). Again, these findings suggest that young Pacific athletes are more likely to internalise pressures to succeed, not just for themselves, but for their families too. Thus, it is vital that family support is visibly exhibited to young athletes when they experience major setbacks in their careers, such as missing out on contracts, not being selected for a representative team, or being unable to provide financial support. However, because young Pacific athletes are more likely to come from lower socioeconomic backgrounds (Statistics New Zealand and Ministry of Pacific Island Affairs 2011), missing out on a lucrative professional sports contract can be a challenging setback for many Pacific athletes and their families.

The Need for A 'Well-Balanced' Life

Participants defined mental wellbeing as having a well-balanced life. A well-balanced life was defined by athletes as having the following factors present in their lives: positive relationships with family, positive relationships with friends, a positive relationship with a girlfriend or partner, performing well on the field, successfully balancing any educational or employment responsibilities and having a strong spiritual connection. In short, these factors are present when everything is going 'pretty well'. The following excerpts describe the notion of a well-balanced life for participants:

> It's when you're happy. Mental, emotional, physical, spiritual, and all that. When you're happy in all those areas you could say you are in a positive mental wellbeing … balanced. An example is when things are good with family, your girlfriend, you're good with God, content, studies are going well, and you're playing well. To me that's positive mental wellbeing. (P11)

> I think a combination of everything. When everything off the field is going pretty well, and you're performing well on the field, and you got a good spiritual connection at the same time. Just having all three in a good balance helps. And if one of them was a bit down it would affect other areas because they're all connected in some sort of way. (P13)

Living a well-balanced life was an important aspect of participants' perceptions of mental wellbeing. The positive correlation between 'balance' and mental wellbeing is relatively well-known within the literature on elite rugby union players (Hodge et al. 2008; Horton 2014; Price 2007). In this case, however, participants defined 'balance' in the context of social activities and hobbies involving family and friends—a stark contrast to the literature, which defines 'balance' for athletes as being able to work towards alternative career options away from sports. Essentially, participants prioritised the maintenance of strong familial and social relationships over their perceived need to work towards alternative career options, despite the fact that many participants were actively working towards an alternative career away from sports. Again, this demonstrates the relational nature of these participants and the centrality of positive social relationships for young Pacific athletes. Of practical significance, there may be a potential to support both mental wellbeing and the development of well-balanced athletic identities by incorporating these social relationships into management approaches. When looking to support the mental wellbeing of a Pacific athlete, management must not only think about what is best for the athlete as an individual, but more importantly about what is best for the athlete in the context of their social relations.

Athletic Performance

Some participants defined mental wellbeing as reaching peak physical fitness and performing well on the field, as illustrated in the following statement:

> [Positive mental wellbeing] is when I'm playing well. And like we have skinfold tests and fitness tests and if my skinfold is going down then I feel real happy and feel like I'm in the best shape to play. (P5)

Participants who prioritised their physical fitness and performance did not entirely neglect other facets of their lives, however:

> [Positive mental wellbeing] is when I'm training well and at my peak and best physical wellbeing. But also maintaining a strong connection with family, having time out with the boys, and spiritually as well, being good with God. Just when everything's going good around you and that all goes on to the field and you perform well. (P16)

Overall, participants noted a positive correlation between mental wellbeing and performance on the field:

> [Positive mental wellbeing] is just feeling relaxed. I can tell when I'm distracted or worked up about something going into a game. So, my best mindset is being relaxed and enjoying myself and the company around me. Remembering we all started rugby to have fun first. So, enjoying yourself and then performance and everything will come after that. (P17)

Performing well in training and on the field was revealed to be a key constituent of positive mental wellbeing for these athletes. While most athletes agreed that performing well was beneficial to their mental wellbeing, a few participants placed significant emphasis on performing well when it came to defining mental wellbeing, which suggests that these players' mental wellbeing and self-esteem may be heavily invested in external performance appraisal. This is a concern, as previous research has linked high degrees of external performance appraisal and performance-based 'perfectionism' to increased mental illness among athletes (Doherty et al. 2016; Lemyre et al. 2007; Rice et al. 2016).

Placing such an emphasis on performance could indicate that some of these athletes are committing, or have committed, to a foreclosed athletic identity without exploring, or having the opportunity to explore, other avenues away from sports (Doherty et al. 2016; Horton 2014; Price 2007). This is not ideal, as identity foreclosure has been found to intensify the negative psychological effect of poor performances, external criticism, injuries and forced retirement (Clews 2015; Harrison et al. 2011; Hughes

& Leavey 2012). There are many studies that explore this phenomenon among non-Pacific athletes, but it would be useful to identify effective strategies to deter the development of foreclosed identities among young Pacific athletes in future research.

Personal Development

Just under half of the participants acknowledged the importance of personal development when defining mental wellbeing. Participants described personal development as the ability to improve themselves and continually achieve new goals. Athletes defined personal development in the context of rugby as well as off-field activities, such as education, spiritual growth and self-confidence. For example:

> I reckon [mental wellbeing] is when you're mentally prepared to do whatever you want … when you're prepared to take risks to better yourself. So, determined and having the freedom to do want you want … like some people have boundaries that surround them and they block themselves from doing what they want and reaching their peaks. So that self-confidence to do what you want is positive mental wellbeing to me. (P14)

It appears evident that participants valued their autonomy and the opportunity to improve themselves on and off the field. Formal education was noted by these athletes as an important aspect of personal development. Participants admitted that their parents and team staff constantly reinforced the need to gain a tertiary degree or apprenticeship, which encouraged them to take their education seriously. These findings imply that current strategies to promote 'back-up' career options, and balanced athletic identities, may be working effectively; and, once again, this reveals the benefits of including Pacific players' parents in player welfare initiatives.

In the context of mental wellbeing, this is an important finding, as personal development has been linked with reduced depressive moods and improved self-esteem and self-confidence for young males and young athletes alike (Goodkind et al. 2012; Rice et al. 2016; Woodruff 2016). These findings highlight the potential to support mental wellbeing through personal development initiatives that build on Pacific athletes' determination to improve themselves. It is crucial to acknowledge that personal development does not inherently occur through participation in sports; however, it is imperative that elite sports have programs in place that facilitate personal development for young athletes (Newhouse-Bailey et al. 2015). Finding effective ways to develop the life skills required to adjust to life at the elite level was also an area requiring further attention.

Sports and Identity: The Athletic Sense of Self

Many of the factors important to mental wellbeing for these athletes appear to be rooted in their intersectional identity as Pacific men, young males and elite athletes. Traditional perceptions of what it means to be a Pacific man, for example, are measured by one's ability to contribute financially, to support others and to make their families proud—attributes that are recurrent in participants' perceptions of mental wellbeing (Macpherson & Macpherson 2009). Other factors contributing to participants' perceptions of mental wellbeing, such as performing well and consistent self-improvement, also align with what it means to be a successful elite athlete. So, there was a strong link between sports and identity for participants in this study.

Strengths, Limitations and Areas for Future Research

This study is the first qualitative investigation in New Zealand examining young Pacific male athletes' definitions and perceptions of mental wellbeing. The findings cannot yet be generalised to all young Pacific male rugby union and rugby league players, given the sample size, and the views expressed by these participants may not be representative of the wider young Pacific male athlete population in New Zealand. Increasing the sample size and extending the recruitment area would address this and could possibly result in different findings. The voluntary nature of this study may also reduce the representativeness of participants, as self-selection bias may be present. Again, further research with a greater sample size would help address this limitation. While the literature and findings from this research confirm that the Pacific identity is prominent among Pacific athletes in New Zealand, ethnic-specific research should be undertaken in the future to improve the rigour and applicability of research findings in this topic area.

Conclusion

Young Pacific male rugby union and rugby league players view positive mental wellbeing as the culmination of several interconnected factors. For these young Pacific male athletes, if one factor suffers then mental wellbeing as a whole suffers, so it is particularly important that athletes are supported during these times and that the 'balance' between these factors is restored. The holistic and relational way that participants viewed mental wellbeing reaffirms the views of Pacific scholarship that states that Pacific peoples view wellbeing in a holistic way, and it highlights the importance of familial servitude and social belonging for these athletes (Alefaio 2009; Bush et al. 2009; Mila-Schaaf & Hudson 2009; Samu & Suaalii-Sauni 2009; Tamasese et al. 2005). While participants prioritised lifestyle balance, their perceptions of positive mental wellbeing, away from family and social relationships, were largely centred on sports. This suggests that some of these athletes may be at increased risk of developing overly salient athletic identities (Doherty et al. 2016; Horton 2014; Price 2007). From the findings of this study and existing literature on the topic, the development of balanced athletic identities that prioritise sports, education, strong cultural ties and positive social relationships appears to be crucial to supporting mental wellbeing and resilience among young Pacific male athletes.

Acknowledgements

Thank you to the Ministry of Health for their financial contribution to this research via the Pacific Health Scholarship. Thank you to the University of Auckland's Faculty of Medical and Health Sciences for their research grant. Ethical approval for this research was granted and obtained from The University of Auckland Human Participants Ethics Committee, Auckland, New Zealand.

References

Alefaio, S 2009, 'Reflections of a practitioner: Purely a journey of the heart', *Pacific Health Dialog*, vol. 15, no. 1, pp. 171–176.

Asselin, ME 2003, 'Insider research: Issues to consider when doing qualitative research in your own setting', *Journal for Nurses in Professional Development*, vol. 19, no. 2, doi.org/10.1097/00124645-200303000-00008

Bathgate, M & Pulotu-Endemann, FK 1997, 'Pacific people in New Zealand', in PM Ellis & SCD Collings (eds), *Mental health from a public health perspective*, Ministry of Health, Wellington, New Zealand.

Besnier, N 2014, 'Pacific island rugby: Histories, mobilities, comparisons', *Asia Pacific Journal of Sport and Social Science*, vol. 3, no. 3, pp. 268–276, doi.org/10.1080/21640599.2014.982894

Bush, A, Chapman, F, Drummond, M & Fagaloa, T 2009, 'Development of a child, adolescent and family mental health service for Pacific young people in Aotearoa/New Zealand', *Pacific Health Dialog*, vol. 15, no. 1, pp. 138–146.

Cadzow, J 2013, 'Tragic story of rising NRL star Mosese Fotuaika', *Sydney Morning Herald*, 26 May, viewed 26 May 2016, www.stuff.co.nz/sport/league/8717606/Tragic-story-of-rising-NRL-star-Mosese-Fotuaika

Chen, CH 2014, 'Prioritizing hyper-masculinity in the Pacific region', *Culture, Society and Masculinities*, vol. 6, no. 1, p. 69.

Clews, G 2015, *Wired to play: The metacognitive athlete*, ZebraMAD, Canberra.

Corbin, J & Strauss, A 1990, 'Grounded theory method: Procedures, canons, and evaluative criteria', *Qualitative Sociology*, vol. 13, no. 3, pp. 3–21, doi.org/10.1007/BF00988593

Craig, E, Taufa, S, Jackson, C & Han, D 2008, *The health of Pacific children and young people in New Zealand*, Ministry of Health, Wellington.

Craig, M 2018, 'White flight: A detailed look at race and Auckland rugby', *New Zealand Herald*, 14 April, viewed 6 September 2018, www.nzherald.co.nz/sport/news/article.cfm?c_id=4&objectid=12029746

Crocombe, RG 1976, *The Pacific way: An emerging identity*, Lotu Pasifika, Suva.

Doherty, S, Hannigan, B & Campbell, M 2016, 'The experience of depression during the careers of elite male athletes', *Frontiers in Psychology*, vol. 7, no. 1069, pp. 1–11, doi.org/10.3389/fpsyg.2016.01069

Dunsford, D, Park, J, Littleton, J, Friesen, W, Herda, P, Neuwelt, P, Hand, J, Blackmore, P, Malua, S, Grant, J, Kearns, R, Bryder, L & Underhill-Sem, Y 2011, *Better lives: The struggle for health of transnational Pacific peoples in New Zealand, 1950–2000*, 9th edn, University of Auckland, Auckland, viewed 7 March 2018, researchspace.auckland.ac.nz/handle/2292/11030

Dwyer, S & Buckle, J 2009, 'The space between: On being an insider-outsider in qualitative research', *International Journal of Qualitative Methods*, vol. 8, no. 1, pp. 54–63.

Fa'alili-Fidow, J, Moselen, E, Denny, S, Dixon, R, Teevale, T, Ikihele, A, Adolescent Health Research Group & Clark, TC 2016, *Youth'12 the health and wellbeing of secondary school students in New Zealand: Results for Pacific young people*, University of Auckland, Auckland.

Field, M 2013, *Polynesian men a global sports commodity*, Fairfax Media, viewed 26 May 2016, www.stuff.co.nz/sport/8718872/Polynesian-men-a-global-sports-commodity

Finau, S & Tukuitonga, C 2000, 'Pacific peoples in New Zealand', in P Davis & K Dew (eds), *Health and society in Aotearoa/New Zealand*, Oxford University Press, Melbourne.

Foliaki, S, Kokaua, J, Schaaf, D & Tukuitonga, C 2006, 'Pacific people', in MAO Browne, JE Wells & KM Scott (eds), *Te rau hinengaro: The New Zealand mental health survey*, Ministry of Health, Wellington, pp. 179–208.

Galderisi, S, Heinz, A, Kastrup, M, Beezhold, J & Sartorius, N 2015, 'Toward a new definition of mental health', *World Psychiatry*, vol. 14, no. 2, pp. 231–233, doi.org/10.1002/wps.20231

Glaser, B 2017, *Discovery of grounded theory: Strategies for qualitative research*, Routledge, New York.

Glaser, B & Strauss, A 1967, *The discovery of grounded theory: Strategies for qualitative research*, Aldine Publishing Co, Chicago.

Goodkind, J, Lanoue, M, Lee, C, Freeland, L & Freund, R 2012, 'Feasibility, acceptability, and initial findings from a community-based cultural mental health intervention for American Indian youth and their families', *Journal of Community Psychology*, vol. 40, no. 4, pp. 381–405, doi.org/10.1002/jcop.20517

Gouttebarge, V, Backx, FJG, Aoki, H & Kerkhoffs, GMMJ 2015a, 'Symptoms of common mental disorders in professional football (soccer) across five European countries', *Journal of Sports Science & Medicine*, vol. 14, no. 4, pp. 811–818.

Gouttebarge, V, Frings-Dresen, MHW & Sluiter, JK 2015b, 'Mental and psychosocial health among current and former professional footballers', *Occupational Medicine*, vol. 65, no. 3, pp. 190–196, doi.org/10.1093/occmed/kqu202

Grainger, AD 2008, 'The browning of the All Blacks: Pacific peoples, rugby, and the cultural politics of identity in New Zealand', PhD thesis, University of Maryland, Maryland, viewed 6 September 2018, drum.lib.umd.edu/handle/1903/8202

Gulliver, A, Griffiths, K & Christensen, H 2012, 'Barriers and facilitators to mental health help-seeking for young elite athletes: A qualitative study', *BioMed Central Psychiatry*, vol. 12, no. 157, pp. 1–14, doi.org/10.1186/1471-244X-12-157

Gulliver, A, Griffiths, KM, Mackinnon, A, Batterham, PJ & Stanimirovic, R 2015, 'The mental health of Australian elite athletes', *Journal of Science and Medicine in Sport*, vol. 18, no. 3, pp. 255–261, doi.org/10.1016/j.jsams.2014.04.006

Hammersley, M 2013, 'Defining qualitative research', in M Hammersley (ed.), *What is qualitative research?*, Bloomsbury Academic, London, pp. 1–20, doi.org/10.5040/9781849666084.ch-001

Harrison, L, Sailes, G, Rotich, WK & Bimper, AY 2011, 'Living the dream or awakening from the nightmare: Race and athletic identity', *Race Ethnicity and Education*, vol. 14, no. 1, pp. 91–103, doi.org/10.1080/13613324.2011.531982

Health Research Council of New Zealand 2014, *Pacific health research guidelines 2014*, Health Research Council of New Zealand, Auckland.

Hodge, K, Lonsdale, C & Ng, J 2008, 'Burnout in elite rugby: Relationships with basic psychological needs fulfilment', *Journal of Sports Sciences*, vol. 26, no. 8, pp. 835–844, doi.org/10.1080/02640410701784525

Horton, P 2012, 'Pacific Islanders in global rugby: The changing currents of sports migration', *The International Journal of the History of Sport*, vol. 29, no. 17, pp. 2388–2404, doi.org/10.1080/09523367.2012.746834

Horton, P 2014, 'Pacific Islanders in professional rugby football: Bodies, minds and cultural continuities', *Asia Pacific Journal of Sport and Social Science*, vol. 3, no. 3, pp. 222–235, doi.org/10.1080/21640599.2014.970428

Hughes, L & Leavey, G 2012, 'Setting the bar: Athletes and vulnerability to mental illness', *The British Journal of Psychiatry*, vol. 200, no. 2, pp. 95–96, doi.org/10.1192/bjp.bp.111.095976

Kessler, RC, Amminger, GP, Aguilar-Gaxiola, S, Alonso, J, Lee, S & Ustun, TB 2007, 'Age of onset of mental disorders: A review of recent literature', *Current Opinion in Psychiatry*, vol. 20, no. 4, pp. 359–364, doi.org/10.1097/YCO.0b013e32816ebc8c

Keyes, CLM 2013, 'Promoting and protecting positive mental health: Early and often throughout the lifespan', in CLM Keyes (ed.), *Mental well-being: International contributions to the study of positive mental health*, Springer Netherlands, Dordrecht, pp. 3–28, doi.org/10.1007/978-94-007-5195-8_1

Lakisa, D, Adair, D & Taylor, T 2014, 'Pasifika diaspora and the changing face of Australian rugby league', *The Contemporary Pacific*, vol. 26, no. 2, pp. 347–367, doi.org/10.1353/cp.2014.0029

Le Va & Te Pou O Te Whakaaro Nui 2009, *Let's Get Real—Real Skills Plus Seitapu—Working with Pacific Peoples*, Le Va, Pasifika within Te Pou, Auckland, New Zealand, viewed 5 September 2017, www.tepou.co.nz/uploads/files/resource-assets/Lets-Get-Real-Real-Skills-Plus-Seitapu-Working-with-Pacific-Peoples.pdf

Lemyre, PN, Roberts, GC & Stray-Gundersen, J 2007, 'Motivation, overtraining, and burnout: Can self-determined motivation predict overtraining and burnout in elite athletes?', *European Journal of Sport Science*, vol. 7, no. 2, pp. 115–126, doi.org/10.1080/17461390701302607

Liamputtong, P & Ezzy, D 2005, *Qualitative research methods*, 2nd edn, Oxford University Press, Melbourne.

Macpherson, C & Macpherson, L 2009, *The warm winds of change: Globalisation and contemporary Samoa*, Auckland University Press, Auckland.

Markser, VZ 2011, 'Sport psychiatry and psychotherapy. Mental strains and disorders in professional sports. Challenge and answer to societal changes', *European Archives of Psychiatry and Clinical Neuroscience*, vol. 261, no. 2, p. 182, doi.org/10.1007/s00406-011-0239-x

Marsters, C 2017, 'Young Pacific male athletes and positive mental wellbeing', Master's thesis, University of Auckland, Auckland.

Mila-Schaaf, K & Hudson, M 2009, 'The interface between cultural understandings: Negotiating new spaces for Pacific mental health', *Pacific Health Dialog*, vol. 15, no. 1, pp. 113–119.

Ministry of Health 2008, *Pacific peoples and mental health: A paper for the Pacific health and disability action plan review*, Ministry of Health, Wellington.

Napier, L 2015, 'Polynesian athletes face stresses and strains in order to give back to families', *Sunday Star Times*, 19 December, viewed 20 December 2016, www.stuff.co.nz/sport/rugby/75254050/Polynesian-athletes-face-stresses-and-strains-in-order-to-give-back-to-families

National Rugby League 2016, *NRL's Pacific strategy grows in Samoa*, National Rugby League viewed, viewed 5 September 2017, www.nrl.com/nrls-pacific-strategy-grows-in-samoa/tabid/10874/newsid/101990/default.aspx

Newhouse-Bailey, M, Dixon, M & Warner, S 2015, 'Sport and family functioning: Strengthening elite sport families', *Journal of Amateur Sport*, vol. 1, no. 2, pp. 1–26, doi.org/10.17161/jas.v0i0.4934

Ng Shiu, R & Vagana, N 2016, 'An unlikely alliance: Training NRL "cultural warriors"', *In Brief*, vol. 2016, no. 10, pp. 1–2.

Oakley Browne, MA, Wells, JE & Scott, KM (eds) 2006, *Te rau hinengaro: The New Zealand mental health survey*, Wellington.

Palinkas, LA, Horwitz, SM, Green, CA, Wisdom, JP, Duan, N & Hoagwood, K 2015, 'Purposeful sampling for qualitative data collection and analysis in mixed method implementation research', *Administration and Policy in Mental Health*, vol. 42, no. 5, pp. 533–544, doi.org/10.1007/s10488-013-0528-y

Panapa, L & Phillips, M 2014, 'Ethnic persistence: Towards understanding the lived experiences of Pacific Island athletes in the national rugby league', *The International Journal of the History of Sport*, vol. 31, no. 11, pp. 1374–1388, doi.org/10.1080/09523367.2014.924105

Price, N 2007, 'Game of two halves: Preparing young elite rugby players for a future beyond the game', PhD thesis, University of Wollongong, Wollongong.

Pulotu-Endemann, F, Annandale, M & Instone, A 2004, *A Pacific perspective on the NZ mental health classification and outcomes study*, Mental Health Commission, Wellington.

Puna, E 2013, 'New Zealand born Cook Islands youth views towards positive mental wellbeing and suicide prevention', Master's thesis, The University of Auckland, Auckland.

Puna, ET & Tiatia-Seath, J 2017, 'Defining positive mental wellbeing for New Zealand-born Cook Islands youth', *Journal of Indigenous Wellbeing*, vol. 2, no. 1, pp. 97–107.

Rice, S, Purcell, R, De Silva, S, Mawren, D, Mcgorry, P & Parker, A 2016, 'The mental health of elite athletes: A narrative systematic review', *Sports Medicine*, vol. 1, no. 1, pp. 1–21, doi.org/10.1007/s40279-016-0492-2

Rickwood, DJ, Deane, FP & Wilson, CJ 2007, 'When and how do young people seek professional help for mental health problems?', *Medical Journal of Australia*, vol. 187, no. 7, pp. S35–S39.

Roberts, CM, Faull, AL & Tod, D 2016, 'Blurred lines: Performance enhancement, common mental disorders and referral in the UK athletic population', *Front Psychol*, vol. 7, p. 1067, doi.org/10.3389/fpsyg.2016.01067

Rodriguez, L & McDonald, B 2013, 'After the whistle: Issues impacting on the health and wellbeing of Polynesian players off the field', *Asia-Pacific Journal of Health, Sport & Physical Education*, vol. 4, no. 3, pp. 201–215, doi.org/10.1080/18377122.2013.836773

Samu, KS & Suaalii-Sauni, T 2009, 'Exploring the "cultural" in cultural competencies in Pacific mental health', *Pacific Health Dialog*, vol. 15, no. 1, pp. 120–130.

Schaaf, M 2006, 'Elite Pacific male rugby players' perceptions and experiences of professional rugby', *Junctures: The Journal for Thematic Dialogue*, vol. 7, pp. 41–54.

Schaal, K, Tafflet, M, Nassif, H, Thibault, V, Pichard, C, Alcotte, M, Guillet, T, El Helou, N, Berthelot, G, Simon, S & Toussaint, JF 2011, 'Psychological balance in high level athletes: Gender-based differences and sport-specific patterns', *PloS One*, vol. 6, no. 5, e19007, doi.org/10.1371/journal.pone.0019007

Schofield, D 2015, '"Despicable" abuse of young Pacific Island rugby talent a blight on the game', *The Telegraph*, viewed 10 September 2017, www.stuff.co.nz/sport/71910425/despicable-abuse-of-young-pacific-island-rugby-talent-a-blight-on-the-game

Schofield, D 2016, 'Revealed: How Pacific Island player welfare is being neglected in rugby's "gold rush"', *The Daily Telegraph*, viewed 10 September 2017, www.telegraph.co.uk/rugby-union/2016/11/16/revealed-how-pacific-island-player-welfare-is-being-neglected-in/

Siataga, P 2011, 'Pasifika child and youth well-being: Roots and wings', in Office of the Prime Minister's Science Advisory Committee (ed.), *Improving the transition: Reducing social and psychological morbidity during adolescence: A report from the Prime Minister's Chief Science Advisor*, Office of the Prime Minister's Science Advisory Committee, Auckland, pp. 153–169.

Smith, JA 2015, *Qualitative psychology: A practical guide to research methods*, SAGE Publications, London.

Statistics New Zealand 2013, *2013 Census Quickstats about Culture and Identity*, Stats NZ, viewed 9 October 2017, www.stats.govt.nz/Census/2013-census/profile-and-summary-reports/quickstats-culture-identity/pacific-peoples.aspx

Statistics New Zealand 2015, *National Ethnic Population Projections: 2013(Base)–2038*, Stats NZ, viewed 10 September 2017 (page discontinued), www.stats.govt.nz/~/media/Statistics/Browse%20for%20stats/NationalEthnicPopulationProjections/HOTP2013-38/NationalEthnicPopulationProjections2013-38HOTP.pdf

Statistics New Zealand & Ministry of Pacific Island Affairs 2011, *Health and Pacific peoples in New Zealand*, Statistics New Zealand and Ministry of Pacific Island Affairs, Wellington.

Suaalii-Sauni, T, Wheeler, A, Saafi, E, Robinson, G, Agnew, F, Warren, H, Erick, M & Hingano, T 2009, 'Exploration of Pacific perspectives of Pacific models of mental health service delivery in New Zealand', *Pacific Health Dialog*, vol. 15, no. 1, pp. 18–27.

Tamasese, K, Peteru, C, Waldegrave, C & Bush, A 2005, 'Ole taeao afua, the new morning: A qualitative investigation into Samoan perspectives on mental health and culturally appropriate services', *Australian and New Zealand Journal of Psychiatry*, vol. 39, pp. 300–309.

Te'evale, T 2001, 'We are what we play: Pacific peoples, sport and identity in Aotearoa', in C Macpherson, P Spoonley & M Anae (eds), *Tangata o te moana nui: The evolving identities of Pacific peoples in Aotearoa/New Zealand*, Dunmore Press, Palmerston North, pp. 212–217.

Teaiwa, K 2016, 'Niu mana, sport, media and the Australian diaspora', in M Tomlinson &T Tengan (eds), *New mana: Transformations of a classic concept in Pacific languages and cultures*, ANU Press, Canberra, pp. 107–131, doi.org/10.22459/NM.04.2016.04

Teevale, T, Lee, A, Tiatia-Seath, J, Clark, T, Denny, S, Bullen, P, Fleming, T & Peiris-John, R 2016, 'Risk and protective factors for suicidal behaviors among Pacific youth in New Zealand', *The Journal of Crisis Intervention and Suicide Prevention*, vol. 37, no. 5, pp. 335–346, doi.org/10.1027/0227-5910/a000396

Tiatia, J 2012, 'Commentary on "cultural diversity across the Pacific": Samoan cultural constructs of emotion, New Zealand-born Samoan youth suicidal behaviours, and culturally competent human services', *Journal of Pacific Rim Psychology*, vol. 6, no. 2, pp. 75–79, doi.org/10.1017/prp.2012.9

Tiatia-Seath, J 2015, *Suicide prevention for Tongan youth in New Zealand*, Health Research Council of New Zealand, Auckland.

Tiatia-Seath, J, Lay-Yee, R & Von Randow, M 2017, 'Suicide mortality among Pacific peoples in New Zealand, 1996–2013', *New Zealand Medical Journal*, vol. 130, no. 1454, pp. 21–29.

Tukuitonga, C 2013, 'Pacific people in New Zealand', in IM St George (ed.), *Cole's medical practice in New Zealand*, 12th edn, Medical Council of New Zealand, Wellington, pp. 66–72.

Vaioleti, TM 2006, 'Talanoa research methodology: A developing position on Pacific research', *Waikato Journal of Education*, vol. 12, no. 1, pp. 21–34.

Vaka, S 2014, 'A Tongan talanoa about conceptualisations, constructions and understandings of mental illness', PhD thesis, Massey University, Palmerston North, viewed 10 September 2017, mro.massey.ac.nz/handle/10179/5777

Vaswani, N 2011, 'Encouraging help-seeking behaviour among young men: A literature review', *Report for the child protection committee*, Glasgow City Council, Glasgow, viewed 7 March 2018, pdfs.semanticscholar.org/700e/7a88d1c848b183cccc47b63927785e40242f.pdf?_ga=2.203886996.565400545.1565517978-1387094338.1564090436

Woodruff, RJ 2016, 'An exploratory study of essential life skills for adolescent elite athletes in South Africa', Master's thesis, University of the Western Cape, Cape Town, viewed 10 September 2017, pdfs.semanticscholar.org/5c07/339d8335bb5aabab53a0e0d077a6e6544787.pdf

World Health Organization 2014, *Mental health: A state of well-being*, World Health Organization, viewed 20 December 2016, www.who.int/features/factfiles/mental_health/en/

Zakus, D & Horton, P 2009, 'Pasifika in Australian rugby: Emanant cultural, social and economic issues', *Sporting Traditions*, vol. 26, no. 2, pp. 67–86.

12

Temporary Futures, Permanent Constraints: Wellbeing of Pasifika Youth in Australia

Lila Moosad

Introduction

Successive Australian prime ministers have invoked sentiments of 'we are family' when discussing the relationship between Australia and Aotearoa/New Zealand. Most recently, it was former Prime Minister Malcolm Turnbull when he first met New Zealand Prime Minister Jacinda Arden in 2017 (McGowan 2017). These sentiments, however, are not borne by regulatory changes that target the entitlements that New Zealand residents who arrived prior to 2001 enjoyed in Australia; these changes deliberately and systematically disadvantage New Zealanders who have moved to Australia since February 2001. This chapter focuses on these changes and their effect on the lives of young Pasifika whose families moved to Australia in search of 'a better future for their kids', as one of the participants in this study stated. The young Pasifika women who were affected by these changes were in the final years of their high school—a critical point in their lives when they consider decisions about their study and employment pathways. As these Pasifika women soon realised, these options were hedged with limitations for them and other young New Zealand citizens who were affected by the post-2001 changes. I use the frame of wellbeing to show how these changes affect their futures in practical and immediate ways. The changes are also salient to a broader wellbeing narrative of belonging and citizenship that is used against Australia's ever-increasing category of temporary residents.

Methodology

This chapter is based on my ethnographic work and comprises the insights of the many young Pasifika women who I met during my fieldwork between September 2015 and April 2017. Many of them participated in various cultural and leadership projects that were initiated by the youth services at the Acacia council in Melbourne's west. The young women were part of a youth committee that I call Pasifika Voices.[1] These projects were often in collaboration with local arts organisations and Pasifika community artists and mentors. The project dates were aligned with the school terms and ended in early December. December signalled the start of a busy month for the young people, with many returning to visit family in Aotearoa/New Zealand or Oceania. Others were kept busy with family commitments in the weeks leading up to Christmas and New Year's Day. We met in February in 2016 and 2017.

The young women ranged from 17 to 27 years in age and were born in Australia, New Zealand and Samoa. They were predominantly Tongan and Samoan, and some were of mixed Pasifika or non-Pasifika heritage. Most were at school or university; others were working or looking for work. During my fieldwork, some of the young women moved into work and tertiary study. The experiences of being Pasifika in Melbourne for these young women were shaped by their transnational experiences and their connections to their communities spread across New Zealand, Melbourne, Samoa and Tonga. While they identified as Pasifika in the context of council projects, they also identified as Tongan or Samoan in other settings, and as Australian, New Zealander and Oceania-born in yet other contexts. Their everyday lives around family, church, work, study and friendship networks varied as well. It was in these overlapping spaces that the contradictions and tensions that were inherent in the young women's wellbeing experiences became clearer. The strengths and

1 Names of participants, organisations and places have been de-identified.

resources that these sites offered were also made visible. In this chapter, I specifically focus on young women whose families moved to Australia from New Zealand after 2001.

My ethnography also includes insights from other members of the Pasifika communities, some of whom were related to the young women in my study. I also spoke to representatives from the service agencies that were working with the young women or Pasifika youth generally. They included Pasifika and non-Pasifika artists, Pasifika researchers, community and religious leaders, social and youth workers and Victorian police force members.

In the following sections of this chapter, I discuss the implications of the changes that the Australian government implemented in 2001, drawing on my fieldwork and the theoretical framework of structural vulnerability. I also discuss the notion of wellbeing, as it relates to the immediate constraints of young people's lives and to the broader notions of citizenship and belonging in Australia.

2001 Changes to Visa Status

Early in my fieldwork, I met Mele and Ema, who were part of the Pasifika Voices youth committee. Some months later, I met Amelia, who was a friend to many young women in the youth committee. Mele's family had moved from Aotearoa/New Zealand to Melbourne in 2008, and Ema's and Amelia's families had moved in 2015. Ema went straight into Year 12 in 2015, which is the final year of high school in Australia. Mele and Amelia completed high school in 2016. I am precise about their dates of arrival in Australia because the regulatory changes that the Australian government introduced in 2001 significantly constrained opportunities for them and the other Pasifika youth who arrived in Australia after 2001.

The 2001 changes were part of the amendments to Australia's *Social Security Act 1991* and were in response to Australia's policy concerns about the increasing numbers of people who were 'born in third-world countries', even though arrivals from Aotearoa were New Zealand citizens and increasingly New Zealand–born (Hamer 2014, p. 110). These anxieties about the 'back door' migration from Aotearoa, which were a legacy of suspicion from the White Australia Policy days, do not reflect the reality of demographic changes in Aotearoa (Mares 2016).

Under the 1973 Trans-Tasman Arrangement between Australia and Aotearoa, there was unrestricted movement between the two countries. Australian and New Zealand officials treated this Trans-Tasman movement into another country as a separate matter to the official migrant intake of their countries. It was an acknowledgement of historical connections and close bilateral ties. Over time, the original arrangement, whereby citizens from both countries could live and work indefinitely in one another's countries with unhampered passport and visa-free entry and all the benefits of permanent resident status, tightened. From 1981, New Zealand citizens were required to present a valid New Zealand passport; in 1986, children born to New Zealand citizens in Australia no longer had automatic citizenship rights; and, in 1994, the Special Category Visa (SCV) was created for New Zealand citizens. This SCV was envisaged as a temporary category, and this classification took on particular significance after the 2001 changes (McMillan 2017). By 2000, the qualifying period to access welfare benefits was extended from six months to two years. These benefits ceased after the 2001 regulatory changes. These welfare restrictions are in contrast to the treatment of Australians moving to New Zealand who automatically became permanent residents with access to welfare and citizenship eligibility after a qualifying period.

The 2001 amendments to Australia's *Social Security Act 1991* have had negative effects on the New Zealand citizens who arrived in Australia after 2001. The new SCV subclass 444 would permit New Zealanders to live and work (and pay taxes) as indefinite and non-protected temporary residents, but without access to the public housing, student loans, disability, health, welfare services and special assistance offered in times of disasters that other permanent residents are entitled to. This visa is issued to New Zealand citizens at the time of entry and is valid for the length of their stay in Australia. A gap has now opened in the level of protection offered through public welfare and health services between the post-2001 arrivals that were issued with the 'non-protected' SCV and the 'protected' SCV holders (pre-2001 New Zealander residents). Unlike the former group, the latter group continues to be entitled to the same benefits as Australian citizens.

A pathway to permanent residency in Australia became available for New Zealand citizens in July 2017 (Mares 2016). However, this is a costly and protracted process that essentially amounts to providing payroll receipts that demonstrate taxable income of at least A$53,900 in the previous five years, as well as to additional application processing costs. Another restriction is that this pathway is only available to New Zealanders who arrive before 19 February 2016 (McMillan 2017). A major reason that Australian permanent residency status and citizenship will remain unattainable for many families is the prevalence of Pasifika workers in low-skilled, casual and precarious work. It is unlikely that many of these workers will average an income in excess of A$53,000 for each of the last five years, and, given the nature of the employment, it is difficult to collate the required documentation.

The people who are designated as 'temporary' residents by the Australian government pay taxes and contribute to the community in many other ways. The altered circumstances that this legal differentiation creates for this group exemplifies the 'dynamics of social exclusion and the limits placed on citizenship' (Quesada et al. 2011, p. 347). The treatment offered by the Australian Taxation Office for purposes of tax liability is consistent with that of a permanent resident; yet, citizens of New Zealand who arrived in Australia after 2001 have a status of 'temporary-ness' in regard to accessing Australian welfare services (Mares 2016). The inconsistencies in this regime are experienced as iniquitous and baffling due to the conveyed sense of movable parts in the regime and due to the seemingly opportunistic shifts of legal interpretation in the nation state's concept of belonging and citizenship. For example, New Zealanders with post-2001 SCVs are denied the services that are provided under the National Disability Insurance Scheme because they are not considered Australian residents under the *Social Security Act*. Yet, they are obliged to pay levies through their taxable incomes towards the scheme because, under the *Health Insurance Act 1973*, they are defined as Australian residents (Mares 2016, p. 137).

The 2001 *Social Security Act* precludes Pasifika youth who fall into the non-protected SCV category from several benefits that are available to those who have permanent residency. These include unemployment benefits, youth unemployment benefits, sole parent benefits, carer payment or allowance paid to carers who look after children or adults with a medical condition or disability, Austudy—which is paid to full-time students—and Special Benefits (Walsh 2015, p. 679). Ema and Amelia felt pressured to quickly find any sort of work after finishing school, particularly since, unlike many of their peers, they could not claim unemployment benefits. Welfare experts consider the Special Benefit as 'the ultimate safety net in the Australian social security system' (Walsh 2015, p. 683); it is paid to people who are ineligible for all other benefits. There is concessionary access to unemployment, youth unemployment and sickness allowance (but only as a one-off payment) for a maximum period of six months for New Zealand citizens who have resided in Australia continuously for at least 10 years. Those who have arrived in recent years are excluded from accessing these benefits, whether they are transitioning from school to work like Ema and Amelia or whether they are in common situations of being retrenched from unstable employment.

Families with unprotected SCVs face added risks related to domestic instability since the 2001 changes to the regulations to remove emergency and public housing access. Under the conditions of their funding, agencies that are funded to provide settlement services for newly arrived migrant communities in Australia cannot work with New Zealand citizens. Youth workers outlined to me that because of the restrictive rules, Pasifika families with temporary visas who experience settlement issues have to be referred to agencies other than the specialist settlement ones. According to the youth workers, the 2001 policy change significantly affects New Zealand citizens in family violence situations who are unable to access housing, financial and legal assistance. They described several examples of New Zealand citizens in family violence situations who are unable to access such assistance in the way that newly arrived permanent residents would be able to. Women (who are predominantly the victims of domestic violence) are unable to return to New Zealand with their children without their partner's approval (Mares 2016) and they often end up remaining in their abusive environments. Non-protected SCV Pasifika youth in need of emergency housing are also not considered a priority group. Youth workers who work with these young Pasifika at risk of homelessness speak of the challenges of being able to secure housing support for them, as well as their reliance on non-government agencies to assist young people and their families who are New Zealand citizens.

Many Pasifika families become aware of these limitations and their consequences only after arriving in Australia. The technicalities of Australia's health, education, social security and immigration laws were not at the forefront of their minds when deciding to move countries. In any case, one's SCV status is recorded electronically rather than in his or her passport on arrival (Kearney 2012). Mele's mother was only vaguely aware of the restrictions, but she found that she needed to clarify its implications when Mele started thinking about studying at university. Similarly, Ema's and Amelia's parents only vaguely knew of the restrictions to their daughters' pursuit of further studies. The 10-year residency requirement attached to the major forms of tertiary education support that is provided through the Australian government excluded Ema, Amelia and Mele from government-supported university places and from accessing the student loans scheme.

Further confusion about what support they could expect also arose from the split jurisdictions for post-school education and training between state and federal governments. New Zealand citizens are eligible to enrol in Victorian state government–funded vocational training, but to access a university course (the federal jurisdiction), they are ineligible to apply for the deferred tuition loans under the Australian government's FEE-HELP scheme. This means that to pursue degree studies, they must pay (prohibitive) upfront fees of up to A$10,000 each year before they start to think about their living costs. Australian citizens, pre-2001 New Zealand citizens and post-2001 New Zealand citizens who have been here for 10 years are eligible for FEE-HELP, which means that they are not required to repay their accumulated tuition debt until their annual income has crossed a threshold of A$55,000. Typically, this would be someone who has graduated into well-paid employment and who could afford to start paying the debt.

Structural Vulnerability

The concept of structural vulnerability, theorised by Seth Holmes (2011), James Quesada et al. (2011) and Philippe Bourgois et al. (2017), critically evaluates the health effect on communities and individuals given their situation within 'socio-economic, political, and cultural/normative hierarchies'—that is to say, hierarchies that are 'overlapping and mutually reinforcing' (Bourgois et al. 2017, p. 300). Quesada et al. (2011) have drawn on the notion of structural violence, which is theorised often in post-crisis neo-colonial societies by anthropologist and physician Paul Farmer (2003), to develop the more nuanced and diffused concept of structural vulnerability. Structural vulnerability removes suggestions of overt violence (the notion of living in a 'failed state'), which facilitates the application of the concept to include a greater range of socioeconomic circumstances, such as urban communities experiencing disadvantages in the rich world. Quesada et al. (2011, p. 341) suggested that structural vulnerability should be viewed as a 'positionality', whereby 'the vulnerability of an individual is produced by her location in a hierarchical social order and its diverse networks of power relationships and effects'. Much of the work on structural vulnerability has been with Latino agricultural workers in the United States, but it is equally applicable to marginalised populations. It analyses and critiques a matrix of factors that work to create conditions of vulnerability for these migrants' health and wellbeing. Structural vulnerability in these communities is generated through a combination that could include racialised stereotyping, social exclusion, immigration status, labour market position, the practical implications of trade agreements between the United States and Mexico, working conditions and political discourses of 'illegal' migrants. The resulting understandings of structural vulnerability, Quesada et al. (2011) argued, have to be incorporated in clinical encounters with vulnerable groups like Latino migrant workers and other excluded minorities.

I use the concept of structural vulnerability to analyse the forces that constrain the lives and wellbeing opportunities of the young Pasifika women as a direct result of the 2001 regulatory changes. I suggest that wellbeing needs to be viewed as a relational and unfolding process. This approach identifies the constraining forces as continuously presenting impediments. It underscores that the social and regulatory limitations that are placed on the young women and their families must be understood as dynamic processes that are continuously recreating the conditions of vulnerability.

Wellbeing

The focus of much of the nascent health literature on Pasifika communities in Australia has been on individual markers of ill health, such as obesity, diabetes, renal disease and cardiovascular and respiratory conditions; it has also covered the experiences of adult (Polynesian) Pasifika in the Australian health system (McCarthy et al. 2010; Rodriguez 2013; Rodriguez & George 2014). The common analytical approach to the Pasifika health issues of these studies is based on a biomedical framework. At one level, the stories that the young women told me of family members with medical conditions like diabetes and cardiovascular disease and of the premature deaths of family members underlined the credibility of this approach. However, a broader concept of wellbeing for young Pasifika women is rarely a feature in these medical and epidemiological studies—one reason presumably being that they are a small subgroup of the population. Along with these medical perspectives, other necessary fields of analysis can be opened through ethnographic and structural approaches. Wellbeing is a contested and ambiguous concept and it is significant that, to capture this notion, rich empirical studies draw on multiple disciplinary and theoretical approaches.

Some biomedical and popular approaches to wellbeing have focused on measuring wellbeing by using a set of categories, and they have assumed universalised experiences. These interpretations have their origins in the Global North (Atkinson 2013; White 2016) and are generally written from the perspectives of those 'already in a position of relative material advantage' (White 2016, p. 5). Generally, these components have focused on the individual as the primary acquirer of wellbeing. This individualised approach to wellbeing, Sarah Atkinson (2013, p. 141) argued, can then be extended to attribute the 'failure of wellbeing' to a result of 'failure of responsible citizenship'. These references to the individual are in parallel to the neoliberal discourse that assigns responsibility elsewhere from broader political, social and economic policies that affect wellbeing.

In the last decade, scholars have turned away from the initial focus on quantitative methods to explore other dimensions of wellbeing through qualitative, mixed methods and careful ethnographic work. As a counter argument to the earlier emphasis on capturing wellbeing through categories, measurements and rankings of many educational, psychological and medical disciplinary approaches, social scientists from anthropology, sociology and geography have reframed the ways of conceptualising wellbeing. These studies draw attention to the complex and relational aspects of wellbeing, shift the focus to the 'socially and culturally constructed' aspects of wellbeing (White 2016, p. 5) and address where and how these constructions emerge and what their outcomes might be. Sarah White's work draws on participant experiences from countries in Africa, Asia and Latin America. This shift in the focus of wellbeing scholarship has produced a rich output of contextual and constructivist findings that have disrupted the conventional and standardising approaches, and it has critiqued the lens from the Global North that has been the primary analytic frame for wellbeing scholarship.

The relational and collective analyses of wellbeing that White (2016), Atkinson (2013) and Atkinson et al. (2012) deliberated are closer to the wellbeing approach that I use in this chapter. White outlined the subjective, material and relational dimensions of wellbeing and further suggested viewing it as a process, paying attention to 'life-course' and incorporating 'reflections on the past and expectations of the future' (White 2016, p. 10).

I argue that for young women like Mele, Ema and Amelia, wellbeing is a relational activity that is shaped and experienced through their interactions with communities, institutions and structures. The spatial and temporal dimensions of wellbeing allow us to understand the connections between the transnational histories of the young women, their complex identities as young women in densely urban settings in Melbourne, their access to social, educational and employment resources and their future aspirations. By highlighting the relational, spatial and temporal dimensions of wellbeing as the units of analysis, the historical, social, economic and political processes that contribute to wellbeing experiences are made visible. Finally, I argue that wellbeing needs to be conceptualised as an ongoing set of social practices, as open-ended rather than fixed, to identify where and how these structural forces stymie young women's pathways to wellbeing. Medical anthropologist, Sarah Willen, similarly argued against abstract and definitional concepts using the notion of dignity as an example. She proposes that 'dignity' needs to be studied as a process: 'The notion of dignity becomes ethnographically visible, and anthropologically meaningful, only in motion: as dignity harmed, denied, violated, or stripped away—or, conversely, as dignity pursued, safeguarded, recuperated, reclaimed' (Willen 2014).

Similarly, I suggest it is through viewing wellbeing as an ongoing set of practices and relationships that we identify its nuances, those factors that act as barriers to wellbeing, and that we identify where and how wellbeing experiences are disrupted. It is in recognising wellbeing as a process that the structural implications of regulatory regimes become visible. In the following section, I focus on the effect of these regulatory changes in the lives of young Pasifika women like Ema, Amelia and Mele.

Stories From the Field

> I'd like to study, but I need money; there's no future for it. It's like for now, when I was in Auckland, I was gonna go study, but then we moved here, it's just changed. (Ema)

When I first met Ema in 2015, she had just finished school without sitting for her final examinations (on the advice of her teachers) and she was unclear about her future prospects. She was unable to return to Aotearoa to pursue her studies because she did not have the financial resources to support herself. She had dreamed of doing theatre studies in Aotearoa before her family moved to Melbourne. Early in 2016, I learned that she was enrolled in a short-term course on leadership through a registered private education provider, with a promise of employment at the end of the course. It seemed a strange choice for a young woman just out of high school—more so that a reserved young woman would be matched to a leadership course as an employment pathway. Ema's experience is not unusual. Deregulation in the education 'industry' created opportunities for private organisations to access government funding, by delivering short-course training that generally took the form of qualifications with low overhead costs for groups who were not well informed about post–secondary education choices. Some training businesses pursued aggressive marketing to sign up individuals to their courses by targeting young people such as Ema in disadvantaged communities, whose information about the educational quality of the courses was limited. The leadership work did not eventuate for Ema at the end of the course. Through her friendship networks, she picked up some shifts at a fast-food outlet. At this point, her attendance at Pasifika Voices became more and more infrequent. After several months of not seeing her, I heard through the other young women that Ema had picked up more shifts at her workplace. 'I don't have many talents, I'm lost', was how she described herself when I first spoke at length with her after she had finished school.

The economic circumstances of Ema's family were precarious. She was one of seven siblings, and her father and older siblings all worked in low-skilled roles. Ema's short leadership course was futile in terms of qualifying her for a good starting point. It gave her no pathway that would advance her beyond the type of job she was doing in the low-skilled segment of the labour market.

Ema's education and employment pathways illustrate the multiple ways in which her life chances and wellbeing are shaped and compromised by structural forces. Constraints on Ema's wellbeing are inherent in her position (Quesada et al. 2011) as an unprotected temporary resident; as a young woman who completed high school without tertiary entry qualifications; as a member of a large family who relies financially on a combined household income; as someone unable to access welfare services and support in Australia; and as a young woman without extensive family networks in Australia. All these elements of Ema's life and their collective effect on her wellbeing may not be immediately evident. The structural constraints on Ema's wellbeing arise from the interconnections and relationality between the immigration policies and the economic contexts in which she and her family were embedded. Ema's position in the social hierarchy—with its political, economic and social networks of power relationships (Bourgois et al. 2017)—created a structural vulnerability that limited her wellbeing potential.

Mele's and Amelia's plans for further study were also shaped by the post-2001 regulations. Mele finished high school in 2016. Her family had moved to Australia when she was eight, which left her not quite qualified for the 10-year residence requirement to access financial assistance for university in Australia. While waiting for the 10-year qualification, she returned to Aotearoa to stay with family and to work and build up her savings. Amelia's family had arrived more recently—in 2015. Like Ema, Amelia's priorities after completing high school were to find work, and she was unable to finance her post-secondary studies. When I met Amelia in early 2017, she was taking a year off so she could work in retail to save money to fund her studies. She was saving up to go to Queensland, where she could stay with relatives and pursue her studies. Though she seriously considered it, she was unable to apply to join the police academy in Melbourne due to her temporary visa status. After navigating the Victoria Police website myself, I was left with a sense of ambiguity about Amelia's eligibility. According to the force's prerequisites for application, SCV holders are eligible, but it is less clear whether non-protected visa holders are.

While Mele qualified for tertiary fee assistance after a wait of 12 months, Ema and Amelia would have to wait until they were well into their 20s before they could access student financial support. Though their families worked and paid taxes in Australia, this marker of citizenship was insufficient to entitle their children access to higher education and training opportunities. For many of the young women, these restrictions to accessing the system of deferred loan finance that the Australian government provided to most qualified school leavers was a common problem. The concept of structural vulnerability shows how the administrative regulation of citizenship benefits profoundly shapes the opportunities for these young women. Ultimately, their vulnerability is based on their location in the 'multiple overlapping and mutually reinforcing power hierarchies' and 'policy level statuses' (Bourgois et al. 2017, p. 300).

Data from recent studies shows that participation in higher education is much lower for young Pasifika with SCV visas when compared to those with permanent resident or Australian citizenship status (Kearney 2012;

Kearney & Glen 2017). This low level of participation is exacerbated by the 10-year wait to qualify for support. These exclusionary processes come at a high cost for Pasifika youth and their families, as well as for the nation and its investment in its youth. As Judith Kearney and Matthew Glen (2017, p. 10) highlighted, the lower levels of higher education participation also have implications for the levels of 'school engagement and educational aspirations of their younger siblings'. A youth worker I spoke with confirmed this, saying that 'for young Pasifika, it is hard to stay engaged knowing there's nothing at the end of high school'. The Australian government's stated position on education is that 'education is fundamental to achieving a fairer and stronger Australia and for many provides a pathway out of disadvantage' (Commonwealth of Australia 2009, p. 9). The implied intention in this official statement is clearly inconsistent with the exclusionary processes that limit the access of many New Zealand citizens settled in Australia to higher education.

Barriers to wellbeing are embedded and interconnected in the socioeconomic hierarchies that structure the everyday lives of young Pasifika. The structural vulnerability of households can escalate rapidly under these immigration regulations. This became strongly evident to me at an information forum for Pasifika who were affected by the 2001 immigration changes. This advocacy event was the initiative of a group of Pasifika women who had participated in a project called 'Our Community, Our Rights', which was organised by a health organisation in Melbourne's west. There was a sizeable turnout for the evening event. During the evening, a young Pasifika woman whose family had moved from Aotearoa for 'a better life' recounted an anecdote that resonated with the audience. She had completed her post-secondary qualifications in early childhood studies through the state government's vocational training system. Because she could not support herself while looking for work in the early childhood sector (and she was ineligible for welfare benefits), she fell back to irregular work in retail and hospitality. She and her family had moved their household between states and cities multiple times in search of stable employment. Matters were further complicated for the family when her brother, who had spent all his adult life in Australia, was deported by the Australian authorities to Aotearoa.

Due to changes to the *Migration Amendment Act 2014*, the state has the power to deport temporary residents (including non-protected SCV New Zealand citizens) who are deemed to be 'of bad character' or who have served a prison sentence of 12 months in Australia (Mares 2016, pp. 146–147). These temporary residents have their visas cancelled automatically, and a visa cancellation on these grounds prevents deportees from returning to Australia. For many families like this young Pasifika woman's, deportations separate families and result in young people returning to countries, in this case Aotearoa, where they have no immediate family support networks or where they have not lived as young adults.

The threat of deportation (with its implications of prolonged detention), separation from family and the uncertainty of starting again in Aotearoa weigh on the Pasifika communities, in which there are close networks among non-protected SCV visa holders. Hoeskstra's (2016, p. 4) work with undocumented migrants in the United States illustrates how deportation threats in themselves enable a hostile environment by provoking 'physical and psychological vulnerability' as much as the actual act of being deported. For the young woman who spoke that evening, the climate created within her community by the draconian application of immigration regulations is one of multiple structural factors (e.g. economic precarity, housing instability and lack of legal redress) undermining her wellbeing.

There were many more stories that evening of families who were unable to access services and support because of their unprotected temporary visa status. A single parent with three school-aged children worried about her children's ineligibility for tertiary assistance. Another parent could not access carer's allowance to take care of a sick daughter. The full implications of their precarious positionality become abundantly clear to families when they need access to financial assistance or support due to 'the vagaries of existence'—serious illness, retrenchment, work accidents and relationship breakdowns (Mares 2016, p. 178). Finally, in case of unexpected hardships and change of circumstances, they are denied access to services that are available to the majority of Australian residents through the social safety net.

The links between wellbeing and immigration status have not been as extensively theorised in Australia as they have in the United States. There are many opportunities for research in this area due to the increasingly higher numbers of temporary residents and the mounting evidence for a portion of the population who is stuck in the segmented layers of the labour force. There are complex patterns resulting from various layers of immigration status and the implications that these have for accessing health care. Scholars in the United States (Cartwright 2011; Heidbrink 2014; Holmes 2011) have ethnographically documented the effects of these immigration status issues on the wellbeing of participants. Recent scholarship by Helen Lee and Makiko Nishitani (2018) takes a step towards addressing this research gap in relation to Pasifika in Australia. Their ethnographic study analyses the complex relationships between the labour market segmentation, economic precarity, residency status and intergenerational disadvantage that is experienced by Pasifika in the Australian agricultural sector. Parallel studies of Pasifika and other communities on perilous temporary visas in Australian cities would be invaluable.

The structural vulnerability concept that was proposed by Quesada et al. (2011) unmasks the connections between the political and economic restrictions of the unprotected SCVs and their effect on the lives of many young Pasifika and their families. These political restrictions further perpetuate stereotypical depictions of Pasifika communities in low-skilled and economically precarious roles that many of the young women in this study referred to. Peter Mares (2016) in his book, *Not Quite Australia,* argued that a large percentage of people who are affected by the 2001 regulations are Maori and Pasifika. For many in the segmented labour market, the complicated and costly steps that are involved in transitioning to permanent residency are out of reach. This leaves young women like Ema and Amelia and their families in an ongoing state of impermanence, with little opportunity to transition out of their low-skilled roles.

The application of the structural vulnerability framework in a political context in which increasingly nativist and fortified immigration policies interlock with cuts to welfare and social services support, while governments benefit from taxation revenue collected from temporary visa holders, is particularly pertinent. For young women like Ema and Amelia, these restrictions result in the transforming of what were initially temporary low-skilled roles into permanent and long-term ones as a way protecting them and supporting their families.

Apart from the disadvantages that are posed by a lack of access to education and welfare support, the post-2001 changes raise larger concerns of wellbeing that are connected to young people's sense of belonging and citizenship. A key result of the changes is the creation of a multi-tiered system that is composed of protected SCV holders, non-protected SCV holders and Australian citizens, and the differences in their entitlements and restrictions.

In the next section, I analyse contemporary dominant and often-contradictory discourses of participation and belonging—discourses that belie the realities for Pasifika youth with non-protected SCV visas. At one point during my fieldwork, I accompanied three of the young Pasifika women and an Acacia council representative to a meeting with federal parliamentarians who constituted the Joint Standing Committee on Migration. As part of their inquiry into migrant settlement outcomes, this group was meeting with representatives from community organisations and individuals in Melbourne. It became apparent in the hearing that the parliamentarians had little interest in investigating the structural issues that some of the young Pasifika women and their families face, resulting from their unprotected temporary visa status.

Structural Wellbeing

Our interaction with the politicians exemplified how mainstream politics and dominant discourses of belonging and participation mesh together, as well as identified the (deliberate) discursive misunderstanding of the effects of regulatory barriers on young people's everyday lives. When I read the entire script of the sessions that the committee had with various representatives on the day we met them, there was a disproportionate focus from the chair of the committee on the 'antisocial' behaviour of migrant youth, visa cancellations for youth who were engaged in 'criminal' activities and the offending patterns of young people from specific cultural communities. His evidence base for his comments appeared to be a tabloid newspaper in Melbourne that reported regularly on the 'crimes' that were committed by 'migrant gangs'. For the political representatives, there appeared to be little perception or empathy that would lead to an acknowledgement of the young people's concerns regarding school and their references to stereotyping, labelling and racial profiling as examples of negative settlement experiences. For a committee whose brief was to consider the settlement experiences of second-generation migrants, it seemed fair to assume that these concerns and those for the educational and economic participation of migrant youth would be of interest. The 2001 changes have deep implications for family and community concepts of belonging and wellbeing, and they leave a sense of ambivalence about citizenship rights (McMillan 2017).

One of the politicians referred to Harmony Day (recognised elsewhere in the world as the International Day for the Elimination of Racial Discrimination) as an example of an event that Pasifika youth could participate in. Harmony Day is held on 21 March every year to celebrate Australia's 'success' as a culturally diverse country, and schools and workplaces commemorate the day by holding culinary and cultural events. The focus on cultural explanations (Viruell-Fuentes et al. 2012; Youdell 2012), such as participation in 'multicultural' events, can operate to gloss over the key structural obstacle that immigration status poses for the young Pasifika who are affected by changes to visa rules; by design, these exclude them from eligibility for various welfare services and educational opportunities. Political processes such as the parliamentary committee's hearings in the public sphere do not serve to inform about as much as to obscure the powerful ways in which power and structural privilege thwart young people's wellbeing experiences and discourage their sense of belonging. Lack of access to education, welfare and employment support adds layers of difficulty to communities who are already disadvantaged in many ways. It diminishes the potential of Pasifika youth to secure their wellbeing; it sustains and inflicts disadvantages that are transmitted between generations.

Medical anthropologist Elizabeth Cartwright suggested that the immigration system in the United States 'is a powerful pathogen' for immigrants from Mexico, through the conditions created by the different immigration categories (Cartwright 2011, p. 475). The 2001 amendments to the Australian social security laws provide a glimpse into the numerous ways in which young women like Ema and Amelia, their siblings and family members are separated from the categories of Australian citizenship and permanent residence and its entitlements. The 'fractured terrain of belonging' that contributes negatively to wellbeing (Cartwright 2011, p. 481) was evident in such stories as the brother, who had been deported despite living his life in Australia; Ema, who was unable to pursue her dream of theatre studies because she needed to earn an income; and Mele and Amelia, who have had to defer their studies. There are numerous other examples of young Pasifika and their families who are constrained by a lack of access to educational and welfare support and by the ever-constant threat of visa cancellation. Yet, for many of the young women who I met, there was no talk of their families returning to Aotearoa in the immediate future. They had warm memories of neighbourhoods, family and friends in Aotearoa, but they and their families planned to live and work in Australia. This clearly demonstrates their commitment and responsibility, which discourse in the public sphere represents as the requirement of the nation state. But, unlike most citizens, Pasifika youth with unprotected visas are confronted with additional structural hurdles that pose significant immediate and long-term consequences not just for their futures, but also for the overall wellbeing of the communities to which they belong.

Conclusion

In this chapter, I have drawn on my ethnographic engagement with young Pasifika women from Aotearoa/New Zealand who moved to Australia with their families after 2001 to illustrate the effect of regulatory regimes on their wellbeing. Using the concept of structural vulnerability, I show how restricted access to economic and educational resources as a result of the regulatory changes shape the wellbeing futures of Pasifika youth. There is currently a sizeable group of young Pasifika in Australia whose futures are determined by these regulatory restrictions and who will grow up without accessing the benefits and rights that young Australian citizens and permanent residents have.

These restrictions raise critical questions about the commitment and the responsibility of the state in taking care of 'its family' while expecting young people to show commitment towards the country that they are living in. The Pasifika population in Australia is a youthful one (Ravulo 2015) and, therefore, government policies on unprotected temporary residents determine life courses from an early age and have far-reaching effects on the life opportunities and potential of young Pasifika.

Maori scholar Linda Tuhiwai Smith (2013, p. 228) stated:

> The future, in one sense, is now. It's not an abstract, theoretical or even visionary picture of what the world may be like in fifty or a hundred years. It is, rather, the potential we hold now, as a society.

To address the wellbeing futures of Pasifika youth who arrived in Australia after 2001, we need to acknowledge the effect of these restrictions on their access to social and economic resources right now.

Acknowledgements

I would like to express my thanks to all the young women from Pasifika Voices who generously invited me to participate in their projects between September 2015 and April 2017, and who shared their stories. My thanks also to the staff at the Acacia council's youth services unit and to the many people from the Pasifika communities who took an interest in this project and made time to share their reflections.

Thank you to Professor Helen Lee, who encouraged me to present my preliminary findings at the Association for Social Anthropology in Oceania meeting in New Orleans in February 2018. Thanks also to Cathy Vaughan, Kalissa Alexeyeff and Richard Chenhall from the University of Melbourne.

This study was undertaken as part of my PhD research, through the Centre for Health Equity, School of Population and Global Health at the University of Melbourne. I am grateful for the Australian Government Research Training Program Stipend Scholarship that funded this study.

References

Atkinson, S 2013, 'Beyond components of wellbeing: The effects of relational and situated assemblage', *Topoi*, vol. 32, pp. 137–144, doi.org/10.1007/s11245-013-9164-0

Atkinson, S, Fuller, S & Painter, J 2012, 'Wellbeing and place', in S Atkinson, S Fuller & J Painter (eds), *Wellbeing and Place*, Ashgate Publishing Limited, Farnham, pp. 1–14.

Bourgois, P, Holmes, SM, Sue, K & Quesada, J 2017, 'Structural vulnerability: Operationalizing the concept to address health disparities in clinical care', *Academic Medicine*, vol. 92, no. 3, pp. 299–307, doi.org/10.1097/ACM.0000000000001294

Cartwright, E 2011, 'Immigrant dreams: Legal pathologies and structural vulnerabilities along the immigration continuum', *Medical Anthropology: Cross-Cultural Studies in Health and Illness*, vol. 30, no. 5, pp. 475–495, doi.org/10.1080/01459740.2011.577044

Commonwealth of Australia 2009, *A stronger fairer Australia*, viewed 5 November 2018, (site discontinued), www.socialinclusion.gov.au/Resources/Documents/ReportAStongerFairerAustralia.pdf

Farmer, P 2003, *Pathologies of power health, human rights and the new war on the poor,* University of California Press, Berkeley and Los Angeles.

Hamer, P 2014, '"Sophisticated and unsuited", Australian barriers to Pacific Islander migration from New Zealand', *Political Science,* vol. 66, no. 2, pp. 93–118, doi.org/10.1177/0032318714554495

Heidbrink, L 2014, *Migrant youth, transnational families, and the state: Care and contested interests*, University of Pennsylvania Press, Philadelphia.

Hoeskstra, E 2016, 'Bodies of resistance: The migrant health justice movement and claims of biocitizenship', paper presented at American Sociological Association Annual Meeting, Seattle, 20–23 August.

Holmes, SM 2011, 'Structural vulnerability and hierarchies of ethnicity and citizenship on the farm', *Medical Anthropology: Cross Cultural Studies in Health and Illness,* vol. 30, no. 4, pp. 425–449, doi.org/10.1080/01459740.2011.576728

Kearney, J 2012, 'Unlucky in a lucky country: A commentary on policies and practices that restrict access to higher education in Australia', *Journal of Social Inclusion*, vol. 3, no. 1, pp. 130–134.

Kearney, J & Glen, M 2017, 'The effects of citizenship and ethnicity on the education pathways of Pacific youth in Australia', *Education, Citizenship and Social Justice,* vol. 12, no. 3, pp. 1–13, doi.org/10.1177/1746197916684644

Lee, H & Nishitani, M 2018, Who are the Pacific farmworkers in Australia?, *DEVPOLICYBLOG,* blog post, 6 March, viewed 30 August 2018, www.devpolicy.org/pacific-farmworkers-in-australia-20180206

Mares, P 2016, *Not quite Australian: How temporary migration is changing the nation*, Text Publishing, Melbourne.

McCarthy, A, Shaban, R & Stone, C 2010, 'Fa'afaletui: A framework for the promotion of renal health in an Australian Samoan community', *Journal of Transcultural Nursing,* vol. 22, no. 1, pp. 55–62, doi.org/10.1177/1043659610387154

McGowan, M 2017, 'Warm relations as Turnbull and Arden stow differences in chilly bin', *The Guardian*, 5 November, viewed 3 December 2018 (story removed), www.theguardian.com/Australia-news/2017/nov/05/warm-relations-as-turnbull-and-arden-stow-differences-in-chilly-bin

McMillan, K 2017, '"Affective integration" and access to the rights of permanent residency: New Zealanders resident in Australia post–2001', *Ethnicities*, vol. 17, no. 1, pp. 103–127, doi.org/10.1177/1468796816656675

Quesada, J, Hart, LK & Bourgois, P 2011, 'Structural vulnerability and health: Latino migrant laborers in the United States', *Medical Anthropology*, vol. 30, no. 4, pp. 339–362, doi.org/10.1080/01459740.2011.576725

Ravulo, J 2015, *Pacific Communities in Australia*, University of Western Sydney, viewed 5 October 2015 (page removed), www.uws.edu.au/_data/assest/pdf_file/0006/923361/SSP5680_Pacific_Communities_in_Aust_FA_LR.pdf

Rodriguez, L 2013, 'The subjective experience of Polynesians in the Australian health system', *Health Sociology Review*, vol. 22, no. 4, pp. 411–421.

Rodriguez, L & George, JR 2014, 'Is genetic labeling of "risk" related to obesity contributing to resistance and fatalism in Polynesian communities?', *The Contemporary Pacific*, vol. 26, no. 1, pp. 65–93, doi.org/10.1353/cp.2014.0005

Social Security Act 1991, *Federal Register of Legislation*, Australian Government, viewed 5 November 2018, www.legislation.gov.au/Series/C2004A04121

Tuhiwai Smith, L 2013, 'The future is now', in M Rashbrooke (ed.), *Inequality: A New Zealand crisis*, Bridget William Books, Wellington, pp. 228–235.

Viruell-Fuentes, EA, Miranda, PY & Abdulrahim, S 2012, 'More than culture: Structural racism, intersectionality theory and immigrant health', *Social Science & Medicine*, vol. 75, pp. 2099–2106, doi.org/10.1016/j.socscimed.2011.12.037

Walsh, T 2015, 'New Zealanders in crisis in Australia: The absence of a social safety net', *New Zealand Universities Law Review*, vol. 26, no. 3, pp. 673–702.

White, SC 2016, 'Introduction: The many faces of wellbeing', in SC White & C Blackmore (eds), *Cultures of wellbeing: Method, place, policy*, Palgrave Macmillan, Basingstoke, pp. 1–44.

Willen, SS 2014, Top of the Heap, *Somastosphere*, blog post, 12 September, viewed 28 June 2018, somatosphere.net/2014/top-of-the-heap-sarah-willen.html/

Youdell, D 2012, 'Fabricating "Pacific Islander": Pedagogies of expropriation, return and resistance and other lessons from a "Multicultural Day"', *Race Ethnicity and Education*, vol. 15, no. 2, pp. 141–155, doi.org/10.1080/13613324.2011.569243

Contributors

Imelda Ambelye is a PhD candidate at James Cook University, in Queensland, Australia. Her fieldwork for her doctoral research was conducted in two villages in Papua New Guinea, evaluating the empowerment and participation of women for community development and social change, comparing mining-affected and non-affected communities. Her previous education was at the University of Goroka, the PNG University of Technology and the University of Queensland.

Doris Bacalzo is a research associate with the Department of Social and Cultural Anthropology, University of Lucerne, Switzerland. She studied biology before pursuing graduate studies in anthropology. She received her MA in Anthropology from the University of the Philippines with an ethnographic study of a Mangyan group in the island of Mindoro in the Philippines, focusing on customary law, indigenous women and gender relations. For her PhD at the University of Lucerne, she looked at the lives of young people and investigated the politics of differentiation, inclusion and exclusion involving children of interethnic marriages among the Wampar of the Markham Valley in Papua New Guinea. She continues to do research among the Wampar and is engaged in a Swiss National Science Foundation–sponsored longitudinal and collaborative project to analyse local inequalities and social relations under the effects of large-scale international projects (copper-gold mine, biomass energy and palm oil).

Laurence Marshall Carucci, Letters and Science Distinguished Professor Emeritus of Anthropology at Montana State University, holds a PhD in Anthropology from the University of Chicago and has conducted more than seven years of community-based research with Marshall Islanders since 1976. The focus of his research has been on issues of social and cultural change among the Enewetak/Ujelang people and the members of other communities who suffered through the Second World War and the subsequent era of United States nuclear testing in the Northern

Marshall Islands. The results of his research appear in numerous articles, book chapters and books, including *Nuclear Nativity*, *The Typhoon of War*, and *Memories of War* (the latter books co-authored with Lin Poyer and Suzanne Falgout). His current research focuses on nineteenth- and twentieth-century historical transformations experienced by Enewetak/Ujelang people in the Marshall Islands and Hawai'i.

Aidan Craney is an Honorary Research Fellow with the Institute for Human Security and Social Change at La Trobe University and an international development consultant. His research looks at youth livelihoods and iterative development practices in the Pacific Islands region. Drawing on his experiences living, working and researching within the region, Aidan's research methods are interdisciplinary and focus on constructing holistic understandings of how social change occurs. He holds a PhD in Anthropology from La Trobe University for his thesis, 'To Be Seen But Not Heard: Youth Livelihoods and Development in Fiji and Solomon Islands', as well as a Master of Social Science (International Development) from RMIT University and Bachelor of Social Work from the University of Melbourne.

Daniel Evans is a PhD Candidate at The Australian National University. He has had a long-term association with Melanesia, having spent over a decade living and working in Vanuatu, Solomon Islands and Papua New Guinea. His past roles have spanned legal sociology and justice system reform. Daniel has worked on a number of bilateral development projects and undertaken various consultancies. His PhD is concerned with male youth in two communities of Honiara, Solomon Islands. He is interested in the intersection between youth and illicit livelihoods, criminality, security, identity, nationalism and the state.

Aaron John Robarts Ferguson is a graduate of Pacific University (Forest Grove, Oregon, United States) with a Bachelor's in Anthropology and History. His research in the Pacific has centred on 'youth futures' among Samoan youth, as well as historical structures of US imperialism in the Samoan Islands. He currently lives in Seattle, Washington, where he conducts health and medical science research and aims to pursue an advanced degree in medical anthropology.

Mary K Good is Assistant Professor of Cultural Anthropology at Wake Forest University in North Carolina, United States. She has recently begun a project on employment, unemployment and decision-making about work opportunities and family responsibilities among Tongan youth. Her other ongoing research projects have focused on the use of new digital media such as online social networks and text messaging by youth on the island of 'Eua in Tonga. Good is particularly interested in the ways processes of global modernity affect youths' understandings of morality, sentiment and competing responsibilities.

Helen Lee is Professor of Anthropology in the Department of Social Inquiry, La Trobe University. Since the 1980s she has conducted research with the people of Tonga, both in their home islands in the Pacific and in the diaspora, particularly in Australia, with a focus on childhood and youth, cultural identity and migration and transnationalism. Her doctoral research on Tongan childhood was published as *Becoming Tongan: An Ethnography of Childhood* (H Morton, 1996). Her other books include *Tongans Overseas: Between Two Shores* (2003) and, more recently, *Mobilities of Return: Pacific Perspectives* (2017, co-edited with Jack Taylor) and *Change and Continuity in the Pacific* (2018, co-edited with John Connell). Her Australian Research Council Linkage Project (2015–19) looked at the impact of immigration status on Pacific Islanders in rural Victoria.

Caleb Marsters is a PhD candidate at Te Wānanga o Waipapa, School of Māori and Pacific Studies, University of Auckland. His field of research centres on Pacific youth, positive mental wellbeing, sports for development and suicide prevention in New Zealand. His PhD seeks to build upon his Master's thesis by conducting further research on strategies to support mental wellbeing among young Pacific males in New Zealand.

Lila Moosad completed her PhD at the Centre for Health Equity, Melbourne School of Population and Global Health, University of Melbourne, in 2019. Her thesis focused on the wellbeing experiences of young Pasifika women in Melbourne and the structural barriers to their wellbeing. Her research interests include the intersections of population movements/visa categories/health, participatory and strengths-based health research and health experiences of minority youth in urban settings. She currently works in the Gender and Women's Health Unit at the Melbourne School of Population and Global Health, University of Melbourne.

Mary L Spencer, PhD, is Dean Emerita, College of Liberal Arts and Social Sciences, and Professor of Psychology and Micronesian Studies, Micronesia Area Research Center (retired), University of Guam.

Jemaima Tiatia-Seath is currently Co-Head of School and Head of Pacific Studies, Te Wānanga o Waipapa, School of Māori Studies and Pacific Studies, University of Auckland. She is of Samoan descent and has a public health background. She was one of six panellists on the New Zealand government's 2018 Mental Health and Addiction Inquiry. Her research interests include Pacific studies, mental health and wellbeing, Pacific suicide prevention and postvention, climate change, youth development, Pacific health inequities.

www.ingramcontent.com/pod-product-compliance
Lightning Source LLC
Chambersburg PA
CBHW050807270326
41926CB00026B/4601

9781760463212